HEBREW HONEY

A Simple and Deep Word Study of the Old Testament

by

AL NOVAK

With Three Indexes of the 545 Words Exegeted

1. English Words.
2. Hebrew Words.
3. Scriptures Used.

Hebrew Honey
COPYRIGHT© 1987
C & D International
Houston, Texas 77068

Published by:
J. Countryman Publishers
P.O. Box 90776
Houston, Texas 77290

Production Agency
Heritage Printers & Publishers
9029 Directors Row
Dallas, Texas 75247

ISBN: 0-937347-08-6

Hebrew Honey
COPYRIGHT© 1965 BY AL NOVAK
LIBRARY OF CONGRESS CARD NO. 64-252876

More Hebrew Honey
COPYRIGHT© 1966 BY AL NOVAK
LIBRARY OF CONGRESS CARD NO. 66-24015

TABLE OF CONTENTS

———•———

INTRODUCTION

Hebrew Honey was first published in 1965. The author, Dr. Al Novak, had a desire to explain many of the Hebrew words (more than 500) contained in the Old Testament. His work was a labor of love that spread over a period of 15 years.

In his colorful career, the author served as a pastor, missionary, naval chaplain and educator. He received his call to the ministry in 1927 and was a graduate of Baylor University. He received his Master of Theology Degree from Southwestern Baptist Theological Seminary.

His tremendous interest in Hebrew, and his desire to explain the interconnection of God's word and its perfect order, makes this book a desirable addition for every serious word student. We are deeply grateful to his wife, Mrs. Al Novak, who has allowed us the privilege of publishing her husband's labor of love. The research, development and explanation of these major Hebrew words of the Old Testament will give you a deeper insight into God's word.

Jack Countryman, President

J. Countryman Publishers

HEBREW HONEY

גּוּר

ABIDE: "Lord, who shall abide in thy tabernacle?", (Ps. 15:1). The Hebrew word for *abide* is _gur_. It has several significations.

One is, to turn aside from one's own way to some other person or place with the idea of lodging there. The happiest person in this world and the next is he who turns from his own way and abides with Him who is "the Way."

Another is, to live as a guest. Most people like to be guests. Precious prospect, precious reality, that of being a guest of the Lord and being under His care and protection.

Still another is to be a client. When a man has the Lord as his Advocate he can never lose, for all things will work together for good.

Yet another signification of this Hebrew word is almost puzzling. It is, to fear, or to be afraid—Ps. 33:8. One who really fears the Lord will run to Him like a prodigal son: confessing, trusting, abiding. _WH elp_

In Jer. 51:38 _gur_ is translated _whelp_. A whelp is still an abider— Ezek. 19:2, lingering near its mother for its nourishment. Man can not live separated from God.

David's flights from enraged king Saul and his armies kept him away from the tabernacle. Hiding in caves, moving stealthily through wildernesses, lonely for home and friends and knowing only temporary safety, David's soul longed for God's house. The religious king reveled in the tabernacle, and that he wanted to "turn aside and abide there forever" became the theme of many of his psalms.

חיל   C BAyiL

ABLE: "Moses chose able men out of all Israel", (Exod. 18:25). *Chayil,* the Hebrew word for *able,* has several shades of meaning.

First, there is strength to enable one to do valiantly—Ps. 60:12. Stouthearted men of the Lord would hardly fear doing anything to advance the Lord's cause.

Next, there is power (Ps. 110:3) that will stir one to move out on campaigns that shall issue in certain victory.

1

Then there is wealth (Deut. 8:18) which can become a tremendously effective tool in the hands of the Lord's men.

Also there is honesty (I Kings 1:52) which is so basically essential in building a great man. This, perhaps more than anything else, fitted Lincoln for great leadership.

Too, there is in this word the idea of entrenchment or fortification to protect a place—Nah. 3:8. How blessed the churches that have strong and honest men in them. These men are appointed of God to be walls and bulwarks—Isa. 26:1.

This root is used to build the name of city—II Sam. 10:16. David won a victory there. Helam (able people), would make a good name for a church or a hymn.

אבר

ABRAM: "So Abram departed, as the Lord had spoken unto him. . .", (Gen. 12:4). *Abram* comes from the Hebrew root *Abar* which has several meanings.

It means to soar or to mount. This is illustrated by Abram's faith—Heb. 11:8; by his daring expedition into the unknown; by his sojourn in a land of promise; by his looking for a city God built. He transcended the average of God's people.

It means wings or pinions—Ps. 55:6; Isa. 40:31. David desired dove's wings for a flight to rest and Isaiah proclaimed that those who waited upon God would have strength and be able to mount up as eagles.

It means protection—Ps. 91:4. Those under God's wings will be spared from snares and pestilences.

So, he who was Abram, "the father of altitude" became Abraham, "the father of multitude". He was an honor to God and a blessing to man.

נשא

ACCEPTED: ". . . The Lord also accepted Job", (Job 42:9). This word *nasa* has much honey in it. There are several significations.

One is to lift up. Man is always in need of a lift—II Kings 25:27. In Job 11:15 the countenance is lifted. In Job 21:12 instruments are lifted to express rejoicing.

Another signification is to bear with or to suffer or to permit—Job 21:3. These characteristics are bound to lead to acceptance.

Then there is the idea of forgiveness of sin. Sin is confessed—Ps. 32:5, the Lord takes it away and accepts the sinner.

This word also means to take a wife—II Chron. 11:21. God took forgiven Job. Christ will take the redeemed which will be followed by a marriage supper.

Also in this word is the idea of applying, e.g., ropes to a city—II Sam. 17:13. It is inspiring to remember that the Lord applied ropes to us, lifted us from the miry clay and set our feet upon solid rock. It is indeed heartening to see a company of stout-hearted Christians apply ropes to a city that has defected and bring it back to God.

עשׂה

ACCOMPLISH: ". . . It shall accomplish that which I please", (Isa. 55:11). A great word in a great text. This ought to inspire God's own to hold forth His Word because He declares it will *asah* (accomplish). This Hebrew word has several significations.

The first is to yield out of one's self. This ought to be first and also enough. The idea is that God is able to bring out of Himself the power; the victory; the solution to problems; the comfort needed anywhere anytime.

God not only causes yields to come out of Himself but also out of other sources. He makes the tree to yield fruit; He gives man power to get wealth. It is still unknown what God can do with His weakest child that goes about planting His Word.

This word also means to appoint—I Sam. 12:6. God accomplished victory by setting forth leaders. He may call out another Abraham and appoint our nation to be greater and to be a greater blessing to all the world—Gen. 12:2. Also, he may appoint the writer or the reader of these words to accomplish the bringing in of His Kingdom.

Also this word means to be done to or to be done with. Many parents and guardians have wondered what God had in store for the child in their care—Exod. 2:4.

קלל

ACCURSED: "But the sinner . . . shall be accursed", (Isa. 65:20). *Qalal,* the Hebrew root for *accursed,* has several black hues.

3

It means lessened and diminished—Gen. 8:11. Sin reduces.

It means to cut down and to afflict—Nah. 1:12. God's curse is like a scythe.

It means unimportant—I Sam. 18:23. A sinner shall discover; or, it shall be discovered to him that he is a cumberer of the ground.

It means an uttered malediction—II Sam. 16:7. Shimei cursed, cf. verse 5.

It means to despise—II Sam. 19:44. Is ever a sinner desired?

This root is considered the same as *qalah*, which means "roasted in the fire"—Jer. 29:22; parched as corn dried by the fire—Josh. 5:11 and Lev. 2:14; loathesome as a disease—Ps. 38:7; and shame—Isa. 22:18. All of these add to the blackness and the blight of the sinner's curse. He shall be tossed like a ball into a large country and left there to die. The chariots of his glory shall be but shame to the Lord's house—Isa. 22:18.

קרץ

ACCUSE: "They brought those men which had accused Daniel, and they cast them into the den of lions, and the lions had the mastery of them, and brake all their bones in pieces . . .", (Dan. 6:24). *Qarats,* the Hebrew root for *accuse,* has surprising explanations.

It means piece or bit—Dan. 3:8. It carries the idea of eating the pieces of anyone or to eat them up piecemeal by slandering and informing against them falsely. These accusers of innocent Daniel (Dan. 6:22) who had done no one hurt but believed in God (Dan. 6:23) were themselves torn to bits by lions. Gossipers who gore with their tongues may be torn by tusks.

It means destruction—Jer. 46:20. The idea is to tear or cut asunder; or to cut off and destroy. So the daughter dwelling in Egypt will furnish herself for captivity.

It means to wink with the eye or bite with the lip—Ps. 35:19. These mischief-makers may gesture by biting with the lips or pressing together the eyelids (like biting with the lips) thus winking and that perhaps behind one's back—Prov. 10:10.

It means to be nipped—Job. 33:6. That is, Job was a piece of clay torn from the earth. The image "being drawn from a potter, who pinches off a portion of clay from the mass in order to form a vessel".

4

בעת

AFFRIGHTED: "My heart panted, fearfulness affrighted me: the night of my pleasure hath he turned into fear unto me", (Isa. 21:4). Isaiah bewails the plight of his people. Desert winds, grievous visions, pangs in the loins, pantings in the heart all affright him. The Hebrew for this word is *Baath* and has color in it.

Job uses it poetically to describe his feelings after his great losses: "Let the blackness of the day terrify it", "Let not his fear terrify me", "Trouble and anguish shall make him afraid". All of us have lost some and we may yet lose greatly. We should desire to have always Job-like trust in God and come to such an end as did Job.

The psalmist used it to describe rightful fear, "The sorrows of death compassed me, and the floods of ungodly men made me afraid"—Ps. 18:4.

The chronicler used it to report that Saul was really troubled when the Spirit of the Lord left him and the evil spirit suddenly seized him so that the servants noted it. One thing far worse than this: to be seized by such spirit for eternity—I Sam. 16:14, 15.

בדד

ALONE: "I watch, and am as a sparrow alone upon the house top", (Ps. 102:7). *Badad* is the Hebrew for *alone* which has several meanings.

It means to separate as from others—Lev. 13:46. In the text given above the psalmist is describing himself as being alone in pouring out a prayer of complaint that his affliction has overwhelmed him.

It means to separate one from all of his impurities—Isa. 1:25.

This root is used to build the Hebrew word for *tin*—Num. 31:22. Smelting has brought the tin out of the ore. What might it take to bring man out of the alloys in which he is found.

It means solitary—Ps. 4:8. *Only* the Lord, no one else anywhere can lay me down in peaceful and safe sleep.

אמן

AMEN: "Let all the people say, Amen", (Ps. 106:48). This Hebrew word has not been translated into English but has been transliterated. It has interesting significations.

5

One is to be trustworthy or sure so that others can lean upon it—I Sam. 22:14. In this passage the word is translated *faithful* and in II Sam. 3:2 it is translated Amon. How many of God's children could be named Amon or how many are there who can be leaned upon when the Lord's work is to be done?

Another is to build upon—Isa. 28:16. Across the centuries there have been "pillars of the church" which God has surely laid "in Zion for a foundation stone." Those sweet souls have been builded into the great Church which we shall see some day as the bride adorned for her Husband. That Church has Jesus for its sure foundation and the Corner Stone.

Still another is sealed covenant—Neh. 10:1. As words fitly spoken are like apples of gold in baskets of silver—Prov. 25:11, so those whose names have been entered into the covenant must be wonderful beyond our conception and about all we can say is "Amen".

יטב

AMEND: "Thus saith the Lord . . . amend your ways and your doings", (Jer. 7:3). The Hebrew word *yatab* has several meanings.

To be well, good, better—Gen. 40:14. Joseph interprets the dreams for the imprisoned butler and baker and requests when it shall be well with them to put in a good word for him to Pharaoh.

To be cheerful, joyous, i.e., in the mind and in the heart—Ruth 3:7. Surely this must be the best amending when one acquires a happy disposition, and only the Lord can do this for one.

To conduct well, to live uprightly—Jer. 4:22.

To do good to anyone, to benefit another—Gen. 12:16. While this illustration of Abram, his sister and Pharaoh may not be one in the best sense, the lesson remains the same: one of the best amendments to life is to do good unto others.

To put in good order, adjust, trim, dress as a lamp—Exod. 30:7. To dress or arrange the hair like Jezebel did when she heard Jehu was coming for a visit—II Kings 9:30. All of us ought to ever put on the best righteousness and arrange for the best manners since we are being read by all.

6

מַלְאָךְ

ANGEL: "He shall give His angels charge over thee", (Ps. 91:11). The word *angel* is used nearly 300 times in the Bible, nearly always carrying the idea of *messenger.* The regular Hebrew word *malak,* translated *angel,* has several meanings.

One sent, a messenger, e.g., from a private person (Job 1:14); or from a king—I Sam. 16:19.

A messenger of God, i.e., an angel—Exod. 23:20; a preacher—Hag. 1:13; an intercessor or priest—Mal. 2:7; a chosen people like a nation—Isa. 42:19.

To perform a ministry, work, service—Exod. 20:9, 10. Since man is made but a little lower than the angels, this meaning of *malak* implies both are to render a ministry, deliver a message.

Message—Hag. 1:13. Here the root word for angel is the same as that used to form the word for the message of that angel.

Malachi—Mal. 1:1. This is a good name for a preacher of God's Word, and is built on the same root as *angel.*

מָשַׁח

ANOINT: ". . . Because the Lord hath anointed me to preach", (Isa. 61:1). It is noteworthy to discover that most of the 150 times this word *mashach* is used in the Bible, the action is by the Lord, for the Lord, or of the Lord. There is not much emphasis on anointing among men, *Mashach* has two meanings.

To draw the hand over, to paint, e.g., with colors—Jer. 22:14. A life set apart to His service is colorful.

To consecrate, e.g., a priest—I Sam. 2:35, Rev. 1:6: "And hath made us kings and priests unto God his Father." A king and then take care of him—Ps. 18:50; 20:6. Man can dedicate himself to God but only God can consecrate him and care for him—I Chron. 16:22.

Samuel was not of Levi's descendants—the tribe of priests—yet God reached over into Ephraim's family for one to replace Eli. There is no way of telling whom God will greatly use.

אָנָה

ANSWER: ". . . For there is no answer of God", (Mic. 3:7). If God does not answer prayers, the prophets will have no vision; seers will be ashamed; the sun will go down; there will be dark-

7

ness; and, divining will be over. But God does answer prayer and the word *anah* has several meanings.

To announce or pronounce as giving out a proclamation—I Sam. 9:17.

To lift up the voice—Song of Sol. 2:10. What sweet music to hear God lift up His voice to His children.

To grant requests—Ps. 3:4; 22:24. After God answered his prayers, David was unafraid of ten thousand who set themselves against him.

To sing—Exod. 32:18; Isa. 27:2. The children call it music with words when their heavenly Father answers their *Abba's*. They send thanks with reverent joy.

ראה

APPEAR: "The Lord appeared unto him (Moses)", (Exod. 3:2). *Raah* is the Hebrew word for appear and is used nearly 100 times. It has several significations.

To see with pleasure—Ps. 106:5.

To see to anything, to look after—Ps. 37:37.

To be certain to practice uprightness. See that you live right. The Lord will see that you live.

To look out anything for oneself—Gen. 22:8. When the Lord appeared unto Moses he was looking for a man and should He appear unto one now, one of the reasons might be this.

To visit—II Kings 8:29. As Ahaziah did visit sick Joram, so should man hope for a visit from the Lord that healeth.

To look upon another as if expecting help from him—Isa. 17:7. When really needing help, man will not look to altars, cities or to anything made with his hands, but will look to his Maker. Inner vision is often sharpened by lack of anything to see with physical vision.

To understand—Isa. 40:5. All flesh shall learn by experience that the Lord hath spoken.

A prophet, a seer—I Sam. 9:9. A seer was one to whom Truth appeared.

Vision—Isa. 28:7. Visibility must remain limitless so God will not be missed when He chooses to appear.

8

Looking-glass—Job 37:18.

Gazing-stock, spectacle—Nah. 3:6. Man's appearance may become just that.

צוה

APPOINT: "The Lord shall have . . . appointed thee", (I Sam. 25:30). The Hebrew word for appoint is *tsavah* which has several meanings.

To erect, to setup or over, to appoint, to constitute as David the spiritual leader and ruler of Israel—I Sam. 25:30.

To decree—Isa. 45:12, e.g., the Lord decreed that the heavens and the earth be made. Also the Lord commands or appoints that man shall have strength—Ps. 68:28.

To charge or to command as a serpent and a sword—Amos 9:4. God has charge of all that may cause Job and fellow-sufferers to endure. Even if by remote control, God uses nature and military might to punish sinners and destroy sinful kingdoms.

To commission—Jer. 23:32. Unless one is commissioned of God, what he shall try will utterly fail.

To set—Isa. 38:1, as a man his house in order before he should die—II Sam. 17:23.

קום

ARISE: *"Arise,* shine; for thy light is come, and the glory of the Lord is risen upon thee", (Isa. 60:1). The Hebrew word for *arise* is *kum* which has several rich denotements.

One is to rise up asking the Lord to come with help—Ps. 3:7; 7:6, so that one is better fitted to go forth with the Light that lighteth every man.

Another is to make an appearance—Job 11:17, which is certainly the first step in evangelizing the world.

This word also means sureness—Gen. 23:17, 20, which is as necessary in bearing the good tidings as it is in the giving forth of light by lighthouses.

It means to be set—I Sam. 4:15, with the idea of being unpliable. Gospel messengers must arise, remain erect and unvaryingly hold forth the Word of life.

Another denotement is to lift up, establish and cause to stand like an altar—I Kings 16:32. All of God's people are to build altars to God so that all of the world might see the light of the one true God.

Still another signification is to exist—Dan. 2:39. This is an example of God's foreknowledge and His revelation of such as He wishes to use. God's people want His kingdom to come into the hearts of all even those in the uttermost parts of the world.

And another is tallness—I Sam. 16:7. God does not measure people according to physical stature but by the heart. He stands tall who rises up to shine for the Lord.

מערכה

ARMY: ". . . Armies of the living God", (I Sam. 17:26, 36). While the word *army* is in the Bible about 100 times, only 13 of them are translated from this Hebrew word *maarakah*. The other Hebrew words translating *army* mean force, strength, might, host, camp and have reference to the armies of man but this one is quite different and has reference to the armies of God. It has several significations.

First it signifies arrangement. God takes men, not against their will but those willing, and arranges them according to His pleasure or according to His needs.

Then it signifies project or preparation—Prov. 16:1. How good when the tongue speaks that which God has prepared the heart to feel. Such a project reveals God's intimate interest and personal work with us. His detailed plans and provided conditions are more powerful than all men's armies.

Also it signifies set in order—Exod. 39:37. This verse is part of a nine-verse sentence listing the articles brought to Moses. Then men were given instructions by the Lord, through Moses, to set them in specified order. The congregation of Israel could worship satisfyingly only if these articles were set in their proper place. God has a meaningful place for everything and everybody. He wants men's lights to shine so that men will glorify Him.

Last it signifies a row as loaves of shew-bread set before the Lord in the temple on a pure table—Lev. 24:6. By this army, whose soldiers are loaves of shew-bread, God provides food for the souls of men, while armies of force, strength, etc., may terrorize the land.

עלה

ASCEND: "Who shall ascend into the hill of the Lord?", (Ps. 24:3). The Hebrew word for *ascend* is *alah* and it has several colorful denotements.

It is used in connection with God, meaning he who is so skilled, or strong, or disposed as to climb on high to God's abode without the help of God. Many stay away from God's place, the drifter, the lazy, the too-busy, the weakling, the failure, because they do not have a vital faith in God.

This next denotement should very properly follow the first. It is used in connection with angels—Gen. 28:12. Because God is high and inaccessible to unaided man, He sent ministering angels down to man and back up to God repeatedly delivering His message and performing miraculous changes.

Another is to grow or shoot up—Gen. 40:10, as blossoms or grapes. Jesus grew in favor with God and men and then ascended to be at the right hand of God. Although undeserving, what *rapport* awaits the child of God who is "growing in grace."

Solomon uses this word—Prov. 31:29, to mean surpassing or excelling. Its use is good, for the daughter has grounds for expecting the mother to surpass her in virtue, knowing that the mother has had more experience "fearing the Lord". The beginner Christian ought to increase "in favor with God and man," until some day, possibly toward eventime of life, the Lord will give him Patmos-isle experiences.

In Job, (5:16), this Hebrew word is translated *hope* to show the poor he hath a foundation to stand on and an opening in his leaden sky through which the soul may rise. His spirit ascends.

בוש

ASHAMED: "I am the Lord your God . . . and my people shall never be ashamed", (Joel 2:27). The Hebrew word for *ashamed* is *bosh* and has several significations.

One idea in it is to be struck dumb. Ezra, having stated publicly that God's hand would be upon them for good, was now ashamed (struck dumb) to ask help of a temporal king. So, he called for prayer and fasting, gathered up gold, silver and vessels and journeyed to Jerusalem through enemy territory. God was upon them and delivered them from harm—Ezra 8:22.

Another idea in this word is to be disappointed—Job 6:20. Jobs

11

"friends" were such failures as friends that the citizens of Tema blushed to see the spectacle they made of themselves. There is a song that says, "There will be no disappointment in heaven."

Still another idea is to be confused, perplexed or troubled—Judg. 3:25. The servants of Eglon were just that as they tarried outside of the locked doors to the parlor where they thought their king was sleeping. Finally in despair they opened the door and found their chief had been murdered.

Another idea in this word is to be dried up—Hos. 13:15. Ephraim deliberately insisted on sinning until there was a drying up of her life. God permitted her citizenry to be captured and dispersed among the heathen. For that nation there was no return or healing even as there is not for the unrepentant soul. There were no wells of water springing up in them. They were dried up, and very much ashamed.

The most shameful idea in this Hebrew root is to disgrace—Prov. 29:15. So diligently the devoted Hebrew parent sought to bring up his children in Godly nurture that both the parent and the neighbors believed the parent disgraced when the child refused to follow obediently.

שָׁאַל

ASK: "Woe to the rebellious children, saith the Lord, that counsel but not of me . . . that walk . . . and have not asked at my mouth . . .", (Isa. 30:2). These people despised the word of God, trusted in Egypt instead and did not ask God's help. *Shaal,* the Hebrew root for *ask,* has strong meanings.

First of all it means to consult—Judg. 20:18. The children of Israel went up to the house of God and asked counsel of God before they set out to do something.

It means to demand—Job 40:7. Moses, Paul and others have taught us by example to humbly pray strongly.

It means to salute—I Sam. 30:21. The salute is a form of asking to show your hand that it does not have a weapon.

It means to beg—Ps. 109:10. This is an intense form of asking.

It means to require—Dan. 2:11. All of God's children have requirements and they ought to be humbly aired in prayer.

It means a petition—Esth. 5:8. A petition may be a crystallized form of prayer. It is spelled out and set down to show that thought had been given it. O that whole churches would sign a petition and present it to the Lord.

It means a loan—I Sam. 2:20. A loan is a prayer whose answer has feet to it. In fact asking for a loan may be the best type of praying after all.

עדה

ASSEMBLY: "Thou shalt gather together the whole assembly of the children of Israel together", (Num. 8:9). The Lord does not want us to forsake the assembling of ourselves together. Proof is in this Hebrew word *edah,* translated *assembly.* It has rich denotements.

It denotes beauty or ornament and is used to name women— Gen. 4:19, 36:2. A church crowd may be an ornament for the Lord, and it is a beauty unsurpassable.

It denotes an appointed meeting or a meeting on purpose— Exod. 12:3. Moses was to gather the people and give them God's message. They came, they heard, were freed from Egyptian slavery and consequently became ancestors of the kingdom of Israel and the Messiah.

It denotes a swarm of bees and there was honey—Judg. 14:8. When the Christian community gathers on purpose to worship and serve the living God, something sweeter than honey is deposited in the lives of those who so gather.

כפר

ATONEMENT: ". . . Whereby an atonement shall be made for him", (Num. 5:8). The Hebrew word for *atonement* is *kaphar* and has several denotements.

One is to cover over, i.e., to overlook, to forgive—Ps. 78:38. Everything shall be done that needs to be done to make the sinner "at-one" with God. Sin will need to be forgiven, covered over, and the Father's wrath neutralized by "paying a fine."

The second is to expiate an offense or a fault—Dan. 9:24. In other words, a complete satisfaction shall be made to the offended. It is to be noted that the sinner does not present Christ's sacrifice as payment to make the satisfaction but God did once and for all for those who believe.

Another is to appease or placate the person offended—Gen. 32:20. As Jacob feared to meet his brother whom he had offend-

13

ed and therefore sent placatory presents in advance of the meeting; so will the convicted sinner fear meeting his God whom he has offended by his sins and he also will seek to offer a present fully satisfactory to the offended One.

Still another is to cancel as one's covenant with death or agreement with hell—Isa. 28:18.

Kaphar is used to build the name of a village because that village gave a covering to people—Song of Sol. 7:11, 12.

This interesting Hebrew word, that spells out so important a doctrine, also denotes fingernail polish—Song of Sol. 1:14. This unusual meaning stems from the idea that oriental females made a powder of camphire leaves, then made the powder into a paste by use of water and put this on their finger nails to give them a much-desired reddish color. The word *camphire* comes from the same root as *atonement*. Well could the sinner pray for a colorful cover for his anemic soul dissipated by sin.

קָשַׁב

ATTEND: "I cried unto thee, O Lord . . . Attend unto my cry . . .", (Ps. 142:6). *Qashab,* the Hebrew root for *attend,* has several meanings.

It means to be attentive—Neh. 1:11. Nehemiah is beseeching the Lord to give his prayer attention with the ear. This attention is to consist of prospering and granting of mercy which was granted in a great measure.

It means to listen—Isa. 32:3. Men may have eyes that see and ears that hear and disposition to heed.

It means to sharpen primarily which may be to have sharp ears and to have ears that are pointed toward the message, a figure drawn from animals. It is inspiring to note eager hearers.

It means to attend with the greatest possible attention—Isa. 21:7. The watchman hearkened diligently with much heed like good watchmen should.

It means to bend the ear—Prov. 2:2. The wise man said to the son, Incline thine ear unto wisdom. How becoming to sons of God when they set the ear toward heaven.

רבה

AUTHORITY: "When the righteous are in authority the people rejoice", (Prov. 29:2). The Hebrew word for authority is *rabah* and has several significations.

One is to be many or numerous—Ps. 139:17. Great is the sum of God's thoughts unto his children and great should be their joy because of this.

To be mighty and powerful—Job 33:12, is another meaning of this word. Here Elihu is pointing up the greatness of Job's sin, the greatness of God and the cause of Job's illness. Job had already acknowledged the might and power of his God and admitted that his hideous suffering and mental anguish had led him to this acknowledgment.

Also this Hebrew root is used to build a name for a great city, the capital of the Ammonites—II Sam. 11:1, 12:27. As the Master's minority becomes a great metropolis they could well rejoice and among other names for their city of joy they might call it *Rabbah.*

It signifies chain about the neck—Ezek. 16:11; Gen. 41:42). How beautifully does this meaning blend with the text given at the first. The righteous are a chain for spiritual benefit in the family, in the church, around the earth and throughout the kingdom of God.

עוּר

AWAKE: "Awake psaltery and harp: I myself will awake early", (Ps. 108:2). The Hebrew word for *awake* is *ur* which has several denotements.

One denotement is to be active and lively as opposed to sleep—Song of Sol. 5:2. The bridal procession is ended, and now the bride is separated from her bridegroom. She goes seeking for him. The search wearies her. Her body must sleep, but not her heart which remains active and lively. This depicts the church that truly loves the Head of the church. Even if the body must stop for rest, the heart will be awake for the primary activity of praising the Lord.

Another is to be raised up as a wind—Jer. 25:32, or a people—Jer. 6:22. God can raise up a whirlwind to bring discomfort to an unrepentant people and cause their whole nation to suffer. If this does not avail, then God can turn to the north (or some other direction) and raise up a people mercilessly cruel to accomplish His pleasure. In light of this, God's people can see how a spiritual awakening must precede the building up of the kingdom of their God.

Then another is to excite or stir up as one's strength and support—Ps. 80:3. A spiritual awakening will come when—and only when—prayers persuade God to send strength and support.

Still another denotement is to brandish as a spear—II Sam. 23:18. Abishai "awakened" his spear and killed 300 enemies of David. When God's people brandish their spear which is "sharper than a two-edged sword," the enemies of the Greater David will be decimated.

To rouse is another denotement. This is illustrated by the eagle in teaching her eaglets to fly and protecting them in training—Deut. 32:11. If God rouses his child from the comforts of his home and sends him afield for Him, He will not only give the child words to say on that mission but will protect and provide.

This Hebrew root denotes keeping watch as those in God's sanctuary—Ps. 134. One watchman calls to another; that one answers, indicating his wakefulness. How becoming for God's people to keep a prayer watch around the clock.

גרז

AXE: "And the house (temple) . . . was built of stone made ready before it was brought thither: so that there was neither hammer nor axe nor any tool of iron heard in the house, when it was in building", (I Kings 6:7). *Garaz,* the Hebrew root from which *axe* derives, has interesting meanings.

It means to cut—Ps. 31:23. Here it is used to mean cut off from the presence of God. The cut is deep in the heart.

The ancients held the root meant to separate one from another by force. Perhaps it is not unapt to say, They gave him the axe.

The root is used to build the name for Mt. Gerizim—Deut. 27:12. Here the idea is exile—separated from the rest of the people and land. On this mountain was built a temple for the Samaritans who were definitely separatists.

16

סרר

BACKSLIDE: "For Israel slideth back as a backsliding heifer", (Hos. 4:16). *Sarar,* the Hebrew root for *backslide,* has several meanings.

It means to be like an intractable animal. One can see the untamed heifer backing off from the rope that holds it, or the rebellious son who is turned over to the city fathers because he will not hearken unto his parents—Deut. 31:18.

It means a perverse shoulder—Neh. 9:29. This is symbolized by refractory animals that strive to shake off the yoke from the shoulder.

It means sad, evil, bad—I Kings 21:4, 5. These, and backslide are good company for Ahab and Jezebel. (See *backsliding,* and *revolt*).

שׁובב

BACKSLIDING: "Return ye backsliding children and I will heal your backslidings", (Jer. 3:22). This Hebrew word *shobab* comes from the root *shub,* which means to return or to convert to a person or things—I Kings 8:33.

When a child of God ceases loving and serving and following after God, he is said to have backslidden because he has turned away from the person of God. (Note: there is no signification in all of this activity of coming to God, or leaving off following God, or becoming a child of God, or being disowned of God. In other words, the prodigal belonged to the father before, during, and after the time he was a prodigal. My son in the flesh is my son before, during, and after the time he is good or bad.)

Shobab also means to refresh—Ps. 23:3 and I Sam. 30:12.

To bring back the captives with rejoicing—Jer. 33:11. This implies that the enemy had those who now were returned.

A rebel—Isa. 57:17, and Jer. 31:22.

נשׂא

BEAR: "He hath borne our griefs ... He bare the sin of many", (Isa. 53:4, 12).

17

Nasa is a great word because it is greatly used of God. Across the sacred pages it is reported that men bore their shame, their parents' sins, reproach, grief, yokes. Also they bore their shields, bows, the ark of God, the table of the Lord, the burden of the people, and carcases. This word is most grandly employed when it says the Lord hath borne for us what we cannot bear (cf. Accept). It means:

To take up, raise—Gen. 7:17. As the waters bore up the ark; as the hand was lifted—Deut. 32:40 (Can not one believe God lifted His hand in a promise to save the world when His Son was lifted on the cross?); as a man was lifted out of prison (II Kings 25:27); as lifting the countenance—Job 11:15; as lifting the eyes to look upon another in love and longing—Ps. 121:12. The Shepherd sets His eyes on His sheep.

To wear as a garment—I Sam. 2:28. Thus did Jesus wear our griefs, our sins.

To endure—Ps. 55:12.

To take upon oneself that which properly falls on another as his portion of sin and sorrow—Isa. 53:12.

To destroy—Job 32:22. Our Lord destroys our sins.

To expiate, or make atonement for—Lev. 10:17.

To forgive sin, to pardon—Ps. 32:4, 5.

To help—Esther 9:3. The Lord gives a lift to the believer.

To apply to e.g.—ropes to a city—II Sam. 17:13. Jesus did just that when He wept over Jerusalem and God does that for the whole world (II Pet. 3:9).

To be exalted—I Chron. 29:11. He that on the cross lifted others from their prisons of sin was at the same time Himself exalted.

נאה

BEAUTIFUL: "How beautiful upon the mountains are the feet of him that bringeth good tidings, that publisheth peace; that bringeth good tidings of good, that publisheth salvation; that saith unto Zion, Thy God reigneth", (Isa. 52:7). *Naah* may be translated by some other word since it means:

To sit or to dwell in rest or in quiet—Hab. 2:5. The Christian who spreads the Gospel will have quiet and rest.

To be proper, suitable, becoming, i.e., to sit well on any one like a garment is suitable to a person or better still, the illustration in religion is "holiness becometh thine house", (Ps. 93:5). Anyone publishing glad tidings is well clad.

Decorous, beautiful like flocks and herds that lie down to rest in the pastures green—Ps. 23:2.

Comely, seemly like "praise becometh the upright"—Ps. 33:1. How beautiful to see the saints in the sanctuary singing.

(Note: There are several Hebrew words translated *beautiful,* e.g., *Phar* (Isa. 52:1) meaning to be adorned, of a high color, etc.; *Yapheh* (Gen. 29:17) meaning appealing in countenance and fair of form; *Tsebi* (Isa. 4.2) meaning desire, beauty.)

יפה

BEAUTIFUL: "Thou art beautiful, O my Love . . .", (Song of Sol. 6:4). Most scholars agree that in this passage the Church is speaking of her Bridegroom, Christ. The Hebrew word *Yapheh* means:

To be bright, to shine probably as a result of splendid deeds and miracles. No wonder beholders call Jesus the Light of the world. Zion shines—Ps. 48:2.

To be fair, comely, beautiful—Ezek. 16:13; 31:7. To be very beautiful—Ps. 45:2. In this passage the word *yapheh* is doubled, thus *yaph-yapheh,* i.e., beauty on top of beauty.

To be excellent—Eccl. 3:11.

A celebrated harbor of the Mediterranean. The name chosen for the harbor, Jaffa, comes from this root. This city is distinguished for its port. Those who have learned to flee to the Lord will likely name the Lord: Yapheh, Yaph-Yapheh—Beautiful, Beautiful-on-top-of-Beautiful.

נשׁא

BEGUILE: "The serpent did beguile me, and I did eat", (Gen. 3:13). The Hebrew word *nasha* means:

To go astray, to go away with the kindred idea of forgetting, neglecting, deserting—Jer. 23:39.

19

To deceive, lead into error, impose on—II Kings 18:29.

To surprise and destroy—Ps. 55:15 (read v 16). This is good reason for likening sin to a serpent.

To seduce, to corrupt—Jer. 49:16.

(Note: Here is an interesting technicality: the second letter in the root of this word *nasha* is made like an English W, with a dot above the right wing tip. There is another Hebrew word *nasa* with the only difference being that the dot is over the left wing tip of the second letter which is similar to an English W. Now, the meaning of the first word is given above, but the meaning of the second is a most pronounced contrast: to lift up as one out of an underground prison, to bear up, to raise up to help make amends for the fallen one (Isa. 53:12) as Jesus does for the fallen race. Exaltation is the primary idea).

נבט

BEHOLD: "Behold, O God our shield, and look upon the face of thine anointed", (Ps. 84:9). The psalmist, longing for the sanctuary, prays to be restored to it where God might behold His anointed. *Nabat,* the Hebrew root for *behold,* has several meanings.

It means to see and know—Ps. 142:4. Here is a basic craving of mankind: to be noticed. The psalmist wanted his heavenly parent to notice him.

It means to respect—Ps. 119:15. Here is another basic craving of mankind: to have the respect of his fellows. The psalmist wanted his God to regard him.

It means simply to look—Job 35:5. Heaven's messenger asked suffering Job to look to the heavens.

It means to behold quietly without doing anything—Hab. 1:13. The prophet exhorts the righteous not to look on evil and to speak up against those who deal treacherously against the righteous. The child of God must *not* behold quietly.

אמן

BELIEVE: "He believed in the Lord and He counted it to him for righteousness", (Gen. 15:6). This is the first time the word *believe* is used in the Bible. The Hebrew word *aman* used here is used in some forty other passages. It means:

To be faithful—Isa. 12:1. Here the idea is to lean upon, to trust in—Isa. 26:3.

To be durable, lasting, permanent, e.g., of waters which never fail—Isa. 33:16. Here the man's life depended on the waters being sure. In the matter of Christian faith, eternal life depends on that faith being of the permanent brand.

To be true—Hos. 5:9. This idea of being true is vitally related to believing. Those putting trust in God will be true to Him. Abraham was.

Architect, artist—believers build a church. They are a portrait on the community's easel.

Covenant—Neh. 10:1. A Testament is a sweet agreement between those who trust one another.

Pillar, column—II Kings 18:16. Needed to build churches.

Amana—II Kings 5:12. A stream which rises in Antilibanus waters the territories of Damascus, and never fails (Isa. 33:16).

פעם

BELL: "And they made bells of pure gold and put the bells between the pomegranates upon the hem of the robe ... to minister in; as the Lord commanded Moses", (Exod. 39:25, 26). *Paam,* the Hebrew root for *bell,* has deep meanings. Christians may be "Bells of Gold".

It means to strike or to pound as an anvil or a bell. A child of God may be chastened, or beat upon by the hand of God and ring true like a bell of pure gold. Job did.

It means to impel, e.g. "the Spirit of God a person," Judg. 13:25. Although Samson was a strong man the Spirit of the Lord moved him like a child would a little bell. The same Spirit moved myriads of others, even Paul, Peter and John.

It means to cause struggle and agitation, Ps. 77:3. David was so driven about by the winds of heaven until he doubted; but victory came.

It means an anvil, Isa. 41:7. God, the Heavenly Goldsmith, may smooth with the hammer some Job who will turn out to be a pretty piece in God's showcase.

21

It means to keep time with the hand or foot—Josh. 6:3. That is, they were to go around once, then twice, then thrice ... So God's servant is to go here and there, preach and teach, sing and pray, read and explain, heal and comfort all the while keeping time to the urgings of God's Spirit: thereby being a "bell of gold".

דוד

BELOVED: "My beloved is mine and I am his: He feedeth among the lilies", (Song of Sol. 2:16). *Davad,* the Hebrew root for *beloved,* has very moving meanings.

It means to boil as a pot or kettle—I Sam. 2:14. Real love does that.

It means to stir or agitate—Job 41:11. Love will move.

It means to love and that deeply—Song of Sol. 1:4. Love moves one more than wine and moves the upright rightly, e.g. the Church for her Christ.

It means a friend, Isa. 5:1. Here the prophet sings of Jehovah, his well-beloved Friend.

It is used to build the name David for the man renowned for his psalms, his territorial accessions, his love for God and his love for his people—I Sam. 16 to the end of II Sam. Did ever a man love like David, except the greatest Lover born a millenium later.

אהב

BELOVED: "...Who was beloved of his God", (Neh. 13:26). "Behold, Thou art fair, my Beloved, yea, pleasant", (Song of Sol. 1:16).

The Hebrew word *aheb* used in these two passages and others means: to breath after, to long for, to desire—Ps. 116.1.

To love—I Sam. 20:17. Jonathan loved David as he loved his own soul.

A friend—loving, beloved, intimate and different from a companion—Prov. 18:24.

In a bad sense: paramour, debauchee—Ezek. 16:33. Contains the idea of idolater. Love, somewhat as fire or water, can be a great blessing and also become a great curse.

22

To love so as to have intercourse and alliance with, as nations—Hos. 8:9. One who loves God will pray and will be allied with Him in redeeming the world.

בקשׁ

BESEECH: "So we fasted and besought our God for this; and He was intreated of us", (Ezra 8:23).

This Hebrew word *baqash* is a strong word for prayer. It means: To seek, to search, to inquire into with the primary idea of touching, feeling out—Gen. 37:15, 16.

To seek the face of, the presence of; to gain an audience with, to see—I Kings 10:24.

To seek the face of God, draw near to Him—II Sam. 12:16.

To find God—Deut. 4:29.

To request, to ask, to seek from any one—Ezra 8:21.

חבשׁ

BIND: "He healeth the broken in heart and bindeth up their wounds", (Ps. 147:3). *Chabash,* the Hebrew root for *bind,* has several meanings.

It means to wrap—Jonah 2:5. As weeds from the deep were wound around the head of him who had fled *from* the Lord so will healing bandages from heaven be bound over the wounds of them that flee *to* the Lord.

It means to repair the breach of God's people—Isa. 30:26.

It means to restrain—Job 28:11. The floods were bound to hold them from overflowing. If this is physical, it is good; if it is spiritual, it is loss.

It means to saddle, as an animal—Gen. 22:3. Abraham saddled his ass and the animal knew not where he was going but was to be directed by his owner. Neither did Abraham know where he was going but he was bound to One who would direct him.

קשׁר

BIND: "As I live, saith the Lord, thou shalt surely clothe thee with them all, as with an ornament, and bind them on thee, as

23

a bride doeth", (Isa. 49:18). God so greatly loved Zion that He promised her rich blessings, one of which was that her people would gather unto her again. She had mourned their departure from her and accused the Lord of forgetting her (Isa. 49:14), but He pledged to not forget her even if a woman forgot her sucking child and that her people would come so close to her that she could bind them about her as a bride doth bind an ornamental girdle about her over her bridal dress. *Qashar,* the Hebrew root for *bind,* has surprising meanings.

It means to conspire—I Sam. 22:8. That is, one will bind himself with others, here not for good reasons but in many cases confederacies are formed for good.

It means to be strong—Gen. 30:42. Often verbs like twisting or binding are transferred to strength and here it is easy to see how a group of God's children (covenanted together) may have strength not of this world.

It means completed—Neh. 4:6. The wall was finished because the people joined the parts together—such parts as each group was working on.

It means bands—Isa. 3:20. So it is very proper for Christians to band themselves together in fellowship and service.

It is used to build the word conspiracy—II Kings 12:20. God's children may want to form a conspiracy against the chief enemy of them all.

It means to be bound—Gen. 44:30. The father's soul was bound to the soul of the child by the strongest ties of love.

נקב

BLASPHEME: "And he that blasphemeth the name of the Lord he shall surely be put to death", (Lev. 24:11, 16). The Hebrew word *naqab* means:

To hollow out, to excavate. To take the name of the Lord thus in vain looks like an attempt to cheapen it.

To bore—II Kings 12:9. A hole, like a purse with holes—Hag. 1:6. Using God's name wrongly in an attempt to bore holes in good money and void it, or to make blessed wages and try to take them home in a bag with holes in it.

To curse, to pierce with words, to cut—Lev. 24:11, 16. From this passage it has been thought by some that God's name is so

24

holy that it should not even be on the lips—Num. 23:8.

Hammer. This idea comes from the root meaning of striking or piercing.

Cavern, cavity—which is the proper name, Nekeb, and given to a city in Naphtali—Josh. 19:33. Could this name be chosen for this city because of a cavern there? Could man be guilty of making a hollow cave out of God's name?

בָּרַךְ

BLESS: "And in thee shall all families of the earth be blessed", (Gen. 12:3). The Hebrew word, *barak,* translated *blessed,* is not kin to, ashere, אַשְׁרֵי (translated *blessed* about a hundred times as in Psalm 1:1). While the latter means *happy,* the former never means that. It means:

To kneel—II Chron. 6:13, as Solomon did for his prayer at the dedication of the Temple.

To invoke God to bless—I Chron. 16:2, as David did the people of his realm. It was predicted of Abraham that many would be blessed because he lived. Could such be expected of all of God's children?

To make prosperous—Gen. 12:2.

To salute, to greet—I Sam. 15:13. This is more than an exchange of the time of the day. It implies a wish or invocation of every good.

Knees—Isa. 66:12. Like children are fondled by their parents on their knees even so doth God comfort His children as told in three verses—Gen. 50:21-23. Pastors ought to comfort God's people.

A pond, pool—II Sam. 2:13. Does not the Lord want each disciple to witness to the fact the Lord gives satisfying draughts? Each Christian ought to be a pool—one an *upper* pool—Isa. 7:3, another a *king's* pool watering kings' gardens, another a *lower* pool for the watering of the lower city—Isa. 22:9.

Benefits, favors, gifts—Gen. 49:25. This is a most fitting eulogy for Abraham. In many scriptures of the Old Testament and of the New Testament there are records to be found of how he was man's blessing. He honored God "and gained glory to himself."

אֲשֵׁר

BLESSED: "Blessed is the nation whose God is the Lord", (Ps. 33:12). *Blessed* is the word for translating several Hebrew words in the Bible. Here it is *ashar* which has some very interesting meanings.

It means to be very happy and the receiver of good fortune.

It means to be straight and is related to the word translated *righteousness.* The happiest people in this world and in the next will be righteous. They have been straightened out before Him in whom there was no crookedness.

It means to guide right. Those are the happiest who have been guided into paths of righteousness.

It means to advance or to prosper.

One derivative means *connection.* Only those branches abiding in the true Vine will bear fruits of joy.

Another is *relation.* The happiest people in this world and in the next are those that are in a proper position in relation to God; to the Church; to the Bible; etc.

פּוּחַ

BLOW: "Awake, O north wind; and come thou south; blow upon my garden, that the spices thereof may flow out", (Song of Sol. 4:16). This passage is a great message on missions. *Puach,* the Hebrew root for *blow,* has colorful facets of meaning.

It means to breathe—Song of Sol. 2:17. The breezes carry fragrances from the garden. The sweet scent of the gospel ought to be wafted from the churches over all the world.

It means to kindle up a fire—Ezek. 21:31, 32. The church must needs have fire inside before warm gospel draughts will be felt outside.

It means to breathe out as the truth—Prov. 12:17. The Christian's business is to breathe the word of life to all nations.

26

It means to pant, i.e., to hasten—Hab. 2:3. Must those lying in darkness wait longer for us to show them the Light?

It means to puff at, as enemies—Ps. 12:5. The Lord promises to set in safety those who are railed at while they pray.

הלל

BOAST: "In God we boast all the day long...", (Ps. 44:8). This Hebrew word *hallal* means:

To be clear, brilliant; to shine.

To boast—Ps. 75:4, 5.

To praise, celebrate, mostly spoken of God—Ps. 117:1. *God* as a word is added to *hallal* in this Psalm and we have the melodic phrase: *hallelujah.* Where boasting might be a sin to us, it can also be a hallelujah chorus.

To commend—Gen. 12:15. This makes a theme for a song.

Renowned—Ezek. 26:17.

To be foolish, mad—Eccl. 2:2; 7:7; Isa. 44:25. Have not diviners, worshippers, and Christians been called mad, drunken, etc., across the centuries as they come forth with their hallelujahs?

עבד

BONDAGE: "Brought thee...from the house of bondage", (Deut. 5:16; 6:12; 8:14; 13:5). *Bondage* derives from the Hebrew root *abad* which has several rich denotements (*serve* also).

It denotes laboring and working as building a city or tilling the ground—Gen. 2:5; Ezek. 48:18. To be bound to such programs is rewarding bondage.

It denotes working for another—Gen. 29:20. Life's sweetest satisfaction issues from the workshop where the Lord is in charge.

It denotes a worshipper, i.e., a humble servant. Daniel was called a servant of God in this sense—Dan. 6:21. Generally this was meant to be a laudatory epithet applied to true worshippers—Ps. 105:6, 42; Josh. 24:29.

It denotes being an ambassador or minister—Isa. 49:5, 6. God's specially called servant was to gather up God's people and also to be light unto them.

It denotes furniture and implements—Num. 3:26; 31; 36. This is a very desirable and distinguished title for God's children who serve Him in His house. Obadiah's name was built on this Hebrew root.

צרר

BOUND: "But the soul...shall be bound in the bundle of life with the Lord thy God", (I Sam. 25:29). The Hebrew word *tsarar* means:

To press, compress, i.e., the soul is drawn up close to the Lord, or drawn with a divine energy that can be felt by him who is drawn.

A bundle—I Sam. 25:29 and Song of Sol. 1:13.

A purse—Gen. 42:35 and Prov. 7:20. Those bound up with God are like pieces of money well guarded and as safe as God.

כרע

BOW: "That unto me every knee shall bow and every tongue shall swear", (Isa. 45:23). *Kara,* the Hebrew root for *bow,* is used variously.

It means to kneel—Ezra 9:5. Heavy-hearted Ezra fell upon his knees and spread out his hands unto the Lord.

It indicates worship—II Chron. 7:3. This made an inspiring scene: bodies bowed in worship of God.

It was the custom in Ethiopia, according to the ancients, for women in labor to bring forth kneeling—I Sam. 4:19. God's kingdom may come sooner on earth if His people fall on their knees in prayer.

It means to cast down as enemies—Ps. 17:13. Every knee (of the good and the bad) shall bow and every tongue confess that Jesus Christ is Lord—Phil. 2:11.

כף

BOWL: "This was the dedication of the altar ... twelve silver bowls ...", (Num. 7:84). The Hebrew word for *bowl* is *caf,* the root of which yields colorful derivatives.

It means to load up or to put on a pack saddle. The dedication of the tabernacle was a great spiritual occasion in the life of Israel and required big men to bear heavy burdens.

It means weight; dignity; responsibility; authority—Job 33:7. Surely the tabernacle had worshippers who had these assets. Certainly the churches of today need such members.

One derivative means palms—Lev. 23:40. Men like these palms are needed for refreshing weary pilgrims.

Another means rock—Jer. 4:29. "Flee to the top of a rock." These rocks were supposed to have hollowed out places in them which served refugees. Peter's name was Cephas, very likely coming from this same root.

נצר

BRANCH: "And there shall come forth a rod out of the stem of Jesse, and a Branch shall grow out of His roots", (Isa. 11:1). *Natsar,* the Hebrew root for *Branch,* has great meanings.

It means to be verdant. The spiritual and physical ministry of Jesus has covered the hills and valleys with a beautiful and glorious green. He is the "Branch of the Lord", Isa. 4:2.

It means to shine. He does shine for He is "the Light of the world".

It means splendor. Such splendor has surrounded the head only of the "man whose name is the Branch", Zech. 6:12.

It means the offspring of God and man. This thing both incredible and believable could happen only to the righteous Branch who was raised unto David—Jer. 23:5.

It means a sprout or shoot. Jehovah revealed unto Zechariah (3:8) that He would bring forth His Servant the BRANCH. Jesus and His Father are One in redeeming the lost world.

אוד

BRAND: "Joshua ... a brand plucked out of the fire?", (Zech. 3:1, 2). *Ud* is the Hebrew word for *brand* and it has colors of courage in it.

It signifies stirring. Joshua was a fire poker that stirred Israel.

It signifies bending. Joshua, was striving to incline Israel after God and quit her backsliding.

It signifies a burden. Joshua, as others of his kind, willingly took on the load of bringing Israel to repentance.

It signifies a robustness. Was Joshua ever stronger than when he declared, "As for me and my house, we will serve the Lord"?

It signifies a cause; a reason; a circumstance. God's courageous leaders have many times been used by the Lord, to be fired as volleys from heaven to cause blessed changes in earth.

כאה

BREAK: "...Broken in heart...", (Ps. 109:16). *Kaah,* the Hebrew verb for *break,* has several meanings.

It means to upbraid by chiding harshly in order to break down.

It means to make sad—Ezek. 13:22. The idea here seems to be that of disheartening.

To be crushed is another idea brought out in Ps. 10:10. This leads to despondency which is a fall down toward despair.

It means to be afraid—Dan. 11:30. This coupled with grief was enough to make withdrawal advisable. The game was too rough, the task too difficult so the participants demurred, "took their dolls and went home".

It means to be frightened or intimidated, "whipped out of the land", (Job. 30:8). This is the principal idea in *kaah,* here translated *viler.*

So, we have the history of many church members: Chided; made sad; broken in heart; grieved; frightened out of God's vineyard.

שבר

BREAK: "The Lord...healeth the broken in heart, and bindeth up their wounds", (Ps. 147:2,3). *Shabar,* the Hebrew root for break, has many meanings.

It means a breach—Isa. 30:13. After a breach in a wall or in a heart, there cometh soon the fall to ruin.

It is used as a metaphor of the wound to the earth. The psalmist seeks God's help for cast off earth with the broken heart.

It means to quench thirst—Ps. 104:11. The idea is that thirst has been broken in its hold. Spiritual thirst may have a strong hold but can be broken.

It is used to tell of broken members of the body—Lev. 22:22. But none of the members broken will cause pain like the heart.

It means to tear in pieces—I Kings 13:26. Talk of a broken heart, here is a man who was torn to pieces by a lion because he had been disobedient to the word of the Lord.

It means destruction—Isa. 1:28. Sinners and they that forsake the Lord shall be broken down—shall be destroyed.

It means corn or grain—Gen. 42:1. The idea is that the grain has been ground in a mill and broken to pieces. God's children may be ground in the mill of afflictions but they are still in God's grainary.

It is used to describe repentance—Ps. 51:17. God will accept the one who has a broken spirit and a contrite heart.

It means astonishment—Jer. 8:21. Astonishment is the breaking of the mind into pieces but the next verse tells there is a balm in Gilead.

It means to measure—Job 38:10. That is, God appointed—measured off—the bounds for the sea. The God that stays proud waves and forbids their going further certainly can stop man.

But the Word that tells of the terrors and terribleness of a broken heart also tells that God is nigh them with a broken heart—Ps. 34:18.

נשׂא

BRING: "Bring an offering and come into His courts...", (Ps. 96:8). "He shall doubtless come again with rejoicing, bringing his sheaves with him", (Ps. 126:6). In other words we are to bring offerings to the Lord in the same spirit and manner that we will lift sheaves that we won by weeping and sowing. For the meaning of the Hebrew word *nasa* see *bear.*

אלה

BRING: "The Lord thy God is with thee, which brought thee up out of the land of Egypt", (Deut. 20.1). This word *bring* is used over a hundred times in the OT as being translated from the Hebrew word *alah* which is used so effectively to express

God's benevolent action toward His children. For its meaning, see *Ascend*.

בָּעַר

BURN: This Hebrew word *baar* is used to describe what happened to Moses' bush which the angel used for a pulpit—Exod. 3:2; the fire of the Lord whose anger was kindled—Num. 11:1; David's deepest thoughts and musings—Ps. 39:3; wickedness lifting up a smoke—Isa. 9:18; the Name of the Lord devouring—Isa. 30:27; salvation burning as a lamp thereby obtaining the peace of God for a city—Isa. 62:1. It means:

To feed upon, to eat, to consume like cattle feeding on grass.

To consume with fire—Ps. 83:15.

To be kindled, inflamed like an oven—Hos. 7:4.

To be brutish—Ps. 94:8. If man can do this in his weakness, the strength of God should keep us from inciting Him to anger. Him we ought to love, obey, and serve with gladness.

To take or put away as a nation—I Kings 22:47; evil—Deut. 17:7; a house or family—I Kings 14:10. This ought to bring nations and those who make up those nations to their knees.

To be stupid—Ps. 49:11.

Conflagration—Exod. 22:6.

קָנָה

BUY: "The Lord...is not he thy father that hath bought thee? hath he not made thee, and established thee?", (Deut. 32:6). *Qanah,* the Hebrew root for *bought,* has instructive meanings.

It means to found and to create—Gen. 14:19, 22. Because He created them, God is possessor of heaven and earth. He paid for creating them.

It means to possess—Prov. 8:22. God bought man in time and possessed him before time and after time.

It means to purchase—Ruth 4:9, 10. Boaz purchased all that was Mahlon's, including his wife. This is a strong word and was the one chosen to show that God purchased people, all of which moved Moses to sing gloriously—Deut. 32:1-43. (Gen. 47:23).

It means to recover—Isa. 11:11. God will raise an ensign for the nations which seek the Root of Jesse and will gather the dispersed from the four corners of the earth, and their dwelling and rest will be glorious.

הוה

CALAMITY: "A foolish son is the calamity of his father", (Prov. 19:13).

The Hebrew word here is *havvah.* It means: To breathe, to blow as a wind and must have an origin wherein sound and sense resemble.

To fall headlong, to strive eagerly—Job 37:6. Here God says to the snow, "Fall (rush down) upon the earth." A foolish son may be the fall of his father.

Ruin, destruction—Ps. 57:1.

As an interjection it means: Woe, Ho, Ah, (sinful nation)—Isa. 1:4. Alas, O, (as an expression of grief)—I Kings 13:30. How many parents have used such interjections when their sons felled them by their foolishness.

קרא

CALL: "Call unto me, and I will answer thee and...", (Jer. 33:3). This is a big word in the Bible. It is found nearly one thousand times. Over one-half of those times it is translated from this Hebrew word *qara* which means:

To cry, to clamor—Gen. 39:14, the sound expressing somewhat the meaning of it.

To call any one to oneself—Gen. 27:1. Early did man begin calling others to him to help him. Even so should we call for God.

To call a solemn assembly—Joel 1:14. To have church. To invite, to bid as to a feast (I Sam. 9:13). This is good for church members who ought to be out urging people to come in for a feast.

To propose an alliance, a call to peace—Deut. 20:10 and Judg. 21:13. No wonder sinners call upon God without whose pardon and alliance there is no peace.

To celebrate, e.g., a name—Ps. 79:6. Here a people have the wrath of God on them because they did not call on His Name.

To read, to recite aloud before an assembly—Josh. 8:34, 35 and Exod. 24:7.

To meet—Gen. 46:29. To meet God is to call upon Him and to call upon Him is to meet Him. This is sweet intercourse.

A partridge—Jer. 17:11. This bird was so called from its cry. That must be a healthy parish where people sound like partridges calling upon their heavenly Parent.

שלח

CAST: "Cast thy bread upon the waters: for thou shalt find it after many days", (Eccl. 11:1). The word *shalach* means:

To send—Gen. 38:17.

To send to do as "bind up the broken hearted"—Isa. 61:1. This was the office of Christ.

To shoot, to throw as arrows—I Sam. 20:20; as fire—Hos. 8:14. Oh, to have churches and messengers who will shoot the arrows of the Gospel and spread the holy fires to the uttermost parts.

To extend, put forth, stretch out, as the woman did her hand to the poor — Prov. 31:20; as the tree its branches—Jer. 17:8.

Dart, javelin, spear used to arm oneself—II Chron. 32:5. Thus a missionary might be considered well armed.

Sprouts, shoots—Isa. 16:8. Thus it can be said of a good church: "her branches are stretched out, they are gone over the sea."

A table, so called from its being extended, spread out—Ps. 23:5. The Lord prepares a table for His children, and they are to prepare a table for all nations and on it serve the gospel.

Table of Jehovah, i.e., an altar—Mal. 1:7.

רדף

CHASE: "One man of you shall chase a thousand: for the Lord your God, He it is that fighteth for you...", (Josh. 23:10). Yes, "the sound of a shaken leaf shall chase them; and they shall flee, as from a sword, and they shall fall when none pursueth." *Radaph,* the Hebrew root for *chase* and for *pursue,* has surprising meanings.

It means to follow—Ps. 23:6. Goodness and mercy follow unremittingly after the Shepherd's flock. Also, one is to follow after righteousness to find life—Prov. 21:21, and the Lord loves them that follow after righteousness—Prov. 15:9. One is to follow peace—Ps. 34:14, but not wickedness—Ps. 119:150. While darkness pursues after enemies—Nah. 1:8; evil pursues sinners—Prov. 13:21. The root is employed to signify following any one—Prov. 12:11, and especially is this profitable if one follows fully after the Lord.

It means to drive away—Isa. 17:13. The nations that spoil and rob shall be rebuked by the Lord and roll like tumble weeds before the whirlwind.

It means to persecute—Job 19:28. The idea is that the pursuit is in order to catch one to persecute. The wicked one goes about like a roaring lion seeking whom he may devour.

יסר

CHASTEN: "Blessed is the man whom thou chastenest, O Lord...", (Ps. 94:12). The Hebrew word *yasar* used here has a pointed meaning and will help one understand Heb. 12:6, which says, "Whom the Lord loveth He chasteneth...". It means:

To correct, to punish with blows—Deut. 22:18.

To admonish or to exhort, i.e., to chasten with words—Job 4:3.

To set right, to instruct—Isa. 28:26. God does operate on this wise in many areas and arenas of life.

Instruction with warning—Ps. 2:10.

Chastisement "of our peace was upon Him", (Isa. 53:5). This, of course, is the most famous use of this Hebrew root, and here the form that is used has the idea of the correcting going on and on.

נצח

CHIEF: "To the chief musician upon Aijeleth Shahar, A Psalm of David", (Heading of Ps. 22). *Natsach,* the Hebrew root for *chief,* has colorful significations.

It means to be famous, to shine, to be eminent and to be conspicuous. An effective worship service may be one-half music. Music leaders generally are prominent in the congregations' programs, even as was David.

It means to superintend—Ezra 3:9. Usually the music director does well in presiding over a choir and a congregation.

It means to lead in music—I Chron. 15:21.

It means to surpass, to excel—Dan. 6:4. The music master ought to excel in knowledge and performance of music.

It means splendor and glory—I Chron. 29:11. Of course this is better when it is for God.

It means purity, sincerity and truth—Hab. I:4. When the life is pure the tones are pure.

It means trust and confidence—Lam. 3:18. How often and how fully are these music men trusted.

It means juice and liquor—Isa. 63:3, 6. While in this passage the setting is not very musical but the Hebrew root means that juice will be pressed out which represents a good musician.

ראש

CHIEF: "And the king called for Jehoida the chief (priest)...he had done good in Israel, both toward God, and toward his house", (II Chron. 24:6, 16). *Rosh,* the Hebrew root for *chief,* has several colorful meanings and I shall use them to at least partially describe the Chief High Priest of all ages.

First it means priest—II Chron. 19:11. The priest was over the people in all matters of the Lord.

It means to be in the highest place—Job 29:25. The Lord sits on the great white throne which is the highest place in heaven and earth.

It signifies the head stone of the corner—Ps. 118:22. Jesus is the Head Stone and around Him is structured the whole of Christianity.

It is used to signify chief spices—Song of Sol. 4:14. The Lord perfumes the halls and temples of man's greatest religion.

It is used to signify the chief joy of God's people—Ps. 137:6. To His followers, Christ is the Chief Joy. Jesus is Zion's Joy.

It means beginning—Gen. 1:1. He was not only Chief but was so in the beginning.

It signifies a former state—Job 42:12. The Lord had a former state in former times before there was time.

It means first born—Gen. 49:3. The New Testament would confirm this as far as the Lord is concerned.

It means first in rank, dignity and excellence—Amos 6:1. He is King of kings and Lord of lords.

בחר

CHOOSE: "Choose you this day whom you will serve...we will serve the Lord", (Josh. 24:15). For the meaning of *bachar* see *Examine.*

בחר

CHOSEN: "He brought forth His people with joy and His chosen with gladness", (Ps. 105:43). "... To give drink to My people, My chosen", (Isa. 43:20). The Hebrew word *bachar* means:

To try, to examine, resulting in that which is tried, proved—Isa. 28:16. The primary idea seems to be that of a rubbing, cutting and scrutinizing—Isa. 48:10.

To select out the best, or to choose the best part of anything—Job 9:14. Did God select us to give the answer in this day and generation?

To choose for oneself—Gen. 13:11. So, God chose us for Himself, not for our sakes.

To like, to delight in—II Sam. 15:15 and Prov. 1:29. Could it be the Lord delighteth in me?

To be acceptable—Prov. 21:3. May both meditations and he who thus meditates be acceptable "in thy sight, O, Lord."

עיר

CITY: "...Put on thy beautiful garments, O Jerusalem, the Holy City", (Isa. 52:1). This Hebrew word *ir* travels over a colorful course to come to mean *city:*

To be hot, to heat, as a baker with an oven—Hos. 7:4.

To run hotly, that is swiftly, as a horse, and comes to designate a wild ass because of his swift unbridled course.

37

Heat of mind, i.e., terror, anxiety—Jer. 15:17. There is terror and anxiety in a great city that exceeds, per capita, that of any community smaller.

A busy, moving throng of men frequenting a place which makes a city—Num. 13:19. This favors a city.

City of God is Jerusalem called—Ps. 46:4. The Holy City—Isa. 52:1.

Watcher, a name given angels keeping watch over the souls of men—Dan. 4:13. What assurance can grow out of the fact that a city of busy, moving angels is set up to protect and provide for God's children.

טהר

CLEAN: "Create in me a clean heart, O God", (Ps. 51:10). *Tahar* means:

To shine, to be bright.

To be or become clean and pure—II Kings 5:12,13.

To be clean morally—Prov. 20:9. This cleanness is to be manifest and conspicuous.

To purify a land from idols which pollute—Ezek. 37:23.

To cleanse the temple—II Chron. 29:15, 18.

To cleanse men from their sins—Mal. 3:3.

Splendor, glory—Ps. 89:44.

Pureness of heart—II Chron. 30:19.

נקה

CLEANSE: "Cleanse thou me from secret faults", (Ps. 19:12). *Naqah* is the second Hebrew word usually translated *clean* and it means:

To be clean in a moral sense and thus be innocent—Ps. 19:13.

To be free from punishments, to be quit and go unpunished—Exod. 21:19; Num. 5:31.

To become clear of an obligation—Gen. 24:8, 41.

To be vacant, empty, i.e., desolate, as of a city—Isa. 3:26.

To pardon—Jer. 30:11.

בקע

CLEAVE: "They thirsted not when He led them through the deserts...He clave the rock also and the waters gushed out", (Isa. 48:21). The Hebrew for *cleave, Baqa,* has several meanings.

It means to divide—Exod. 14:16. God's providence often calls for tremendous operations.

It means to lay open—Isa. 48:21. That without which man would otherwise perish, God may break out.

It means to hatch—Isa. 34:15. So it is quite correct to say, Hatch up an idea. Meditation precedes incubation.

It means to break in upon as a city—II Kings 25:4. It may become necessary for the righteous to pray until God's power converts sinful Ninevehs.

It means valley—Deut. 8:7. Marvel: God founds valleys by cleaving mountains. Nothing is impossible with God.

דבק

CLEAVE: "Therefore shall a man leave his father and mother and shall cleave unto his wife", (Gen. 2:24). *Dabaq* means:

To adhere, to be glued, to stick—Jer. 13:11.

Silent from reverence and awe—Job 29:10.

To follow, i.e., cleave to a person so as to go where he goes—Ruth 2:8, 21.

To be attached, devoted, to hang upon and thus express love—Deut. 10:20. Those so in love with God make great Christians and on them a church can be built.

Made fast, permanence in adhesion—Job 38:38. Can anyone pluck God's children out of God's hand?

Soldering, welding, i.e., of metals—Isa. 41:7.

Joints of a coat of mail—I Kings 22:34. Had the fatally wounded king kept all of his armour in place and welded together, he might have lived. The Christian is to keep all of his armor on, in place, and welded together: salvation, faith, righteousness, etc.

All of these pieces come from the Lord, and only the Lord can weld them into a whole.

לבש

CLOTHE: "My soul shall be joyful in my God; for He hath clothed me with the garments of salvation", (Isa. 61:10). *Labash* used here is found some fifty other times. One may be clothed with cursing, with trembling, with strange apparel, with desolation, etc. The root of the word means:

To put a garment on oneself—Lev. 6:10, 11.

To put on splendor and majesty—Ps. 104:1.

To be covered with shame—Job 8:22. There are pastures clothed with flocks—Ps. 65:13 and raiment of those slain—Isa. 14:19.

There is a two-fold use of this word in Job 29:14: I put on righteousness and it put me on, i.e., without I am clothed with righteousness as a garment, and within it fills me wholly. Also, in Judg. 6:34, this word is used to report that the Spirit of the Lord puts on one, i.e., to fill him, to come upon him.

בוֹא

COME: "O, come let us worship and bow down; let us kneel before our Maker", (Ps. 95:6). The word *come* is found in the Bible nearly 2,000 times. The Hebrew word *bo* is found some 1,000 times and means:

To go or come in, to enter as a bride unto her husband—Josh. 15:18. How fitting and fine for the church as the bride to go in unto her husband, the Lord, and bow down and worship.

To go out and to come in, spoken of one's daily life—I Sam. 29:6. This is the way a reputation is established.

To go out and to come in before a people so as to lead them—II Chron. 1:10. Solomon led Israel closer to God in this fashion.

To go in and out in order to have intercourse—Josh. 23:12. God wants us to come in unto Him. To that end were we made. God would be lonely without us.

40

To come to a person, attain unto him, be more equal to him—II Sam. 23:19. They who company with the Lord may become more like Him. "We are a part of all whom we have met."

To walk, to live—Ps. 40:7. Those coming to Him ought to live for Him and walk with Him.

To be brought to one—Lev.14:2. Let the High Priest bring those unto Him whose leprous sin needs cleansing.

נחם

COMFORT: "...Thou, Lord hast holpen me and comforted me", (Ps. 86:17). This Hebrew word, *nacham,* has a sound that helps express the meaning of it: to sigh, to pant, to groan. It means:

To lament, to grieve, and this emotion leads to having pity for others, like in Jeremiah 15:5, where the Lord is reported as having compassion. The sighing is also expressed in Psalm 90:13.

To repent—Exod. 13:17. To grieve in regard to one's own deeds is to repent, to sigh—Gen. 6:6, 7.

To aid—Isa. 12:1. This is comfort indeed when God comes to our side—Isa. 49:13. Singing will replace crying when the Lord comforts Zion and turns her deserts into gardens—Isa. 51:3. Jehovah is the only one who can do this—Isa. 52:9.

Nehemiah—Neh. 1:1, 8. This man was helped and comforted by his God so much that his name is "aided of Jehovah."

דבר

COMMAND (COMMANDMENT): "And he laid his hands upon him, and gave him a charge, as the Lord commanded...", (Num. 27:23). The words *command* and *commandments* are found in the Bible about eight hundred times. In most cases the translation is from *tsavah,* for the meaning of which, see *Appoint.* The Hebrew word to be considered here is *dabar* and means:

To set in a row, to arrange in order, to connect.

To lead, to guide, to drive as flocks to pasture. It is easy to conclude that God does all of this for us through His commandments.

To follow, to be behind. Here is the idea that once God sets His Words, His law, His program in order, it is the principal business of His children to follow fully as did Caleb—Num. 14:24, and get as great a blessing as did he.

To arrange in order, to speak, to set words in order—Prov. 25:11, Exod. 6:29.

To promise—Deut. 19:8. There is a close relation between command and vow.

To sing—Judg. 5:12. Why should not all Christians join with Deborah and sing as God protects His own?

To ask in marriage—Song of Sol. 8:8. Divine commands are issued to those who are the bride of heaven.

Thing, affair, business—Esth. 6:1. A great business: God orders and man obeys.

A cause—Josh. 5:4. There is reason for God's commands.

A suit of law—Exod. 18:16. God the great Law-giver is at the same time heaven's Attorney and man's Advocate.

Floats, rafts—I Kings 5:9. God's words become life rafts to men sinking in sin. Here in Kings is the report on how cedar logs from Lebanon were drawn to sea, fixed in rafts, and floated to be used to build the temple for the Lord. In Latin, *sermo* and *dissero* is an arrangement of words, which arrangement, if it has God's blessing upon it, may be the means of saving souls.

גָלֵל

COMMIT: "Commit thy way unto the Lord; trust also in Him; and He shall bring it to pass", (Ps. 37:5). "Commit thy works unto the Lord...", (Prov. 16:3). For the meaning of the Hebrew word *asah,* translated *commit* in Lev. 5:17 and in many others, see *accomplish*. The Hebrew word *galal* used in these two passages means:

To roll, e.g., stones—Gen. 29:3. Just as the well was opened by rolling away the stone, so may one's life become a well of water springing up if sin is rolled away.

To roll away, to roll off of anyone—Josh. 5:9. Note it is the Lord that does the rolling off of reproach.

To roll off of oneself onto another—Ps. 37.5. This may read: devolve thy way, thine affairs, upon Jehovah.

Wheel, ring, whirlwind, scroll, skull, ball—all of these and more

42

grow out of this widely extended Hebrew root. Also in the word is the imitation of the sound connected with these objects.

Heavy business, weighty, worthy or worth notice is in the wagon-like weight of this sound-full word. Iniquities are all of that and more, so that when the Lord begins rolling them from the back of the praying penitent, all of these heavy objects will likely come into mind.

שׁיחַ

COMMUNE: "Stand in awe and sin not: commune with your own heart upon your bed and be still. Selah", (Ps. 4:4). The most often used Hebrew word translated *commune* (Gen. 18:33) is *dabar*. For its meaning see *command. Siach,* which is used in the quoted passage means:

To bring out, to produce like sprout and bloom.

To speak, to speak to some one or to something—Job. 12:8.

To sing—Ps. 145:5.

To praise, to celebrate—Ps. 105:2.

To lament, to complain—Ps. 55:17.

To meditate—Ps. 143:5 and Isa. 53:8. Thinking about God's work and surveying the Suffering Servant makes one say, who shall declare it? Job was given to meditation and devotion before God—Job 15:4.

Bush—Job 30:7. There was great communion between man and His God at a bush when Moses saw it ablaze.

חָבַר

COMPANION: "I am a companion of all them that fear thee, and of them that keep thy precepts", (Ps. 119:63). Much is involved in a fellowship with God's people. *Chabar,* the Hebrew root for *companion,* has several meanings.

It means to join together—Exod. 28:7. God's grace binds His children together.

It means to form a league or an alliance—II Chron. 20:35-37. While this did not turn out good, experiences report that blessings accrue to him who forms a partnership with God and with His people.

43

It means a wife—Mal. 2:14. Jesus chose to call God's people the bride and Himself the Bridegroom.

It means an associate—Job 41:6. Fishermen formed partnerships and God's workmen do the same.

It means a society—Hos. 6:9. While this is in an evil sense here, there are holy societies of God's chosen meeting in churches.

It means a charmer—Ps. 58:5. A magic charmer was one who bound others to himself so closely that he could direct them. So does Jesus for His followers.

סבב

COMPASS: "Thou art my hiding place; thou shalt preserve me from trouble; thou shalt compass me about with songs of deliverance. Selah'', (Ps. 32:7). "...But he that trusteth in the Lord, mercy shall compass him about'', (Ps. 32:10). *Sabab* means:

To turn back after anyone, to follow—II Kings 9:19. To have goodness and mercy to follow one all the days of life is to have much, if not all.

To be conferred, turned about—I Kings 2:15. This is heaven's degree conferred on undeserving man.

To go about continually like a watchman—Song of Sol. 3:3. One is safe when God causes deliverance and mercy to guard him.

To surround like a river surrounds a land—Gen. 2:13. Or, like the brothers' sheaves gathered around Joseph's, to do reverence to his—Gen. 37:7. I think I would like to do reverence to deliverance and mercy from God that surround me.

To surround in order to protect and defend—Jer. 31:22. Here the word is used to describe a new thing: a woman protecting a man.

Turn of things, course of events as proceeding from God—I Kings 12:15. God orders, God ordains. He has mercy on whom He will have mercy.

Circuit, on every side round about—Deut. 12:10. The old-fashioned circuit-riding preacher went 'round and 'round looking after the churches. Even so, and much more grandly does God look after His own.

Neighbors, those round about—Jer. 48:39. Salvation and mercy make wonderful neighbors.

Environs, circumjacent, places round about—Jer. 33:13. With such environs as promised by Psalm 32:7, 10 a Christian ought to grow in life and service for his God.

רחם

COMPASSION: "He hath made His wonderful works to be remembered: the Lord is gracious and full of compassion", (Ps. 111:4). "Full of compassion" is found here and in Ps. 78:38; 86:15; 112:4; 145:8. The Hebrew word *racham* means:

To love—Ps. 18:1.

To cherish, to soothe, with the primary idea lying in a gentle emotion of mind—Exod. 33:19.

A carrion-vulture, because of its tenderness to its young.

Womb—Isa. 46:3, Job 24:20.

Damsel, female, from the womb as peculiar to the sex—Judg. 5:30. So, God the Father, strong and mighty, is also gentle like a mother.

The inner parts, as the seat of gentle affections—I Kings 3:26.

Favor, mercy—Ps. 40:11. Compassion becomes most exciting when it precipitates favors to one. "God so loved the world that He gave His only begotten Son..."

ידה

CONFESS: "When the heaven is shut up...because they have sinned against thee; yet, if they pray toward this place, and confess thy name, and turn from their sin...". (II Chron. 6:26). The Hebrew word *yadah* means:

To cast, e.g., a stone—Lam. 3:53. To broadcast, to proclaim the Name of the Lord is to meet one requirement for reopening a shut-up heaven.

To profess, to confess with the hand thrown out, to bare one's sins—Ps. 32:5.

To give thanks, to sing—Ps. 30:12. The person is moving into the atmosphere where he might get the blessing promised.

To point out oneself as guilty, to accuse, to incriminate—Dan. 9:4, 5. Then, and likely only then, will one be in a position to receive blessings from God.

כטח

CONFIDENCE: "For thus saith the Lord God,...In returning and rest shall ye be saved; in quietness and confidence shall be your strength", (Isa. 30:15). "In the fear of the Lord is strong confidence", (Prov. 14:26). The Hebrew word *betach* means:

To trust, to confide, to place hope. He that does these things in the Lord utterly shall have blessings beyond count.

To cast oneself or one's cares upon any one—Ps. 22:8. This notable passage reports in prophecy Christ's complete trust in His Father; and we have the same Father.

To be confident, to feel secure without fear—Judg. 18:7, 10, 27. The people of Laish were secure and quiet until the children of Dan smote them. The people of God are secure against any and all who would disturb. "Behold, God is my salvation; I will trust and not be afraid...", (Isa. 12:2).

Tranquility—Job 12:6. There may appear to be a want of care and caution on the part of God's children who enjoy a great security.

כון

CONFIRM: "For thou hast confirmed to thyself thy people Israel to be a people unto thee for ever", (II Sam. 7:24). To confirm is a big assignment for religion. It has been misunderstood in some circles. Here the Hebrew word *kun* means:

To set upright, to establish—Ps. 40:2. The Lord does it.

To adjust, to direct (as arrows)—Ps. 7:12. Like an arrow, he is confirmed who is well placed in the bow and directed at a certain goal. Life then has an aim.

To found, as a sanctuary—I Kings 6:19. To set up an altar—Ezra 3:3. This is biblical confirmation.

To fix, to fill with hope—Ps. 57:7. A grand result of confirmation.

To be certain, to be sure—I Sam. 26:4 and 23:23. Assurance comes to those confirmed of God.

A small cake, a wafer—Jer. 7:18. From the Hebrew root comes the word used here. This is a good title for him who has been confirmed of God in the things of God for God's glory. He becomes a spiritual wafer for a society that hungers for the better.

בּוֹשׁ

CONFOUND: "Our fathers trusted in thee:...and were not confounded", (Ps. 22:4, 5). For the meaning of *bosh,* see *ashamed.*

בּוֹשׁ

CONFUSION: "Let me never be put to confusion", (Ps. 71:1). For the meaning of *bosh,* see *Ashamed.*

קהל

CONGREGATION: "...The congregation of the Lord...", (Num. 16:3, 4). *Congregation* derives from a Hebrew root *qahal* which has interesting meanings.

It means to call together or to convoke—Num. 8:9; 20:8. The Lord spoke to Moses saying, "Call the people together to watch water flow from the stricken rock".

It means a nation or a company of nations—Gen. 35:11. There are, after all, only two nations in the world. One is God's nation.

It means a preacher—The Title of Ecclesiastes. *Koheleth,* by which the book by Solomon is designated, means a convoker who addresses a public assembly in a discourse on human things. The orator called the assembly together in a certain place.

יד

CONSECRATE: "Consecrate yourselves today to the Lord", (Exod. 32:29). This little word *yad* means:

Hand—II Kings 15:19.

The hand to aid anyone—I Sam. 22:17. When we consecrate ourselves, it means we give a hand to the Lord.

The hand of the Lord is upon one to aid him—Ezra 7:28.

47

The hand of the Lord upon one in the sense of the Spirit being upon one so as to make him a prophet—Ezek. 1:3.

A pledge of fidelity, a promise—II Kings 10:15. We use the hand to express our promise to God. We may give the hand to God's prophet or minister.

Submission to the Lord expressed by giving the hand—II Chron. 30:8.

Bounty, liberality—I Kings 10:13. That is, the open hand signifies that everything is given.

Near—Judg. 11:26. That is, at hand, by the side of, near. The consecrated will be near the Lord.

בִּין

CONSIDER: "O that they were wise, that they understood this, that they would consider their latter end", (Deut. 32:29). *Bin* means:

To discern, to perceive—Prov. 7:7. This is a good verse on selection of company.

To feel—Ps. 58:9. If a pot can feel thorns, why can man not feel sin?

To understand, to be acquainted with—Ps. 19:12. We need to give earnest consideration to our errors.

To be wise, intelligent—Job 42:3. One who considers will approach unto things too wonderful to know.

Between, i.e. difference between—Mal. 3:18. Here as elsewhere, there is the thought of separation.

Umpire, champion, go-between—I Sam. 17:4, 23. Certainly this is not far removed from thinking and making decisions.

תַּנְחוּמוֹת

CONSOLATIONS: "Are the consolations of God small...", (Job. 15:11). *Tanchumoth* comes from the root *nacham* and means:

To grieve, to have pity, to have compassion—Ps. 90:13. Here it is hoped and urged for the Lord to come near and have compassion.

48

To console—Isa. 54:11. Here consolation comes from a promise of security.

To comfort, including the idea of rendering aid—Isa. 51:3. That is consolation indeed when the Lord offers aid to His children since we need help along with sympathy. The Father's compassion has swift feet and a train of excellent blessings following after.

חזק

CONTINUE: "Yea, also I *continued* in the work of this wall...", (Neh. 5:16). This strong word *hazak* means:

To bind fast, to gird tight, e.g. bands, ligatures—Isa. 28:22. Nehemiah was tied to the word of the Lord—Neh. 5:15.

To hold fast, to cleave, like the tree held Absalom—II Sam. 18:9.

To make strong and firm, like the binding and girding of muscles and loins makes one stronger—I Sam. 17:50. Oh, to have men thus girded continuing in the Master's work.

To help is an idea in this work—II Chron. 28:20. Oh, to have crowds so given in the service of the Lord.

To be established, confirmed—II Kings 14:5. This sort of workman will get God's work done. He will persevere. Like Sears, Roebuck and Company, he will continue in business.

Continuing in strength and spirit—Isa. 8:11. Just as God's hand and His Spirit impel me, so will I keep on keeping on in His work.

Hezekiah, strength of Jehovah—Isa. 1:1. A good name indeed will I possess, if I continue in the building up of God's Kingdom, although in a small measure, this is one of the qualities built into this name.

דכא

CONTRITE: "The Lord saveth: such as be of a *contrite* spirit.", (Ps. 34:18). THis Hebrew word *dakka* means:

To break in pieces—Ps. 8:11. Note the Lord is the one who did this to Egypt, not Pharaoh with an oration or by punishment.

To crush—Isa. 3:15. Just so, must the sinner be ground and beaten down before the Lord can save.

49

To be bruised and smitten—Isa. 53:5. Jesus the Head was thus bruised, should sinners go free who desire to be members of His body?

To be humbled—Jer. 44:10. Unless all pulpit and pew members are humble, how shall they expect their God to bless?

To wound severely unto sickness—Isa. 53:10. This same verse promises prosperity from the Lord, but *after* the wounding.

דֶּרֶךְ

CONVERSATION: "To him that ordereth his *conversation* aright will I shew the salvation of God." (Ps. 50:23). Here *derek* means:

To tread—Isa. 63:2.

To enter a place by walking into it—Mic. 5:5. Sweet converse that, when we walk in "The Way."

To bend—Jer. 9:3. Here the people are bending their tongues like bows.

Double way—Prov. 28:18. The sense is that one is perverse in his double way, or is a double-tongued person who is perverse.

A journey—I Kings 19:4.

A path—Gen. 3:24.

The mode or manner of one's life—I Kings 16:16.

A coin—Ezra 2:69. This is a *daric,* a gold coin. The connection with conversation could be in the saying that "money talks."

שׁוּב

CONVERT: "The law of the Lord is perfect converting the soul", (Ps. 19:7). For meaning of *shub* see *Backsliding.*

מִקְרָא

CONVOCATION: "Six days shall work be done but the seventh day is the Sabbath of rest, an holy convocation", (Lev. 23:3). *Quara* means:

To call to any one—even loudly cry—Judg. 18:23.

To cry for help—Ps. 22:3. When a church is called together,

50

it is to bring in God's Kingdom in that place by the will of God.

To proclaim like a herald—Isa. 40:6.

To call one to himself—Gen. 27:1. In public worship God is calling His people to himself.

To convoke a solemn assembly—Joel 1:14, i.e. to have church.

To propose an alliance—Deut. 20:10. God's people do well when in an alliance with God.

To read aloud or to recite before an assembly—Josh. 8:34, 35. This occurs at church.

יכח

CORRECT: "Happy is the man whom God correcteth", (Job 5:17). "For whom the Lord loveth He *correcteth*", (Prov. 3:12). *Yakach* means:

To be in the sunshine, to be clear, to appear. A Child of God ought to enjoy this sort of correction.

To argue, to show, to prove—Job 13:15. God can prove His point.

To argue down, confute and convict—Job 32:12. We need convincing regarding sin.

To rebuke, to reprove, i.e. to chasten with words—Job 6:25. God's children ought to kiss the chastening rod and be glad.

To reform by chastening—Job 5:17. This reformation is good for the whole world.

To judge, to decide—Isa. 11:3, 4. No wonder the Lord said, "Come let us reason together", (Isa. 1:18).

Jachin, one whom God makes firm or founds by correcting—Gen. 46:10. Oh, to have more solid timber for building churches.

שחת

CORRUPT: "The earth also was *corrupt* before God", (Gen. 6:11). *Shachath* means:

To destroy—Gen. 9:11. To corrupt is to destroy wickedly.

Compassion—Amos 1:11; wisdom—Ezek. 28:17.

To act wickedly—Deut. 9:12. Here the people left God's way.

To destroy one's way is to corrupt or pervert it. This becomes wickedness in a high place—Gen. 6:12.

To lay waste—Exod. 8:20.

A pit—Ps. 7:15. A miry cistern becomes a pit-fall for those who are victims of treachery, plots, corruption. Corruption in high places will put somebody into the very low places.

Grave—Ps. 30:9, and to perish in it—Job 33:28. Corruption is sin and how many has it put into the grave.

יעץ

COUNSEL: "I will bless the Lord who hath given me counsel", (Ps. 16:7). *Yaats,* used in this verse, is the root on which *Counsellor* is built—Isa. 9:6. It means:

To advise—Prov. 11:14. Advice is everywhere sought and everywhere given, but Jesus is the only perfect Advisor.

A minister of state—I Chron. 27:32. Our Lord is the Minister of State of the whole world.

To determine, to decree—Ps. 62:4. The encyclic command of the Head of the church is found in Mat. 28:19, 20.

To care for—Ps. 16:6, 7. This Counsellor is not only able to prescribe, but also to fill the prescription.

To guide—Ps. 32:8. The Lord gives a holy gesture to his humble servant in the council chamber.

To predict—Num. 24:14. This Counsellor can give perfect advice because he foresees his client's doings.

To decide—I Kings 12:28. This is the climax of a counselling service: The confused seeker is enlightened and makes a decision. He has listened to his Lord and has taken his advice.

עצה

COUNSEL: "The Lord of hosts which is wonderful in *counsel.",* Isa. 28:29. This heavy word *etsab* means:

To advise—Ps. 119:24.

Plan or purpose—Isa. 19:3. When God advises, He has a most holy purpose in mind, and woe unto him who heeds not.

Prudence and wisdom—Isa. 11:2. Here the Branch which came out of Jesse is this wisdom, and eternal welfare is his who accepts this advice.

Building materials—Jer. 6:6. Children of God who take their Father's advice make fine timbers for building churches. Christ, their Head, is called Counsellor—Isa. 9:6.

יעץ

COUNSELLOR: "His name shall be called Wonderful, Counsellor, The Mighty God...", (Isa. 9:6). For the meanings of *yaats,* the Hebrew root for *Counsellor,* see *counsel,* and page 52.

מראה

COUNTENANCE: "A man of God came unto me, and his *countenance* was like the countenance of an angel of God", (Judg. 13:6). *Mareh* describes a very influential quality and means:

To be well fed. Ofttimes a countenance that makes a favorable impression is associated with being well fed, while leanness of body and soul and spirit are thought of together.

Sight and vision—Exod. 3:3.

Appearance and looks—Exod. 24:17. A man's face tells who he is.

Form—Dan. 10:18. One's form supplements his face in making a total countenance. No wonder a Christian can be known by his walk.

Mirror—Exod. 38:8. How much there is in this one Hebrew word used by the Lord's scribe to tell the total looks of a man. The looking glass tells and so does one's countenance.

Crown of ornament—Jer. 13:18. Head dress is very important to many, but countenance is important to all.

אמץ

COURAGE: "Be strong and of a good *courage"*, (Josh. 1:6, 9, 18). *Amatz* is a firm word and means:

To be alert and active, to be swift-footed and strong in the feet, as if to stand against the enemy.

Alertness of mind and an undaunted spirit, as opposed to feeblemindedness and sinking knees.

To prevail over anyone or over unfavorable situations—Ps. 18:17.

To repair or restore a building—II Chron. 24:13. Oft times man's spirit needs the same.

To set fast, i.e. make strong—Ps. 80:17. When the Lord sets fast a man's heart, it will not fail any sooner than a fast color will fade.

To resolve, to make oneself firm or to be steadfastly minded— Ruth 1:18. Ruth firmly set her course of spirit and action.

Amaziah—II Kings 12:32 (whom Jehovah strengthens). A church can be built out of Amaziahs.

ברית

COVENANT: "Behold, I will send my messenger...even the messenger of the *covenant*", (Mal. 3:1). *Berith* is a great word in a great verse and means:

To reach across, like a cross bar—Exod. 36:31. God's covenant is like a strong cross bar across the heavens reaching from eternity to eternity, all the while protecting man under it.

A bolt for fastening a gate—Judg. 16:3. The covenant locks and unlocks the door to heaven. Whoever has Jesus can go into heaven.

A league between private persons and friends—Isa. 18:3; between parties contracting marriage—Mal. 2:14.

Promise of God—Isa. 59:21.

Precepts of God—Jer. 11:2.

Messenger and introducer of the new promise—Isa. 42:6. This must be Jesus.

כסה

COVER: "Blessed is he whose transgression is forgiven, whose sin is *covered"*, (Ps. 32:1). *Kasah* means:

To pardon, to forgive (when used in relation to sin)—Ps. 85:2.

To put on something, or to cover oneself—Prov. 12:16. Ever and always will men want to cover their shortcomings: Adam in the garden using leaves and sinners today using Christ's blood.

To hide, to conceal—Prov. 12:23.

To wrap oneself up—Isa. 59:6. Here people were trying to cover their sins with works, in vain; but no wonder, since such sins had separated them from their God whom they desired very much.

A present given as a penalty or as an atonement—Gen. 20:16. This is the brightest color in this colorful word. Jesus becomes such atonement for all sinners. He is given as the ransom price. He redeems those penalized who appropriate Him by faith.

A garment—Deut. 22:12.

עטה

COVER: "Who coverest thyself with light as with a garment: who stretcheot out the heavens like a curtain", (Ps. 104:2). *Atah,* the Hebrew root for *cover,* is used in various ways.

It is used to cover oneself, how indescribable the action in the verse quoted above.

It means to wrap up or to roll up—Jer. 43:12. Nebuchadnez-zar wrapped himself up in the land of Egypt as a shepherd in a cloak but God wraps the heavens and His people around Him.

It means to become languid or to faint—Song of Sol. 1:7. The fair bride (Church) was seeking her Beloved (Groom) so ardently that she fainted. Her mind was covered with darkness. God's mind was never covered with darkness but with light.

It is used to describe rain as blessings that cover the man who loves and dwells in the sanctuary—Ps. 84:6

ברא

CREATE: "In the beginning God *created...*", (Gen. 1:1). *Bara* is used in the first verse in the Bible, and properly so, since it has much to do with all things that come to be. It means·

55

To produce—Gen. 5:1. God, and God only, could, can or ever will be able to make or change man.

To create something new—Gen. 2:3.

To beget, to be born—Exod. 21:30. Here is a record of a man being who was not. So it is in the creative work of God. *Bara* says whatever God wanted, He willed it; and it came forth out of the womb of the mind that willed it. This is exclusive with God.

עקלקל

CROOKED: "Such as turn aside to their crooked ways", (Ps. 125:5). This long and crooked word *aqalqal* means:

To twist, to wrest—Hab. 1:4.

Winding—Judg. 5:6. This means side roads or devious and unfrequented by-paths. A man is really lost, when he is not on the main road which is He who said "I am the Truth."

Tortuous—Isa. 27:1. This is an epithet of a serpent and well might be applied to the crooked man.

מעקשים

CROOKED: "I will make darkness light before them, and *crooked* things straight." (Isa. 42:16). Here the long crooked word *maaqashshim* means:

To turn the wrong way. His is a crooked and wearisome road who turns the wrong way.

To pervert—Mic. 3:9. Perverseness is a sin, and more than that, it is a crooked one.

A perverse mind or perverseness in mind—Prov. 11:20. This kind of a mind will lead him who has it in many crooked and painful paths. He needs to have the mind of Christ.

False speech—Prov. 4:24. Here crooked language becomes a manifesto on a crooked man with his crooked mind.

כתר

CROWN: "And the king loved Esther above all the women...so that he set the royal crown upon her head", (Esther 2:17). Esther deserved a crown for her effective intercession for her people. *Kathar,* the Hebrew verb for crown, has different shades of sense.

One is going in a circle waiting and delaying—Job 36:2. Job's wisdom shone as a crown for his head.

One is to surround—Ps. 142:7. The righteous compass about to make a beautiful crown for any assembly.

Another is to be adorned as with knowledge—Prov. 14:18. Knowledge in a head is crown splendid for that head.

Another is chapter—II Chron. 4:12. The chapiters were brass columns about a man's height resting on tops of the pillars supporting the great building. There are men supporting churches who outshine polished chapiters.

רנן

CRY: "My heart and my flesh cry out for the living God", (Ps. 84:2). Nearly five hundred times the word *cry* is found in the Bible. About a dozen different words are translated *cry,* but of them all *rannan* seems to be the most colorful and is found in a powerful text. It means:

To give forth a tremulous sound, like music—Prov. 29:6. This sound resembles the whining of a mast in the wind, and have not men sounded like that when they were filled with the Holy Ghost? This sound also resembles that of a roaring torrent. Does not man who is having a Jacoban wrestle with the Lord sound like that?

To shout or to utter cries of joy—Job 38:7. There is shouting all up and down when stars and sons of God both praise the Lord.

To praise someone—Ps. 51:15.

Ostrich—Job 39:13. This Hebrew word is employed to label this bird because the bird makes a continuous whirring sound with its wings, or because of a continuous wailing cry as if needing something. Oh, that man would be more like the ostrich in this respect; then would he "pray without ceasing."

כוֹם

CUP: "My cup runneth over", (Ps. 23:5). There are five different Hebrew words used in the OT all of which are translated *cup.* One of these is *kos* which is used about five times as much as all the others put together and it has several denotements.

It means a receptacle or vessel. At once this brings to mind many pictures where the cup plays a large part physically and/or morally, e.g., Matt. 20:22; 26:39.

It probably means a pouch for storing valuables—Ps. 116:13. A cup with salvation in it becomes a treasured purse.

It means a lot or portion—Ps. 11:6; 16:5. Although it is a dread to drink some cups that are served there will be delight by and by as it was for our Lord.

It means a Pelican according to ancients. This reminder is timely to those who have seen this bird with the pouch under his throat—quite sizable. Those who hunger after the spiritual might wish to own a receptacle of such size.

רפא

CURE: "For thus saith the Lord...I will cure them and will reveal unto them the abundance of peace and truth", (Jer. 33:4, 6). This is a great text and context and *rapha* is a great word. For its meaning see *Heal*.

ארר

CURSE: "Ye are cursed with a curse: for ye have robbed me, even this whole nation...saith the Lord of hosts", (Mal. 3:9). *Arar* means:

To detest—Mal. 2:2. One thinking upon what this means would soon be flying to God and begging for reconciliation.

To abhor—Num. 22:6. To partly conceive what it would mean to have God so abhor us that He would order that we be disposed of, would cause one to fall upon his face before Him from Whom he has stolen.

To become infamous and accused—Gen. 3:14. This ought to prevent one from incurring the wrath of God.

A plague caused by a certain water—Num. 5:22. God can heal and God can hurt.

Ararat—Gen. 8:4. Note when God chose to destroy the earth with water, He led Moses to name the highest place by this awful word. What word could be used to describe the low places?

58

כרת

CUT: "The Lord will cut off the man that doeth this...", (Mal. 2:12). There is another Hebrew word, *garaz,* translated *cut* in II Chron. 26:21. "He was cut off from the house of the Lord," which means a shorn land, a desert. This word *karath* means:

To cut down trees—Deut. 19:5.

To cut and to destroy persons—Deut. 20:20.

To be cut off from one's city or country, i.e. driven into exile—Zech. 14:2. When God's sword of wrath cuts, it cuts deep indeed.

Death—Exod. 31:14. The Godless are not deathless.

To fail—I Kings 2:4. This is a type of death.

To be separated—Josh. 3:13. Jesus said He was the vine and that we were the branches. When we become separated from Him, or are never joined to Him vitally, then are we dead in trespasses indeed.

To withdraw—I Sam. 20:15. This is a smooth cutting off, but perhaps more painful.

Executioner, a Cherethite—II Sam. 15:18. (See I Sam. 5:4).

גדע

CUT OFF: "All of the horns of the wicked also will I cut off; but the horns of the righteous will be exalted", (Ps. 75:10). *Gada,* Hebrew for *cut off,* has several meanings.

It means to cut down as felling a tree—Isa. 9:10. When the kingdom of the Prince of Peace is set up, enemy kingdoms will be cut down.

It means to demote or break down—Isa. 14:12. This one that said he would be like the most High—Isa. 14:14, is made the most low.

It means to reduce blessing and power—Ps. 75:10. God will break the power of the wicked but give power to the prayers.

It means impetuousness—the king God uses to get victories for His people—Judg. 6:8. Gideon's name is built on this root and it was he who received signs of God's favor.

59

חוּל

DANCE: "Let them praise his name in the *dance.*", (Ps. 149:3). *Chul* is translated *dance* fifteen times in the OT and it means:

To whirl in a circle—Judg. 21:21.

To be whirled like a whirlwind—Jer. 23:19.

To writhe or twist oneself with pain—Isa. 13:8.

To quake or tremble—Deut. 2:25.

To be strong—Job 20:21. Quite often the idea of strength comes from the idea of twisting and binding. Of course he who dances before the Lord will get strength.

Sand—Exod. 2:12. Likely comes from the notion of rolling and being whirled by the wind.

In Isa. 30:16 *chagag* is used and translated dancing, and it means a sacred leaping in celebrating a holy day—Exod. 5:1; to reel or be giddy like a drunkard—Ps. 107:27.

Raqad used in Eccl. 3:4, another Hebrew word for dancing, and means to leap, to skip for joy or because of fear—Ps. 114:6.

בָּגַד

DECEIT: "They have dealt treacherously (deceitfully) against the Lord", (Hos. 5:7). The Hebrew for *deceit* is *Bagad* which has several colorful meanings.

It means to deal treacherously—Lam. 1:2. Captive Jerus was in a miserable condition because she had been treacherously dealt with. More, she had leanness—Isa. 24:16.

It means a bed coverlet—I Sam. 19:13. The idea being that though the bed may not be clean, it may be hiding something and the viewer may not know it.

It means a robe or outer garment—Gen. 39:12. It is not easy to tell what may be underneath.

It means to spoil—Isa. 21:2. The spoiling takes place without the spoiled knowing it. Is not the man foolish who thinks he will get by taking blessings from Him with Whom he has dealt faithlessly?

It means to deceive—Exod. 21:8. One who deceives his spouse

is like an unclean bed under a coverlet or a filthy man in a robe.

To deal falsely—Prov. 11:3. Perverseness is untrueness.

פתה

DECEIVE: "Take heed to yourselves that your heart be not deceived, and ye turn aside, and serve other gods, and worship them", (Deut. 11:16). This verse is in the midst of a great sermon of Moses to Israel and this work "deceived" derives from *patha* which has very colorful meanings.

It means to open—Job 31:27. The idea is that the heart is open like that of a child and the enticer stealthily moves in.

It means to expand. That is, one's mind is so spread out that the seducer can do his ugly work. There is enough tolerance for Satan's teacher to get in.

It means to persuade—Prov. 25:15. The teacher may be able to pry open the mind of his pupil with his personality or skill and then sway him.

It means to delude—Prov. 24:28. The lips are opened for the purpose of flooding the listener with words meant to deceive. (Note: All of the above could be used positively by ministers of the gospel).

It means to let oneself be enticed—Jer. 20:10. The "familiars" watch for one's halting in order for a chance at prevailing against him. Satan, like a serpent, may be coiled at one's doorstep.

פרש

DECLARATION: "And all the acts of his power and of his might, and the declaration of the greatness of Mordecai...are they not written in the book...", (Esther 10:2). *Parash,* the Hebrew root for *declaration* is very rich with the main idea being *exposition.*

It means to show distinctly and specifically—Lev. 14:12. The object of the pulpiteer was to show the mind of the Lord to the people.

It means to cleave or to divide. The faithful teachers will rightly divide the Word of Truth.

It means to separate or to distinquish. God's Word will more likely be appropriated when it is separated into distinct portions all the while appearing to be a part of the whole.

It means to spread out. The teacher needs to spread out God's word on the table for the hungry souls before him.

It means to distend like the feet in riding a horse. Great good is accomplished when divine revelation is stretched out so people can see the many rich colors in it.

It means accurate plainness—Ezra. 4:18. The meaning must be very plain so that a plain person swishing in a spacecraft may read and profit.

באר

DECLARE: "On this side Jordan, in the land of Moab, began Moses to declare this law...", (Deut. 1:5). As Moses declared the law in finer detail, greater depth and more colorful dimensions he employed *Baar,* a Hebrew root with several meanings.

It means to dig, e.g. a well. At the end of the fortieth year of Moses' leadership of Israel, he dug into God's word and found promises, happenings on the journey, God's anger at the disobedience of the people and much more.

It means to dig in or engrave—Deut. 27:8. God commanded that His law be written plainly and to last across generations.

It means to expound—Deut. 1:5. Not only did the willing scholar dig in for himself but also dug out for other people in order that they might understand. Moses dug a spiritual well for himself and also for others.

This verb root is used to signify a well—Gen. 26:19; a well of heroes—Num. 21:16-18; a well of an oath—Gen. 21:31. Moses was a well of God's word springing up like a fountain; he was the hero of Israel; he made an oath for the honor of God and for the welfare of Israel.

ספר

DECLARE: *"Declare* His glory among the heathen...", (Ps. 96:3). This is a great word for preachers, teachers, soul winners and witnesses. *Saphar* means:

To insculp or grave on stone or on hearts of men—Ps. 45:1. One declaring for God is indeed a scribe. Secretary—II Sam. 8:17. What a humbling honor to be God's secretary.

Muster master—Jer. 52:25. Could preachers and teachers of the Lord be so honored as to be roll callers for Him.

To number, to count, to take a census—2 Chron. 2:16.

To tell, to narrate—Ps. 2:7. This is the occupation for a Christian.

A writing or a letter—II Sam. 11:14. This sounds like the New Testament. God's men are to become epistles.

A book—Exod. 17:14. All sermons and lessons taught make us a book in God's library which has been checked out and read by those that want to know the Lord.

קָדַשׁ

DEDICATE: "So was ended all the work...for the house of the Lord. And Solomon brought in the things which David his father had *dedicated*", (I Kings 7:51). *Qadash* is a great word on sanctification and majestic cleanliness. It means:

To keep pure and clean that destined for sacred use—Exod. 29:21. No wonder Paul said bodies presented to the Lord should be kept clean—Rom. 12:1, 2.

To be regarded and treated holy—Lev. 22:32.

To be consecrated—Exod. 29:43.

To appoint or to institute—Joel 1:14. God does the cleansing and using but man is to dedicate for such use.

To consecrate with rites or to dedicate with ceremony—Exod. 13:2. How appropriate to have a dedicatory service for a baby.

To pronounce holy—Jer. 1:5. The Lord does the pronouncing and calls people into His service.

עָמַק

DEEP: "O Lord, how great are thy works! and thy thoughts are very deep", (Ps. 92:5). The Hebrew word *amaq* has several deep meanings.

It means to be unsearchable—Ecl. 7:24. The wisdom, the knowledge, the judgments and the Gift of God are all past finding out.

It means a wonder—Isa. 7:11. The Lord said for us to ask for something from the ever-mysterious deep.

It means profound living—Jer. 49:8, 30. Fishing in the deeps; dwelling without care; prudently practicing wisdom—Jer. 49:7, 31; these please God.

It means sinful revolt—Isa. 31:6. Sin has a deep dye that makes profound revolters slaughter—Hos. 5:2.

It means valley—Ps. 65:13. These low lands are good for the culture of grains; or, may be clothed with flocks and resounding with songs.

It means deep people, I Chron. 12:15. Shallowness is a bane. God wants His people to be moved deeply in their worship and plow deeply in kingdom building.

גָּנַן

DEFEND: "As birds flying, so will the Lord of hosts defend Jerusalem; defending also He will deliver it; and passing over He will preserve it", (Isa. 31:5). *Ganan*, the Hebrew root for *defend*, has interesting meanings.

It means to cover—II Kings 20:6; 19:34; Isa. 37:35 (all three verses read the same). The idea being that of a mother hen that protects her own. Note that it is saved, first of all for the Lord.

The root is used to build the word for gardener—Neh. 10:6. The Lord defends His hosts like the gardener does his flowers or the sower his grain.

In Neh. 12:4 the root is used to make a word meaning priest. A true priest of God will forever defend his flock.

So, if we go back to Isa. 31:5, we have the Lord as Priest and Husbandman, going by Heaven's aircraft over Jerusalem on reconnoitering and defending missions.

עָנַג

DELIGHT: "And call the sabbath a delight", (Isa. 58:13). *Oneg* is a delicate word but it helps to bring out another of the facets of the energy and experience in delight. It means:

To live delicately and effeminately. (Spoken of females who draw attention by ogling and other coquettish gestures). Many

64

have felt attraction to the sabbath who love the Lord of the sabbath.

To be delicate and tender—Jer. 6:2. Unregenerate man has pronounced Christianity effeminate, while Christians find it inexpressibly delectable.

To delight oneself and be satisfied—Isa. 66:11. Jerusalem and her God are rivers of delight.

To sport oneself over any one or any thing—Isa. 57:4. This is in a bad sense; but that which can afford the greatest pleasure, can also cause the greatest pain. One is so highly exalted in spiritual things that he may be in a position to sin greatly.

חפץ

DELIGHT: "But his *delight* is in the law of the Lord", (Ps. 1:2). *Chaphats* means:

To bend—Job 40:17. There are noble men who bend their wills to God's will like the cedars bend to the wind.

To be favorably disposed or inclined—Song of Sol. 2:7; 3:5. Many talk as did Isaiah, "Here am I, Lord, send me."

To love—Gen. 34:19.

To desire—Mal. 3:1. Desire ought to be a delight.

To wish or to will—Job 31:16.

Preciousness—Isa. 54:12. Delight is a precious gem itself.

A business, a cause, or a weighty matter—Isa. 53:10. Here God's cause becomes a pleasant affair and a prosperous one.

Hephzibah, a symbolic name for Zion in which the Lord delighteth—Isa. 62:4. Could the Lord ever call our church that?

For more on this word see *Pleasure.*

נצל

DELIVER: "He trusted on the Lord that he would *deliver* him", (Ps. 22:8). "O keep my soul and *deliver* me", (Ps. 25:20). *Natsal,* Hebrew for deliver, has several meanings.

It means to take away—II Chron. 20:25. The idea is to snatch away, as a treasure. Jesus was taken away from the scoffers and

65

scorners even after they put Him in a sealed and guarded tomb. The Lord will *deliver* us thus.

It means to spoil—Exod. 3:22. Whatever the Lord gets of me or of mine will be saved.

It means to preserve—Exod. 14:14. God preserved His son before, during, and after the entombment. We are His sons, too.

It means to deprive of—Gen. 31:9. God's redemption program deprives hell and Satan's kingdom of citizens.

It means to escape or hide oneself—Deut. 23:16. While we cannot deliver ourselves, it is comforting to know of a refuge such as the Lord is.

חלץ

DELIVER: "The righteous is delivered out of trouble, and the wicked cometh in his stead", (Prov. 11:8). The righteous will be delivered not only from trouble but also from death, v. 4. *Chalats,* the Hebrew root for *deliver,* has other meanings.

It means to draw off, as a shoe—Deut. 25:11; hence, to be free as from an ill destiny to sing with the redeemed.

It means to withdraw or to pull out—Hos. 5:6. While here the Lord is withdrawing Himself, He usually is snatching His elect as brands from the burning in order to save them from eternal fire. (Compare II Pet. 3:9; Ezek. 33:11).

פלט

DELIVERER: "...Thou art my help and my deliverer; make no tarrying, O my God", (Ps. 40:17). *Palat,* the Hebrew root for *deliverer,* is a great and colorful word.

It means to be slippery and smooth, hence, to slip away or escape—Ezek. 7:16. Everyone mourning for his iniquity will be glad for a way of escape.

To be wholly and forever delivered is another meaning—Job 23:7. When the Lord, our holy Judge, sets us free it is for always and in all ways.

It means to bring forth as a foetus from the womb—Job 21:10. Unless one is born he will be dead: physically or spiritually.

It means to escape by flight—Jer. 50:28. Man needs fly from

sin, Satan, hell and the wrath of God; and fly to the bosom of the Lord.

It means deliverance—Ps. 32:7. When we have God we have deliverance, and we shall call Him our hiding place, as did David.

This root is used to build a name—I Chron. 4:42, Pelatiah, which means: Whom Jehovah delivers. I would be proud to wear this name.

It means one escaped—Gen. 14:13. How we ought to sing since we have escaped (Heb. 2:3) and have so great a Deliverer.

יקע

DEPART: "Be thou instructed, O Jerusalem, lest my soul depart from thee; lest I make thee desolate, a land not inhabited: (Jer. 6:8). To be alienated is an awful end to any Jerusalem. This is one meaning of *yaka,* translated *depart* in this verse. There are other meanings.

It means to be out of joint—Gen. 32:26. When people are dislocated in relation to God their situation is serious.

It means to hang, as on a cross—II Sam. 21:12, 13. The Philistines hanged Saul and Jonathan. Jesus was hanged on a cross and clearly indicated God departed from Him.

ירד

DESCEND: "...And behold the angels of God ascending and descending on it", (Gen. 28:12). *Yarad,* the Hebrew root from which *descend* is derived, is variously used.

It is translated "brought down"—Isa. 14:11, in the passage telling of Lucifer's fall and how "hell from beneath is moved for thee to meet thee."

It is used to signify going down to a well—Gen. 24:16; into Sheol, Ps. 55:15; into a grave—Prov. 1:12.

It is used to describe impoverishment: those on high are cast down and the poor become lenders—Deut. 28:43.

It signifies leading—Judg. 7:4. Angels of God may lead one to heaven but Lucifer may lead one to hell.

It means to carry—Gen. 37:25. Angels can carry people.

This root is used to build *Jordan,* the principal river of Palestine that begins at the foot of Antilibanus and ends in the Dead Sea.

It makes an interesting study to apply all of the above significations to both good and bad angels.

חמד

DESIRE: "The Desire of all nations shall come", (Hag. 2:7). *Chamad* the Hebrew for *desire* has several meanings.

It means to covet—Mic. 2:2. Here it tells how fields which were coveted were taken by violence. Therefore we can better understand why this word was chosen to tell of Him whom the nations have laid hold upon by faith.

It means to delight in and take pleasure in—Ps. 68:16.

It means Precious—Ps. 19:10. In this passage the word shows its strength even to those not Christians.

It means acceptable—II Chron. 21:20. Here it reports that a king who reigned eight years was desired by no one. Generations across two thousand years declare that the King of kings is desired.

It means idol—Dan. 11:37. Here the context teaches that the desire of the women was some idol worshipped by the Syrian women, perhaps Astarte, or Anaitis. Women have taken leading parts in worshipping.

It means savory—Dan. 10:3. Oh, taste and see that the Lord is good.

(Note: Another colorful Hebrew word for *desire* is *chaphats* which is derived under *delight.*)

אבד

DESTROY: "But if they will not obey, I will utterly pluck up and destroy that nation, saith the Lord", (Jer. 12:17). This strong word *abad* (the Hebrew word for *destroy)* which was employed by God's great prophet has several meanings.

It means to be lost, to wander about like sheep—Ps. 119:176. So many times are we reminded in Scripture that the Lord is our Shepherd and He does not want us to die.

It means to perish—Isa. 27:13. But Jesus says, "Whosoever believeth in Him shall not perish."

It means to consume away, like the burning fat of lambs—Ps. 37:20.

It means to be without a hiding place—(Ps. 142:4. The Lord will, for those who will not trust Him, hide the hiding place.

It means to be miserable—Prov. 31:6. Wretched is he who doth not always trust in the Lord and obey Him.

It means place of destruction—Prov. 27:20; Job 26:6. The meaning of this word is close to that of Sheol—Prov. 15:11.

(Note: For meaning of another Hebrew word translated *destroy* in Gen. 6:17, see the word *Corrupt).*

מות

DIE: "The soul that sinneth it shall *die",* (Ezek. 18:4, 20). This word has some drab colors and colors of warning in it. Those who see them surely will turn from sin to Him who gives everlasting life. *Muth* means:

To be sterile, desert—Gen. 47:19. No sinner can be fruitful for the Lord.

To perish or be destroyed—Hos. 13:1. Here sin, offence, exalting self, trembling, and death are put side by side.

To slay—Judg. 16:30. Just as Samson slew many, so will sin slay many.

The world of the dead—Job 28:22. Who wants to go to a world like that.

Deadly disease, plague and pestilence—Jer. 15:2; 18:21.

Destruction and ruin—Isa. 25:8. Notice of this ought to cause sinners to repent and turn to the Lord.

בין

DISCERN: "That I may discern between good and bad", (I Kings 3:9). Used in Solomon's prayer, this word *bin* has some nice distinctions. For its meaning see *Consider.*

למד

DISCIPLE: "Bind up the testimony, seal the law among my disciples", (Isa. 8:16). This Hebrew word comes from the root *lamad* which means:

To beat, to chastise, to train, to teach beasts—Hos. 10:11, also, to teach men to war—I Chron. 5:18. A disciple of Jesus needs just these things to help bring in the kingdom of His Master. Discipline is basic in Christianity.

To accustom—Jer. 10:2. Learn not the way of the heathen, but become accustomed to the way of the Lord. Get used to His yoke; it is easy and light.

To teach—Ps. 71:17. One taught of God in his youth will serve God all of his days, even to old age.

To practise, the tongue for instance—Isa. 50:4; one day be eloquent for the Lord. A learner and follower of the Lord is a disciple and has peace—Isa. 54:13.

המם

DISCOMFIT: "And the Lord discomfited them...and slew them...and chased them...and smote them", (Josh. 10:10). As to how the Lord may *discomfit* is found in *hamam,* the Hebrew root for the word.

It means to put in consternation—Exod. 14:24. The Lord troubled the Egyptians by taking off their chariot wheels just as they had roared into what was to become their high water grave, divinely opened for them.

It means to drive—Isa. 28:28. God may drive His enemies like the horseman drives his cart over the threshing floor.

It means to vex—II Chron. 15:6. God may disturb with adversity.

It means to destroy—Deut. 2:15. When the Lord's hand is against His enemy destruction may be near.

חתת

DISMAY: "Be not afraid, neither be thou dismayed", (Josh. 1:9). *Chathath* means:

To break—Isa. 7:8. What suffering must come to a nation or to a person that is broken.

To be broken with fear—Deut. 31:8. To flee for fear is natural—Jer. 10:2.

To terrify—Job 7:14. One can be frightened because of his dreams.

To confound—Jer. 1:17. When a person is mixed up, he knows not what to do and becomes afraid.

מרה

DISOBEY: "Thus saith the Lord, Forasmuch as thou hast disobeyed the mouth of the Lord...", (I Kings 13:21).

This bitter word has a bitter meaning and leads to a bitter end. The context here shows that a disobedient person will not even be buried in the cemetery with the faithful. *Marah* means:

To be perverse, to rebel—Ps. 78:8. Such people resist and rebel by striking and fighting with their hands—Ps. 5:10.

To reject a divine command—Num. 20:24. The repulsion in this is really repulsive. It carries the idea of smiting on the mouth him who gives the orders.

To oppose—Job 17:2. He who obeys not his Lord is against Him.

To be bitter—II Kings 14:26. This condition follows, surrounds, and accompanies disobedience.

פזר

DISPERSE: "...There is a certain people scattered abroad and dispersed among the people...", (Esth. 3:8). This is good for Christians, a certain people, to be scattered abroad among all nations. *Pazar,* the Hebrew root for disperse, has several uses.

In Prov. 11:24 it means to be liberal or to distribute largely. Today, at Glorieta, New Mexico, a wealthy philanthropist said, "I've scattered my money in so many places, I'm afraid it won't do any good". But those who know Laura Sampson will report: she has done much good to many in several places.

In Jer. 3:13 it is used to tell of one roving about: i.e., he has scattered his ways.

71

In Ps. 89:11 it is used to report that the enemies have been scattered.

In Ps. 53:5 it is used to tell of a scattering of bones. It would likely mean an extending of God's kingdom if we would present ourselves for expending in the kingdom of God.

עשׂה

DO: And the Lord God said unto the woman, "What is this that thou hast done?", (Gen. 3:13). This word *asah* is used here for the first time in the OT and is used over 1,000 in all, the last being: "And ye shall tread down the wicked; for they shall be ashes under the soles of your feet in the day that I shall do this, saith the Lord of hosts", (Mal. 4:2). So many of the times it says something like this: "And Noah did according to all the Lord commanded him". (Gen. 7:5).

For the meaning of this word see *Accomplish.*

לקח

DOCTRINE: "My doctrine shall drop as the rain...because I will publish the name of the Lord", (Deut. 32:2, 3). Interesting meanings are found in *laqach,* the Hebrew for *doctrine.*

Its primary meaning is to take—Num. 21:25. This is to seize or to lay hold on. It is not much doctrine until it is seized upon by the heart, soul and mind or, until the doctrine seizes the one possessing these.

It means to admit or to listen to—Ps. 6:9. Here the Lord listens to the supplicant and in Prov. 24:32 the audience is reversed.

It means to receive, as a benediction from God—Num. 23:20. Also, it means to receive by ear and perceive—Job 4:12.

It has the idea of assumption—Gen. 2:15. Here man was to take the garden from the Lord and assume responsibility along with it. When one receives the Lord with His train of doctrines he also receives responsibilities.

It means to be captivated—Prov. 7:21. Thrills follow the reception of God's word. The auditor's mind is bound.

This root carries the idea of the learning process, Prov. 9:9. The teacher gives and lives; the pupil receives and lives.

72

In Deut. 32:1 graphically does the great teacher plead that the great doctrine of God be received and acted upon even as it had been in his own life.

שׁלט

DOMINION: "One like the Son of man came...and there was given him dominion, and glory, and a kingdom, that all people, nations, and languages, should serve him: his dominion is an everlasting dominion...", (Dan. 7:14). *Shalat,* which is the Hebrew root for *dominion,* has several facets of meaning.

It means to rule—Neh. 5:15. It usually means to rule over people. This would be desired by all of us—to be ruled by the "Son of man".

It means to have power given over anything—Eccl. 5:18-19. In the New Testament the Son of man was given power in heaven and in earth—Matt. 28:18.

It means to be ruler—Dan. 3:2. The One named in our text will be ruler of more than a province: it will be all "people, nations, and languages."

A derivative of this root carries the idea of an empire that will rule over other empires, kingdoms and dominions—Dan. 7:27. The Son of man shall be King of kings and Lord of lords.

Sultan comes from this root and means sovereign. The sultanship was the title of the office of the ruler of the Turks at one time but that office was abolished in 1922. The text heading the study of this root says the dominion of the Son of man shall be an *everlasting* dominion.

פתח

DOOR: "Be ye lift up ye everlasting doors", (Ps. 24:7). There is much depth and width and height to this word *petach.* It means:

To open. To open the mouth in a parable—Ps. 78:2. This is good grounds for the request in the text. To open the ear—Isa. 50:5. The people must have wanted a hearing. To open the hand—Deut. 15:8. The request was being made that the doors be open at the only source for blessings needed. To open the granaries and expose the grain for sale—Amos 8:5. God's granaries have something God's people need. To open, as a flower—Song of Sol. 7:12).

73

To let loose, to set free, e.g. captives out of prison—Isa. 14:17. God's children are free indeed and love to sing, "Be ye lift up ye everlasting doors."

To engrave, to carve, to plough the earth—Isa. 28:24, wood— I Kings 7:36, gold—Exod. 28:36. These meanings and scriptures certainly add to the meaning of these doors; and, no wonder there was prayer for their lifting.

Insight, instruction—Ps. 119:130. These are teaching doors. The very word used by the singer, as he was led of the Lord, tells us so. We ought to be such doors.

Whom Jehovah sets free, Pethahiah—Ezra 10:23. Door, with this meaning, is a good name for a child of God.

דלה

DRAW: "...And also drew water enough for us and watered the flock", (Exod. 2:19). This is prose but there is poetry in *dalah,* the Hebrew root for *draw.*

It means to draw as understanding—Prov. 20:5. From one life is drawn that which enriches another.

It means to deliver—Ps. 30:1. The sinner is praising Him who lifted him out of the mire of his sin, set his feet on a rock and put a new song in his mouth.

It means a door—Ps. 141:3. The lips form a door for the mouth.

It is used to describe weavers' threads—Isa. 38:12. Threads being pulled from the loom are a sign death is coming—the end of the work.

This root is used to build a name for a man whom Jehovah delivered—Neh. 6:10. This would make a wholesome entry on the church roll.

חלם

DREAM: "Your old men shall dream dreams...", (Joel 2:28). The root for *dream* is *chalam,* is used over one hundred times in the Old Testament, and means:

To be fat. Perhaps this idea grows out of the fact that persons who are fleshy are inclined to sleep and to dream.

To be strong, sound, robust—Job 39:4. Certainly unhealthy persons would not be as apt to have healthy dreams for the Lord, for mankind, and for themselves.

To receive a message from God under divine inspiration—Num. 12:6. Prophets have dreamt across the centuries, and we hope prophets will continue to do so until Jesus comes.

To restore to health—Isa. 38:16. Those whom the Lord makes to really live will likely dream dreams for Him.

גָּרַשׁ

DRIVE: "I will do marvels...behold, I drive out before thee the Amorite, and the Canaanite...", (Exod. 34:10, 11). *Garash,* the Hebrew root for *drive,* has several meanings.

In the above passage, part of which is quoted, it means to make way (for the people led by Moses who are to have the promised land).

It means to feel cast out—Jonah 2:3, 4. Jonah was expelled from company with God, and this because of his disobedience.

It means deprivation—Gen. 3:24. Man lost Eden.

It implies punishment—Gen. 4:14. Cain was driven off because he was a murderer.

It means a violent release—Exod. 11:1. Pharaoh thrust Israel out of his domain and they set out for the promised land.

It means to produce—Deut. 33:14. Here God's sun and moon cause fruitage and in other reports we learn God caused spiritual results.

נָטַף

DROP: "Son of man, set thy face toward Jerusalem, and drop thy word toward the holy places, and prophesy...", (Ezek. 21:2). *Nataph,* the Hebrew root for *drop,* has great significations. (In the Aramaic, Arabic and Ethiopic languages this common root is translated *percolavit* in the Latin; which is our word *percolate* and could represent a preacher).

It signifies rain—Job 36:26-28. God makes small drops of water to pour down upon man abundantly. These distilled drops could well portray the Gospel Tidings.

It signifies prophecy—Mic. 2:6. How sweet and instructive the prophecy that fell from the lips of the prophets.

In Exod. 30:34, this Hebrew word means sweet gum like candy. These freshly distilled drops flow spontaneosly from trees. In our great preachers we have trees like that.

In Song of Sol. 4:11, this word is employed to describe the honey that falls from the lips of the Church into the mouth of the Bridegroom.

This root is used to build the proper name, Netophathite—II Sam. 23:28, 29, for a gentile who distilled drops (words) from his lips. Could faithful ambassadors of the King be called by this name?

אלם

DUMB: "...He is brought as a lamb to the slaughter, and as a sheep before her shearers is *dumb,* so He opened not His mouth", (Isa. 53:7). *Alam* is a very instructive word.

It means to bind or to tie. Jesus was bound to a great program. Redemption's ropes tied Him to the cross. He chose deed instead of dialogue.

It means to be silent—Ezek. 33:22. The Lord opened not His mouth for saints, time, eternity and God would come to His defense.

It means to be lonely and forsaken. He who espouses a great cause may lose companions, especially if He walks down the corridors of death with a cross upon His shoulder.

A colorful use of this root is made in the inscription to Ps. 56. It has been translated, "The silent dove among the strangers". Jesus was this.

עפר

DUST: And Abraham answered and said, "Behold now, I have taken upon me to speak unto the Lord, which am but dust and ashes", (Gen. 18:27). *Aphar,* the Hebrew root for *dust,* has some particles of gold in it.

It means, in the passage above, the lowness and frailty of human nature. There is a hymn, which says, "We are as worms of the dust".

It is used to foretell that we will return to the dust—Gen. 3:19; and go down as it were into the sepulchre—Ps. 22:29.

It is used to tell of a people like the dust of the earth innumerable—Num. 23:10.

In the tropical sense it means to bow in silence and await God's help—Lam. 3:29.

In Job 28:6, we have "dust of gold". Those that are an honor unto God and a blessing to earth are really "dust of gold" as well as dust of earth from whence they came.

יָשַׁב

DWELL: "I will dwell in the house of the Lord forever", (Ps. 23:6). This Hebrew word *yashab* is used some four hundred times in the Old Testament, and, no wonder, for it has so much in it. It is used to speak of God's people dwelling in a place, of the ark of God the Lord dwelling in a place (I Chron. 13:6) and even of God dwelling on earth (I Kings 8:27). It means:

To be seated, as a judge to dispense justice—Ps. 9:4. In the New Testament we are taught that God's people will judge with the Great Judge.

To be seated as a king on a throne—Ps. 9:7, 8. This meaning is appropriately set forth in a Psalm for it is something to sing about. The Lord will make all of His children kings—Rev. 1:6.

To hold possession of a place by sitting down on it—I Sam. 13:16. God's children will not only be in God's house but will own the place. They will be allowed squatter's rights.

To sit down with anyone in order to associate with him—Ps. 1:1. David sang when he looked forward to sitting in company with the Greater David. So should we sing out, using Psalms 23 as the text.

To remain, to stay, to abide—Gen. 29:19. There is not found a scripture that reports the house of the Lord to be a temporary dwelling place. There is not a tension of transiency in heaven, but an air of permanency.

To inhabit—Gen. 13:12. This word means that we will have the privilege of setting up house and living in God's place.

To marry—Hos. 3:3 and Ezra 10:2. This stems from the idea of letting dwell with oneself, that is, to marry. There will be no marriage in heaven, but Jesus will be the bridegroom and the church will be the bride. The Lord will let us dwell with Him in the house which He has prepared for us. This will be far better.

Jashobeam—I Chron. 11:11. This is the name of one of David's chief officers and means "dwelling in quiet." This is a fitting name for a man in so important a position. It is a good name for a pastor.

אכל

EAT: "Thy words were found and I did eat them; and Thy word was unto me the joy and rejoicing of my heart...", (Jer. 15:16). The Hebrew word for *eat* is *akal* which has other meanings and is used in several colorful situations.

It means to devour—Ezek. 3:1. The prophet is commissioned to eat the whole roll of a book and then speak to Israel. People hunger for Bible study.

It means to dine—Gen. 43:16. Joseph ordered a great meal so that the re-united family may feast together. All of God's children will one day dine with the Greater Joseph at the marriage supper.

It means to taste—Deut. 4:28. God's word is sweet—Ps. 119:103 and taste reveals that God is good—Ps. 34:8.

It means to enjoy—Job 21:25. Many shout joyful amens when served portions of God's word by faithful preachers.

Some eating situations: Having a sacrificial feast before Jehovah; To eat up anyone piecemeal by slander or by accusing falsely; To listen so that the spoken words are being eaten; To eat up a people by high rent or taxes; To consume a people by war; A fire, famine, disease, wrath of God may consume.

אבן

EBENEZER: "Then Samuel took a stone, and set it...and called the name of it Ebenezer, saying, Hitherto hath the Lord helped us", (I Sam. 7:12). *Aban,* the Hebrew root from which *Ebenezer* comes, has several meanings.

Basically the root means to build or to found. Our faithful forbearers sang, "Here I raise mine Ebenezer..." all the time building and founding churches.

It also means to prop or to support. One church member sang in the presence of the others, "Here I raise my *support*..."

Rather commonly this root means a stone—I Sam. 17:40. Once a stone for a foundation—Isa. 28:16; once precious stones for ephods and breastplates; once a stone ore—Job 28:2. Men, rugged men in rugged days, were saying, Here I am, rather rough, but willing to build a church or any other institution with noble purpose. Those stone ores produced silver and gold.

It means to weigh, that is, ancients used stones in balances for weighing.

In Jer. 18:3 this root is used to describe a potter's wheels.

In very unusual circumstances it is used to signify a bathing stone for infants—Exod. 1:16. The midwives used the hollowed-out stones for bathing the new-born infants.

Perhaps the greatest use made of this root is to signify the Lord's help—Isa. 7:12. No wonder that Israel, when she went out against the Philistines to battle, pitched beside Ebenezer.

עדן

EDEN: "For the Lord shall comfort Zion...and He will make her wilderness like Eden, and her desert like the garden of the Lord; joy and gladness shall be found therein...", (Isa. 51:3). *Adan,* the Hebrew root for *Eden,* is full of meaning.

It means to live delicately, sumptuously and voluptuously—Neh. 9:25. Our first parents took advantage of this and sinned.

It means pleasures, only in the plural—Ps. 36:8. How many of God's children testify they drink delights from God's rivers. While Saul clothed the daughters of Israel with delights—II Sam. 1:24, the Greater Saul clothes God's children with infinitely greater delights and that for eternity.

This root seems to have had the general signification, to be soft, lax, pliant and to waver. This might be expected of those like the first pair, who in luxury sinned.

This root is used to build the name for a very pleasant region in Asia—Gen. 2:10-14, in which was placed the gardent of our

79

first parents, and the name of a region in Mesopotamia or in Assyria—II Kings 19:12.

בחיר

ELECT: "Behold my servant whom I uphold; mine elect, in whom my soul delighteth; I have put my spirit upon him: he shall bring forth judgment to the Gentiles.", (Isa. 42:1). The Hebrew word *bachir* has great and deep meaning, for which see *Chosen.*

ערה

EMPTY: "And she hasted, and emptied her pitcher into the trough...", (Gen. 24:20). *Arah,* the Hebrew root for empty, has several meanings—one of which is directly connected with the supreme sacrifice of Jesus—Isa. 53:12.

It means to uncover—Zeph. 2:14. All was torn from the walls and fences and the frame was left bare. Jesus had all torn off of Him: possessions, earthly authority, life.

It means to raze—Ps. 137:7. The edifice, Jesus, was demolished but rose again the third day.

It means to lay bare with the idea of discovering the foundation—Mic. 1:6. When the man of Jesus was shorn away by sin the God of Him shone more.

It means to empty—Gen. 24:20. Christ's life was poured out on Calvary—Isa. 53:12. Those who pour out their lives on His altar might be called Emptied Pitchers.

It means to spread oneself abroad like a flourishing tree—Ps. 37:35. Christ's efficacious ministry is spread abroad as far as believers are found.

בקק

EMPTY: "Behold the Lord maketh the earth empty, and maketh it waste", (Isa. 24:1); "Israel is an empty vine" (Hos. 10:1). *Baqaq* is the Hebrew for *empty* and it has colorful meanings.

It means to pour out as the blessings out of a land—Isa. 24:1. The should of the word imitates the meaning. Our land could lose its blessings like a bottle can be emptied.

It means desert—Naham 2:10. Our sins may cause God to desert us, depopulate our country and turn it into a desert.

The root is used to build the name for Balak, that empty-headed king who denied God and defied Israel, etc.—Num. 22.

חנה

ENCAMP: "The angel of the Lord encampeth round about them that fear Him, and delivereth them", (Ps. 34:7). The Hebrew word *chanah* means:

To bend, to bow down, and thus be favorably disposed.

To pitch a tent—Gen. 26:17. One is favorably impressed with a place to let oneself down and camp there. Certainly we would that God would dispatch His angels to be tenting about us, and that not with hostile design to besiege us, but to bless us.

To defend—Zech. 9:8. This is real security for the believer.

To dwell—Isa. 29:1. This is the climactic meaning of this word. This variety of signification is the best, namely, that angels abide with us and about us.

חזק

ENCOURAGE: "David encouraged himself in the Lord", (I Sam. 30:6). for the meaning of *chazaq* see *Continue.*

צרר

ENEMY: *Tsarar,* (whose derivatives are nearly always plural), means:

To bind, to roll up in a bundle—Hos. 13:12. The word is used here in a bad sense, but for a contrast see I Sam. 25:28.

To press upon—Num. 33:55. Certainly enemies can become pricks in the side which can crowd one into a corner.

To be in distress—Jer. 48:41. This alludes to pangs of a woman in her pains.

A stone—II Sam. 17:13. Enemies are rocks of stumbling in a man's path. While care must be taken lest a man dash his foot against a stone, the same stone may become a step to higher character.

אֹיֵב

ENEMY: "Out of the mouth of babes and sucklings hast thou ordained strength because of thine enemies, that thou mightest still the enemy and the avenger", (Ps. 8:2). *Oyeb* means:

To persecute, to hate. The primary idea seems to be that of puffing and blowing upon anyone as an indication of anger—Ezek. 23:22. It would be difficult to hear the still small voice of God in such an atmosphere.

To be an adversary—I Sam. 18:29. In a degree, he is shackled who has an enemy.

A load, a burden. While this is only a probable meaning, it fits well, since man's enemies are his burdens.

Destruction—Job 18:12. While this is another probable meaning, it is true one's enemies may lead to his destruction.

A clamorous and unclean bird of prey—Lev. 11:14. Hawks make the worst enemies of the best fowls.

רָאָה

ENJOY: "That he should make his soul enjoy good in his labor", (Eccl. 2:24). For the meaning of *raah* see *Appear*.

רָחַב

ENLARGE: "Enlarge the place of thy tent...spare not, lengthen thy cords, strengthen thy stakes", (Isa. 54:2). *Rachab* means:

To become wide like chambers—Ezek. 41:7; like a heart—Isa. 60:5; like borders of a kingdom—Exod. 34:24. All of these can well be applied to a church or to its members.

Great—Ps. 25:17. A church becomes greater in its influence when it lengthens its cords.

A street—Gen. 19:2. A church in enlarging its ministry is ever to keep in mind this idea of being a street for the people.

A market place—II Chron. 32:6. This was a broad place in front of Oriental cities where things were exposed for sale. The church is a market place for the Gospel.

The area before the house of God—Ezra 10:9. Make it large. A well—Gen. 26:22. Something about a church ought to remind people of a well of water.

A river—Gen. 36:37. Here *Rachbat* means a river of flowing water. A church ought to be that for the thirsty nations.

Rehabiah, whom Jehovah makes free and happy—I Chron. 23:17. This makes a good name for a church.

בקר

ENQUIRE: "One thing have I desired of the Lord, and that will I seek after; that I may dwell in the house of the Lord...to enquire in His temple", (Ps. 27:4). *Baqar* is the Hebrew for *enquire* and has colorful meanings.

It means dawn—Ps. 5:4. At the breaking forth of the morning light the psalmist will talk with God. (There is a rather famous and fine coffee named *Bokar*.) Prosperity and happiness are associated with morning—Job 11:17. When the sun cleaves the sky, prayer is sent on high.

It means to cleave, to lay open, to plough. As oxen plough fields—Amos 6:12, so will man labor to discover the beauty of the Lord—Ps. 27:4.

It means to search—Lev. 13:36. Man will search the scriptures for eternal life.

It means to think upon, to look at or to meditate—II Kings 16:15. Putting all these meanings together we have the pilgrim, early in the morning, meditating and praying; searching God's word and sensing prosperity and happiness.

בוא

ENTER: "In the selfsame day entered Noah...into the ark", (Gen. 7:13). (See Isa. 2:10; Exod. 33:9; Isa. 3:14). *Bo* means:

To go or come in unto, as a bride into her house especially built for her—Josh. 15:18. Think of the Church on entering heaven.

To confer—Josh. 23:12. This conference is for forming a confederacy between God and His children.

To be rendered—I Kings 10:14. Praises and services become profits and revenues unto the Greater Solomon. (Is this why music is said to be rendered?)

To come up to, to be equal to—II Sam. 23:23. How the sons of God ought be humbled to think they will become like the Son of God.

To come to pass, to be accomplished—I Sam. 9:6. When the eight were safe in the ark of Noah, something great did come to pass. When a person enters the kingdom of God, it is a great accomplishment.

To walk, to live, to associate—Ps. 26:4. What associations will come to pass when God's children come into the place prepared by the Greater Noah?

עתר

ENTREAT: "His prayer also, and how God was entreated of him...", (II Chron. 33:19). *Athar* means:

To burn incense, to smoke with perfume, to breathe odors. All of these are to be done to a divinity, and most favorably. This is a type of prayer.

To supplicate—Gen. 25:21. One pleads with God on another's behalf.

To hear and answer—II Sam. 21:14. This is an illustration of answered prayer.

To be abundant—Prov. 27:6. Here, the word translated deceitful means abundant. Abundant are the kisses of the enemy, but faithful are the wounds of a friend. He who entreats would like for mercy, grace, etc., to abound.

קנא

ENVY: "For wrath killeth the foolish man, and envy slayeth the silly one", (Job 5:2). " A sound heart is the life of the flesh, but envy the rottenness of the bones", (Prov. 14:30). "Wrath is cruel, and anger is outrageous; but who is able to stand before envy?", (Prov. 27:4). *Qana* means:

To be jealous, e.g., of a female rival—Gen. 30:1. This is such excitement that it causes one to become very red. This jealousy may be expressed in anger—Deut. 32:21. God is a severe avenger of defection from Himself—Deut. 5:9.

To envy—Ps. 37:1. Those who have sought and found the king-dom of God and have had all needs added, are not to want what sinners might have.

To be zealous, to possess ardor—II Kings 10:16. This idea of the Hebrew word is to be desired. It can result in love—Song of Sol. 8:6.

שׁוה

EQUAL: "To whom then will ye liken me, or shall I be equal? saith the Holy One", (Isa. 40:25). *Shavah,* the Hebrew root for *equal,* has colorful meanings.

It means to be of like value—Prov. 8:11. God is so precious that He is not even to be compared to all the gems He put in the treasury of the earth.

It means to resemble—Prov. 26:4. There is no one to whom God can be likened because His ways and thoughts are above all others.

It means a plain or king's dale—II Sam. 18:18. "Plain folks" means people that are ordinary and common, having possessions and principles like the bulk of the masses. Not so with God who is perfect and owns everything including the gold and silver and the "cattle of a thousand hills".

It means to put forth fruit—Hos. 10:1. God is the only one who can put forth fruit physically and spiritually.

It signifies calmness and quietness of mind—Ps. 131:2. There is no variableness with God whose mercy endures forever. There is no one anywhere who in the least approximates Him.

It means to put or to set—Dan. 5:21. If there is any pushing around done, God does it.

שׁגה

ERR: "But they also have erred through wine, and through strong drink are out of the way; the priest and the prophet have erred through strong drink, they are swallowed up of wine, they are out of the way through strong drink; they err in vision, they stumble in judgment.", (Isa. 28:7). *Shagah* is used three times in this verse and means:

To wander, to go astray—Ezek. 34:6. Sheep go wandering in the mountains where dangers are many, and during that time the sheep are of no good to the shepherd.

To sin, to transgress—I Sam. 26:21. David became a fool when he sinned. The fool hath said in his heart, (probably also with his life) that there is no God.

To seduce—Job 12:16, 17. Seduction is a great sin and he who leads another astray is guilty of it.

מלט

ESCAPE: "Whoso pleaseth God shall escape from her; but the sinner shall be taken by her.", (Eccl. 7:26). A study of *malat* helps to understand Heb. 2:3 which asks "How shall we escape if we neglect so great salvation?" It means:

To be smooth like cement, mortar—Jer. 43:9, and therefore more rapidly slip away.

To deliver, or give counsel leading to one's deliverance—I Kings 1:12. The way of life's preservation is to please God by accepting His plan of salvation.

To scarcely be saved as by the skin of the teeth, as if there were no soundness of body—Job 19:20. But Job did escape, for God had limited satan's persecution program. The Arabs have a proverb: "He escaped with his head," which means he saved his life.

Whom Jehovah delivers is the meaning of the name Melatiah in Neh. 3:7 which name is a derivative of this Hebrew root. Old Testament Christians could be called Melatiahs.

סור

ESCHEW: "One that feareth God and eschewed evil.", (Job 1:1) *Sur* means:

To turn away from something, i.e. to fall away from the worship of it, like unto a people who rejected God—I Sam. 12:19. This would be commendable apostasy: to reject and fall away from evil?

To rebel—Hos. 7:14. This would give license to rebel against and to protest the evil policies, principles and practices in our land.

To abandon—I Sam. 28:15, 16. Evil, like any other leaven, would die or dry up if given no meal to work in.

To desert—I Sam. 16:14. If sin be deserted while it is little, it will perish for the want of nourishment, or at least be a harmless and weak dwarf.

To depart from—Deut. 17:20. This means to violate a law by departing from it. Sin needs violation or breaking.

To avoid—Job 1:1. This is the best policy of him who would walk in paths of righteousness for His name's sake.

To remove or to make depart, to cause to deflect from intended course, to drive out—I Sam. 28:3. This is the Christian's climactic action against sin.

ישׁב

ESTABLISH: "He withdraweth not his eyes from the righteous; but with kings are they on the throne; yea, he doth establish them for ever, and they are exalted.", (Job 36:7). This is a great text telling how God's people will be settled and *yashab* is a great word in it, and for its meaning see *dwell*.

Another Hebrew word translated *establish* is *kun,* and for its meaning see *Confirm*.

קדם

ETERNAL: "The eternal God is thy refuge and underneath are the everlasting arms", (Deut. 33:27). *Qadam* tells of the greatness of God in the direction of time. It means:

To go before, to precede—Ps. 89:14. God set the precedent in preceding.

To get before anyone, to anticipate—Ps. 119:147, 148. This passage could be translated, "I rise early with the dawn." In other words, he was the first one up. The splendor of our great God dawned upon all before there were any dawns.

To go to meet anyone—Ps. 79:8. When we, (or the first Adam) come into the world, there is God.

Front—Ps. 139:5. God is, was and shall be in front and after all things and all creatures.

Beginning, origin—Isa. 23:7. Our God is the Originating God.

Eastward—Gen. 25:15. This is a good name for a person. Man and civilization has always gone Westward, originating in the East—originating with God.

One before God—Ezra 2:40. This name was given a minister.

עוֹלָם

EVERLASTING: "And Abraham planted a grove in Beersheba, and called on the name of the Lord, the everlasting God", (Gen. 21:33). *Olam* means:

Perpetuity—Isa. 35:10. Perpetual joy will be upon the heads of the ransomed and sighing and sorrow will be gone for ever.

Grey antiquity—Through all the days of old, God redeemed and cared for His children (Isa. 63:9).

Bright and unending future—Ps. 18:50. God is showing mercy to David and to David's seed, which includes us.

Eternity—Ps. 90:2. The true notion of eternity is expressed by *olam* in those passages referring to the nature of God. God was always before the mountains were made, and will always be after those same mountains melt with a fervent heat—II Peter 3:10.

רע

EVIL: "So that the Lord could no longer bear because of the evil of your doings...", (Jer. 4:22, 23). The word *ra* is used about four hundred times in the Bible and means:

Worthless—Lev. 27:10. Think of people loving that which is worthless—Mic. 3:2.

Noxious and hurtful—Gen. 37:33. Could Jacob love the animal that rent his son to pieces; yet men love that which is hurtful.

Ill-favored—Gen. 42:3. These lean-fleshed animals were ugly, and so is evil.

Unfortunate and ill—Isa. 3:11. It shall be ill with the evil.

Sad and sorrowful—Prov. 25:20. Evil brings sorrow as a part of its retinue.

Depravity and wickedness—Gen. 6:5. It takes a great power to uproot evil in the heart of man.

Noise—Exod. 32:17. Evil seems always to be loud.

שׂגב

EXALT: "Behold, God exalteth by his power", (Job 36:22). *Sagab* means:

To be lifted or raised up—Job 5:11. Job was conscious of the fact that God elevated people.

To be inaccessible, like a city—Deut. 2:36. When satan goes about like a roaring lion, seeking whom he may devour, it is good to be out of his reach.

To be safe and secure—Prov. 18:10. God's name is a tower to which Christians may repair and be protected.

To strengthen, make powerful—Isa. 9:10.

To defend—Ps. 20:2. When God exalts a man, it at once becomes his greatest defense.

To become great—Job 8:7. While the root here may be *sagah* or *saga*, instead of *sagab*, the primary idea still seems reasonable, viz., if a man ever becomes great, it will be because God exalts him.

רוּם

EXALT: "Be Thou exalted, Lord, in Thine own strength: so will we sing and praise Thy power", (Ps. 21:13). On exalting the Lord, the scriptures put by far the heaviest emphasis on the Lord exalting Himself rather than man exalting Him. Can the drop of rainwater raise the sea's level? Can the candlelight add to the brightness of the noon-day sun? In this text as in 34:3; 57:5, 11; 99:5, 9 and others, the Hebrew word *Rum* has several meanings.

It means to lift up oneself proudly—Dan. 11:36. David and we have seen other gods rear their heads on the horizon and pray that our God will show Himself.

To erect as a monument—Gen. 31:45. The prayer is that God will set up a marker to show His presence and power. He may use His leaders to build a church or some person to build a Sunday School class.

It means to become powerful—Ps. 57:1-6. Many powers on earth exert their damping pressure on man until that man prays that God will come forth in His might.

It means to celebrate—Dan. 4:34. Man is to sing and praise and honor God's power.

גבה

EXALTED: "Behold, my servant shall deal prudently, he shall be exalted and extolled, and be very high", (Isa. 52:13). *Gabah,* the Hebrew for exalted, has several derivatives and colorful meanings.

It means tall—I Sam. 10:23. Whereas Saul was head and shoulders taller than his fellows, Jesus was worlds and heavens taller than any man.

It means to be encouraged—II Chron. 17:6. When one's heart is lifted up he takes courage in the ways of the Lord.

It means to be high, lofty, powerful—Eccl. 5:7. Although a man will have many empty words when he dreams, yet a dreamer is a powerful man.

It means haughtiness—Isa. 2:11. There is such a fine line between pride and honor. This Hebrew root is used to signify either.

It means exalted—Isa. 52:13. It is divine compensation to know that in this verse and in many others the suffering Servant has been elevated to so high a degree of dignity and glory.

כחן

EXAMINE: "Examine me, O Lord, and prove me;...", (Ps. 26:2). This is a great prayer studded with this great word *bachan* which means:

To prove—Ps. 7:9. God tries men by sending calamities upon them.

To examine into man's faith and discover doubt—Mal. 3:10. Man's giving tests the man, and at the same time tests God's promises.

To rub, like trying a metal by rubbing it upon a stone—a lapis Lydius or touch-stone.

A watch-tower—Neh. 3:26, 27. Only proved material should go into a watch-tower. Men who become watchmen at the gate should be carefully examined. A man examined and called of God

90

to the ministry is an asset to the kingdom.

Trial, proof—Isa. 28:16. In this passage the proved becomes a foundation stone. On such, churches can be built knowing that only Jesus is the perfect, the precious, and the corner stone.

גאה

EXCELLENCY: "God...His excellency is over Israel, and His strength is in the clouds", (Ps. 68:34). *Gaah,* the Hebrew root for Excellency, is used contrastingly.

On the good side, it is used to tell of the glorious triumph of God—Exod. 15:1, 21. It is employed to tell how God rideth in His excellency on the sky—Deut. 33:26.

On the other side it is used to point up man's pride—Jer. 48:29, 30. Ungodliness went before this pride and a fall followed it.

Also it signifies an ornament—Deut. 33:29. This ornament for Israel is the Lord.

It is used to signify a neck-chain—Ps. 73:6. Ancients believed that pride's seat is in the neck. Here it showed first and most.

It is used to build a name for one who had the majesty of God in him—Num. 13:15. Geuel, an unusual name; an unusual man.

אדר

EXCELLENT: "O Lord our Lord, how excellent is thy name in all the earth", (Ps. 8:9). To tell of God's greatness is quite an undertaking, but help can be gotten from this word *adar* which means:

To be ample, large, great, splendid, powerful.

To be magnified and to be glorious—Exod. 15:6. Strength adds to God's glory.

To be honorable—Isa. 42:21. Add honor to all named above and it will help his excellency show forth.

A month of the year—Esth. 3:7. This month comes in the spring when the flowers bloom and there is so much splendor every-where. This signification of the word helps one to grasp some of the meaning of *excellent.*

Chief-judges—Dan. 3:2, 3. This gives another shade of meaning to *excellent* and has in it the idea of authority.

A mantle—Mic. 2:8. A wide cloak, draping from shoulders, always denotes some excellence.

Diligence—Ezra 7:23. This adds to one's greatness.

A coin of pure gold—I Chron. 29:7. Often a king's image was placed on these finest coins to show forth his majesty and excellence. Now, the very name of the coin is used to express excellence.

נגד

EXPOUND: "And the Spirit of the Lord came upon him, and he gave change of garments unto them which expounded the riddle", (Judg. 14:19). While the context here is not most suitable, the meanings of *nagad,* the Hebrew root for *expounded,* are most instructive. The unfathomableness of the life of the "unspeakable gift" is always a riddle both to the preacher and his auditory.

Nagad means simply to tell the story as did Ruth to Boaz—Ruth 2:11, and most grand results may follow.

It means to shew forth—Ps. 92:2. Show the facets of the Gospel gem for there are those who have not seen them.

It means to flow as a fiery stream—Dan. 7:10. The minister's message is to run thus and that "in front of", "in the presence of", "in the sight of" (Exod. 34:10), people.

All of the above activity which is denoted in the root is to take place also in the presence of the Lord—I Sam. 12:3.

The one leading in this activity becomes a leader of the people—I Chron. 13:1. He is a man after the Lord's heart and will be made captain over the Lord's inheritance. The Messiah became the perfect example of such a leader—Dan. 9:25. *Nagad,* the root, is used to build the title for Him.

כהה

FAIL: "He shall not fail nor be discouraged, till He have judgment in the earth: and the isles shall wait for his law", (Isa. 42:4). Jesus shall not fail and the several reasons why He will not are found in the meanings of *Kahah,* the Hebrew root for *fail.*

His light shall not go out—Isa. 42:3.

It shall not even be darkened—Zech. 11:17.

His eye shall not be dim—Deut. 34:7.

He shall not have the spirit of heaviness but of praise—Isa. 61:3.

He shall not be timid—Ezek. 21:12.

He shall not be restrained—I Sam. 3:13.

"He shall not fail."

כלה

FAINTETH: "My soul fainteth for thy salvation...I hope in thy Word", (Ps. 119:81). *Kalah* means:

To finish—Exod. 39:32. The sinful soul which is so unready, unprepared, and incomplete, longs for that which is perfect, even the salvation of the Lord.

To be spent—Gen. 21:15. The sinner is willing to cast his whole incomplete life on the Lord, for he knows he will get an abundant life in return. This is an eternal bargain, and that is why David and all the chosen after him are willing to be consumed or destroyed if only eternal salvation can be gained.

To pine—Deut. 28:32. Ours is a religion that affects the emotions. Its subjects cry after their Lord.

A bride or a spouse—Song of Sol. 4:8. In this life, a man's life comes nearer completion when it becomes one with his wife. In eternity, man's life is never complete unless united with God by faith.

טוב

FAIR: "And at the end of ten days their countenances appeared fairer...", (Dan. 1:15). *Tob* is used here to describe how Daniel and his three friends stood well before the king after the abstinence test was over. For its meaning see *merry*.

יפה

FAIR: "Thou art all fair, my love; there is no spot in thee", (Song of Sol. 4:7). (Note also Song of Sol. 1:15; 1:16; 4:1; 6:10). For the meaning of *yapheh* see *Beautiful*. This word with its variety of significations so adeptly portrays the church's graces.

אמן

FAITH: "But the just shall live by his faith", (Hab. 2:4). The word *faith* is found only twice in the authorized version: here and in Deut. 32:20. There are compounds such as *faithful,* and *faithless,* found some thirty times. In each case *amen* is the Hebrew word, and for its meaning see *Believe.*

נפל

FALL: "And the Spirit of the Lord fell upon me, and said unto me, Speak; Thus saith the Lord...", (Ezek. 11:5). *Naphal,* the Hebrew root for *fall,* has several meanings.

This root is used to express falling from a horse—Gen. 49:17; falling into a pit—Ps. 7:15; falling in battle—Isa. 10:4.

This root is used to report seeing of visions sent from God in sleep—Num. 24:4. This divine precipitation will quicken the soul.

It is used to describe the falling of the countenance—Gen. 4:5, 6. Sorrow, disappointment and other depressants will cause this.

It means to descend, as divine revelations from heaven, Dan. 4:28; as the Spirit of God upon any one—Ezek. 11:5. This is the primary requisite of a pentecostal revival.

It means to end, i.e., how the thing will fall out—Ruth 3:18.

It means expression of emotion, as falling upon one's neck in embrace—Gen. 33:4.

It is used to describe prayer, i.e., the falling of one's supplications before the Lord—Jer. 42:2.

It means to desert, to fall away, to go over to another party—Jer. 37:14.

It means an abortion—Job 3:16. A premature birth, or miscarriage is to fall from the womb too early.

כשל

FALL: "O Israel, return unto the Lord thy God; for thou hast fallen by thy iniquity", (Hos. 14:1). *Kashal* does not have in it the idea of death or condemnation or damnation because of sin, but means:

To totter, reel, faint—Jer. 50:32. When God's children sin, they become a feeble folk in influence.

To stumble and become useless—Lev. 26:37. Valiant men march in paths of righteousness.

To be miserable and unhappy—Ezek. 33:12. "Blessed (happinesses) are the pure in heart for they shall see God." Sin makes the unsaved and the saved miserable.

To fail—Lam. 1:14. Backsliding Israel, walking in iniquity, will stumble and cannot arise of her own strength and will fail in every undertaking for her God. Romans 12:1, 2, says we are to present ourselves to God for service; but must be transformed, and in no way conformed to the world.

רחק

FAR: "The Lord is far from the wicked", (Prov. 15:29). "Salvation is far from the wicked", (Ps. 119:155). *Rachaq* means:

To recede—Job 30:10. In the ebb and flow of society, it is sad when friends recede. It is life's greatest tragedy when God recedes from one's life; and what should be said of the man who recedes from God? This shade of meaning could be transitive, and we would have: to repel.

Distant, remote—Ps. 22:11, 19. This is the prediction that God would forsake His Son. The sins of others removed God into the distance for Christ. Our sins will remove God out of our midst—II Chron. 7:14.

To put far away—Ps. 103:11. This is a good signification, because we want our sins removed as far as the east is from the west, but not our God.

Departing—Ps. 73:27. Can one picture God departing? He will so do for the wicked. Then what can the wicked do? Reason with God and have his sins washed as white as snow—Isa. 1:18. Christ is the Advocate for this trial.

אב

FATHER: "Thy first father hath sinned, and thy teachers have transgressed against me", (Isa. 43:24). *Ab* is a meaningful word full of instruction.

It means forefather or ancestor and could be translated in the above verse "earliest forefather" indicating the antiquity of iniquity.

It means founder—Gen. 17:4, 5. There are two words in Abram: *Ab,* father and *am,* people.

It means Creator—Isa. 64:8. God is the source and the origin of man.

It means to be a nurse—Isa. 22:21. Jerusalem and other cities need a nursing-father to be a blessed benefactor.

It means a prophet and a master—II Kings 2:12. Those who, like Elijah, become great teachers may be called fathers of learning or of the church, or even of the community.

It means companion—Job 16, 17 (espec. 17:14). Through his trials and to the grave Job claimed God.

פחד

FEAR: "Wherefore now let the fear of the Lord be upon you.", (II Chron. 19:7). *Pachad* means:

To tremble, to be in trepidation—Isa. 12:2. While fear can make a man tremble, trust in the Lord will save a man from that fear.

To be on one's guard—Prov. 28:14. We ought continually to walk circumspectly, having our conversation in heaven.

Terror—Isa. 2:19. If God inspires terror, that will lead one to trust and reverence Him like Isaac did—Gen. 31:53, then such terror becomes a blessing.

An attendant, a life-guard. This idea is in the root of the Persian language. It is good to consider here, since we know that man likely does more because of fear than because of love or because of any other emotion.

ירא

FEAR: "Better is little with the fear of the Lord than great treasure and trouble therewith", (Prov. 15:16). *Yarah* means:

96

To reverence, to trust—Exod. 14:31. When the people saw the great works of God they trembled and believed.

To tremble for joy—Isa. 60:5. This is enough to cause astonishment. People of all nations were converted to the Lord. The heart was afraid and swelled with joy.

חגג

FEAST: "For we must hold a feast unto the Lord", (Exod. 10:9). God's people gathered up offerings and went to the house of the Lord to celebrate with a feast. *Feast* derives from the Hebrew root *chagag* whose denotements are given under the word *Dance*.

רעה

FEED: "And I will give you pastors according to my heart which shall feed you . . . ", (Jer. 3:15). *Feed* derives from the Hebrew root *raah* which has rich denotements. *Shepherd* also derives from this root.

It denotes looking upon and beholding with pleasure—I Sam. 16:11. This is a basic characteristic of a good shepherd.

It denotes leading—II Sam. 5:2. David led his people in paths of righteousness by still waters to tables of plenty.

It denotes feeding by preaching—Prov. 10:21. The preacher's lips and the lips of the righteous shall speak words that will be food for the souls of many.

It denotes grazing—Isa. 65:25. The shepherd will lead his sheep to a good pasture and will induce them to eat.

It denotes being a companion—Prov. 13:20. The shepherd will be in and out among his flock: suffering with them and rejoicing with them; having experiences in common with them.

לחם

FIGHT: "The Lord shall fight for you, and ye shall hold your peace", (Exod. 14:14). *Lacham* means:

To eat, to consume—Deut. 32:24. Why should a child of God fear, when such disposition shall be made of his enemies?

Man-eater is the basic meaning of the Persian root comparable to *lacham*. This is used to describe a fierce warrior.

To contend or fight together—I Sam. 17:10. While the Philistine did not win his contest, God has never lost one of His.

To besiege—Judg. 5:8. When there is something to be won or taken, as a land flowing with milk and honey, we must have the Lord to fight for us.

אֵשׁ

FIRE: "Then the Lord rained upon Sodom and upon Gomorrah brimstone and fire from the Lord out of heaven.", (Gen. 19:24). *Esh* means:

Fire of God—I Kings 18:38. Like lightning did fire fall from heaven and burned up the wetted-down sacrifice of Elijah.

The anger of God—Deut. 32:22. The lowest hell, the earth, and the foundations of the mountains were to burn because God was provoked.

Destruction—Job 15:34. A destroying fire will consume the hypocrites and the bribers.

Scorching heat—Joel 1:19. There is enough about God destroying by fire in the Old Testament to believe that the prophecy in the New Testament, that the world will be destroyed by a fervent heat, is coming as sure as the flood came. (See: Ps. 106:18 where we are told the wicked were burned up by a flame after they fell into a great hole.)

פָּרַח

FLOURISH: "Those that be planted in the house of the Lord shall flourish in the courts of our God", (Ps. 92:13). *Parach,* the Hebrew root for *flourish,* is very colorful.

It is used to report that leprosy broke out—Lev. 13:12. Even as sin breaks out, or a plague—Lev. 14:43.

It is used to report that judgment springs up—Hos. 11:4. Judgment will be the day of reckoning for a Hosea who has been forsaken by his wife and for the church that forsakes God.

It is used to report that the wicked flourish—Ps. 92:7. Wickedness outgrows weeds.

It is used to report that God's people flourish—Ps. 92:12-15. Those whose partner is God will prosper.

It means prosperity—Isa. 27:6. God prospers those who plant their investments in the house of the Lord.

It means to fly—Ezek. 13:20. The Lord's people grow so fast that God caused them to fly out of the arms of the hunters that hunt them.

This root also means progeny—Job 30:12. There is a breaking forth from the womb. The church flourishes when there is travailing in Zion and souls are born into the kingdom of God.

גדר

FOLD: "We will build sheep-folds here for our cattle and cities for our little ones", (Num. 32:16). *Gadar,* the Hebrew root for fold, has interesting meanings.

It means to wall around anyone—Job 19:8. This was to obstruct his way, shut him in and prevent his going out.

It means a walled place or an enclosure—Ezra 9:9. Here in Ezra's tremendous prayer of confession of sin and request for revival, God promises to build a wall around Judah and Jerusalem to fold His people.

This root is used to build a name for a city of a king—Josh. 12:13. The Holy City, with its walls of jasper will house the King of kings—Rev. 21.

אחר

FOLLOW: "Surely none of the men . . . shall see the land (that floweth with milk and honey) . . . Save Caleb . . . and Joshua . . . for they have wholly followed the Lord", (Num. 32:11, 12). *Achar* means:

To remain—Gen. 32:5. Those that remain with the Lord shall always have the victory.

To linger—Judg. 5:28. Those who linger around the Lord will get blessings like Jacob did when he spent the whole night at it.

To tarry late—Prov. 23:30. The word carries the idea that waiting with the Lord may bring Great Blessings.

The last—Ps. 139:9. This seems to smack of the sense of humility.

נבל

FOOL: "The fool hath said in his heart, There is no God", (Ps. 14:1; 53:1). *Nabal,* the Hebrew word for *fool,* has several meanings.

It means to wilt, to fade—Ps. 18:45. A man who talks like that is well described in this subordinate meaning of the word.

It means to fail, to come to nought, to become a corpse—Ps. 79:2. The man must really be dead in his sin.

It means to act wickedly—Prov. 30:32. Anyone who is blessed and denies the existence of his benefactor is indeed wicked.

It means to esteem lightly—Deut. 32:15. This is a step toward despising.

It means to disgrace, to treat with contumely—Nah. 3:6. It is certainly casting filth upon God to say He is not.

It means shameful deed, crime—Judg. 19:23, 24. It might be expected that those thus constituted might thus do.

It means punishment—Job 42:8. A fool shall receive fool's wages.

צוה

FORBID: " . . . The Lord thy God hath forbidden thee", (Deut. 4:23). For the meaning of *tsavah* see *Appoint.*

כפר

FORGIVE: "But he, being full of compassion, forgave their iniquity and destroyed them not", (Ps. 78:38). *Kaphar* is one of the great words of the Bible. For its meaning see *Atonement.*

נשא

FORGIVE: "Yet now, if thou wilt forgive their sin—and if not, blot me, I pray thee, out of thy book which thou hast written", (Exod. 32:32). Moses, in his great intercessory prayer, chose a great word for forgive: *nasa.* For its meaning, see *Accepted* and *Bear.*

יָצַר

FORM: "The Lord God formed man of the dust", (Gen. 2:7).
Yatsar means:

To fashion, to make—Gen. 2:8, 19. This was the fashion of the
hour of all hours. This was the style and never to be changed.

To destine, to appoint for or to anything—Isa. 44:21. God made
man for a reason—for himself.

To form in mind, to devise, to meditate—Jer. 18:11. Back in
the hall of eternity God planned man.

תֹהוּ

FORM: "And the earth was without form", (Gen. 1:2). *Tohu*
means:

A desert—Deut. 32:10. No life there.

Desolation—Isa. 24:10. No one lived there.

Worthless and empty—Isa. 41:29. This is true from our point
of view and from God's.

עָזַב

FORSAKE: "I will not fail thee, nor forsake thee", (Josh.
1:5). *Azab* means:

To let go free—II Kings 14:26. There seems to be in this word
the idea of abandoning—Exod. 23:5.

To leave, to quit—Gen. 2:24. Here a son leaves his parents and
joins the company of another.

To entrust one to another's charge—Gen. 39:6. God will never
leave his children with baby-sitters. God keeps the nursery.

Deserted—Isa. 6:12. Man may desert a piece of land, but God
will never desert man.

To withdraw favor from anyone—Ruth 2:20. The Lord will not
withdraw favor from his children.

נָטַשׁ

FORSAKE: "The Lord our God be with us . . . let him not leave
us, nor forsake us", (I Kings 8:57). *Natash,* the Hebrew root for

101

forsake, has several meanings.

It means to let go or to leave to oneself—I Sam. 30:16. The godless horde was let go their own way. They chose to eat, drink, dance and run through with spoil taken from God's people and they suffered elimination. Impenitent sinners' way leads to eternal death.

It means to let alone or let lie as a field—Exod. 33:11. We should want to pray the prayer quoted at the head of the study of this word lest the Lord let the mission fields, the church fields, the field of our soul grow over with obnoxious weeds of sin.

It means to permit—Gen. 31:28. One facet of forsake is to permit one to have his way but the prayer in I Kings 8:57 indicates desire to go some other way.

It means to cast—Ezek. 29:5. Here the idea is that one will be let go with force. Those wanting to walk in the way of the ungodly will one day be cast into hell with them.

It means to spread abroad as an army—I Sam. 4:2. Impious people must learn from this that the enemy, if permitted will set itself in array against them.

It means to loose as a rope—Isa. 33:23. O God, loose not thy ropes around us as a nation; as a church; as a family; as one soul.

מצא

FOUND: "Seek ye the Lord while He may be found", (Isa. 55:6). *Matsa* means:

To come to—Job 11:7. Seek the Lord while he can be attained unto.

To acquire—Gen. 26:12. Search for God while he is obtainable.

To fall in with, to be in the company of—Gen. 2:20. This is a high reason for wanting God and desiring the Desire of the nations.

To suffice—Num. 11:22. It is most wonderful to find God when he satisfies every noble desire. He is all-sufficient for all.

יסד

FOUNDATION: "Behold, I lay in Zion for a foundation a stone, a tried stone, a precious corner stone, a sure foundation:

he that believeth shall not make haste", (Isa. 28:16). *Yasad* means:

To found, to lay the foundation of a building—Ezra 3:12. In Christ, the Rock, was the idea of building—building a kingdom.

To establish—Ps. 119:152. There is an everlastingness to this edifice.

To support oneself—Ps. 2:2. This foundation will not need a lift or a prop. It is sure. It is firm. It will not become sodden with water—Exod. 12:9.

Beginning—Ezra 7:9. Just as the first day begins a month, so is Christ the beginning of the Christian era with its blessings. And the beginning of much else besides which will last through eternity.

שִׁית

FOUNDATION: "If the foundations be destroyed, what can the righteous do?", (Ps. 11:3). *Shith* is the Hebrew root of the word foundations in this text. *Shith* has many very colorful significations.

It means to set in place as persons to keep a watch or to guard. God's work will have strengthened stakes and lengthened cords if men can be found to watch and tend it with their best.

It means to constitute. Churches are constituted.

It means to put in array as an army. Christian soldiers may go forth to war being well armed from head to foot.

It means to found, that is to found the world upon columns— I Sam. 2:8. God's kingdom program can well be founded on the pillars of the churches.

It means to lay the hand upon anyone—Gen. 48:17. God, through His Spirit lays hands on men for Himself.

It means to lay the hand with anyone, that is join hands in doing something—Exod. 23:1.

It means to put on something, i.e., garment. Put on Christ.

חדל

FRAIL: "Lord, make me to know mine end, and the measure of my days, what it is; that I may know how frail I am", (Ps. 39:4).

103

Chadel means:

To cease from labor—I Sam. 2:5. Man is always to face up to the fact that he cannot do anything.

To cease to be—Exod. 9:34. There is only a step between man and death.

To leave off, to desist—I Sam. 9:5. Frailty may cause man to beware of doing.

To forbear, to not do—I Kings 22:6, 15. When frailty is consulted, indecision and hesitancy result.

Destitute, despised, forsaken—Isa. 53:3. This is the most touching picture of frailty.

A place of rest, hades, the region of the dead—Isa. 38:11. This helps to explain the remark: "There are dead members on our church roll." Those members have not been led to have strength for work.

נדיב

FREE: " . . . And uphold me with thy free spirit. Then will I teach transgressors thy ways and sinners shall be converted unto thee", (Ps. 51:12, 13). *Nadib* means:

To show oneself willing—Neh. 11:2. The spirit of God must voluntarily brace one if he is to teach sinners effectively.

To offer oneself spontaneously—I Chron. 29:9. Never is it known when and on whom the Holy Spirit will descend. He does not come when man orders or requests, but there is revival when He does come.

Volunteer service—II Chron. 17:16. Just like soldiers offering themselves for sacred service in kingdom work, so might it please the spirit of God to volunteer. When He does, success is assured, but until then it is best to gather in an upper room and pray for days if necessary.

Abundance—Ps. 68:9. When He comes, it is in abundance, because He is great. Great things happen when He comes.

אהב

FRIEND: " . . . a friend that sticketh closer than a brother",

(Prov. 18:24). *Ahab* is a great word and its meaning is given under *Beloved*.

פרה

FRUIT: "And he shall be like a tree planted by the rivers of water, that bringeth his fruit in his season . . .", (Ps. 1:3). *Parah* means:

To bear—(The primary idea seems to be to carry along: hence, *carriage* or *fahren* in German and *sedan* or *aphiryon* in Hebrew.)

A heifer—Hos. 4:16. Reference made here is to a backsliding heifer describing Israel as a people sliding back. In other words, Israel did not bear the burden for the Lord. She did not pull together in the work of the Lord. She backed out of the yoke.

Kernel—Neh. 7:57. Perida, who bore children, was fruitful and was named *kernel*. Those bearing the yoke with their Lord will be like kernels of grain in the Lord's great field.

Blossoming—I Kings 4:17. Paruah, whose son was Jehoshaphat, was said to have blossomed in her son. One blossoms in kingdom work when he is instrumental in causing another to be born into that kingdom.

A region producing gold—II Chron. 3:6. Parvaim could be the name given to the people bearing fruit for the Lord.

כבם

FULLER: "For He is like a refiner's fire, and like fullers' soap", (Mal. 3:2). The Lord can full the sinful hearts. *Kabas,* the Hebrew root employed to describe the Lord's action as a Fuller, has several meanings.

It means to tread upon—Isa. 7:3. Garments were washed by trampling them with the feet in a vat of water. Testimonies tell that in the cleansing from sin one feels like God trampled upon the heart in bringing about conviction.

It means to purify, as the heart from iniquity—Ps. 51:2, 7. David applies for a cleansing to the Fuller whose soap can wash the vilest clean by a unique process—Jer. 2:22 which must precede salvation—Jer. 4:14.

מלא

FULNESS: "The Earth is the Lord's and the fulness thereof", (Ps. 24:1). Much is the Lord's for *mala* means:

To be full—Ps. 144:13. Consider several verses in this context to discover much that belongs to God.

פרד

GARDEN: "I made me gardens and orchards, and I planted trees in them of all kinds of fruits: I made me pools of water . . .", (Eccl. 2:5). *Garden* derives from the Hebrew root *parad* which is very colorful.

It means to expand or to spread out—Ezek. 1:11. In this case it was wings, perhaps for flying away. In a garden is a good place to stretch the mind, eyes, soul and body.

It means to separate or be separated—Prov. 18:1. Here is a wise man who went aside from the crowd to seek wisdom and to intermeddle with it. In Hos. 14:4, it is used to tell of a man that went aside to be with a harlot but for the child of God it would mean to go aside to talk and walk with the Lord.

It means to be scattered—Esth. 3:8. God's people were scattered in the king's many provinces but God's people today are scattered all over God's world—in some places very sparsely.

It means a park, a paradise or a place elevated and cultivated—Song of Sol. 4:13; Neh. 2:8; Eccl. 2:5. This word *paradees* corresponds to the Greek *paradeisos* which was applied to pleasure gardens and parks with wild animals around the mansions of Persian monarchs. But they had it not as well as children of God.

אסף

GATHER: " . . . The Lord spake unto Moses, Gather the people together, and I will give them water", (Num. 21:16). *Asaph,* the Hebrew root for *gather,* has interesting meanings.

It means to collect or assemble a people—Exod. 3:16, for the purpose of getting a word from the Lord or for some other good reason.

It means to be hospitable to another—Josh. 20:4. A friendly

106

church or Bible class will be receiving all kinds of people: helpless, helpful and in need of help.

It means a collector—I Chron. 16:5. This root is used to build Asaph's name. His duty was to collect psalms, records, praises. How valuable a choirmaster and a secretary are to a church.

It means a mixed multitude—Num. 11:4. What a privilege God's servants have gathering in the halt, the maimed, the poor and rich, the blind and the ones who can see spiritually in order that the Lord's house may be filled.

קבץ

GATHER: ". . .With great mercies will I gather thee", (Isa. 54:7). *Qabats,* the Hebrew root for *gather,* has several meanings.

It means to collect—II Sam. 3:21. Here Abner collects the people together. God would that none should perish but that all would come unto Him.

It is strangely used to mean the gathering of iniquity—Ps. 41:6. Matter was collected for slander.

It means to assemble—Isa. 60:4. The sons and daughters of the Lord flow together unto Zion in the light, splendor and peace God sheds upon her.

It means to take up with the hand. God handpicks those He wants around Him. No man can come unto the Lord except the Lord draw him—John 6:44.

It means to gather up with tenderness—Isa. 40:11. In how many merciful ways does God gather His lambs.

It means to cause to be assembled—Ezek. 38:8. God uses various means to bring the redeemed to the land of the redeemed.

It means a heap or a hoard—Josh. 21:22. This root is used to build the name for a city, Kibzaim, which means two heaps. It certainly must be the desire of men everywhere to be in the Lord's heaps. The old expression, "there were heaps of people at church", is not far wrong.

דּוֹר

GENERATION: "But Judah shall dwell forever, and Jerusalem from generation to generation", (Joel 3:20). Judah with her

Jerusalem shall be blessed round and round; on and on. As to how this is timed shall show up in the study of *dur*, the Hebrew root for *generation*.

It means to dwell—Ps. 84:10. (In the quoted text above another Hebrew root is used for *dwell*). Here in Psalms the idea is moving in a circle, going round and round with the wicked only to dissipate into dishonorable disintegration. But Joel writes that the Lord promises Zion a never-ending life of bliss.

The root is used to express the idea that man lives long enough to be replaced by others in about 30-35 years and they in turn to be replaced in about the same length of time. Hence, we have rounds and rounds of people, never running out and this is called *generations*.

This root is used to build a name for a city—I Kings 4:11. Certainly Jerusalem shall be a "continuing city" (Heb. 13:14), with rounds and rounds of blessings.

ענה

GENTLENESS: "Thy gentleness hath made me great", (Ps. 18:35). This word *anah* is used here to describe the gentleness of God. It means:

To suffer, to be afflicted—Ps. 116:10. There was a gentleness about Christ, when He was afflicted, that has made Him great.

To humble one's self—Exod. 10:3. Humility, gentleness, and affliction were all three together in Christ.

To subdue by force—Judg. 19:24. When the Lamb was taken by force, He opened not His mouth.

To fast—Lev. 16:31. The soul is afflicted by fasting; would this make it gentle?

To submit, to dedicate—Dan. 10:12. Gentleness rears her beautiful head when one submits himself to be buried with Christ by baptism, to suffer with Christ, and give himself to Christ.

To be distressed, to be miserable—Ps. 25:9. This kind of a person is of a humble mind, and prefers rather to bear injuries than to repay them. Instead of returning evil for evil, the Lord prayed for those who persecuted Him unto death.

Mildness, clemency—Ps. 18:35. Anyone appropriating the clemency of God and the mildness of God will be great. Those who humble themselves will God lift up. Those who take the lowest seats will be asked to come up higher.

נפש

GHOST: "She hath given up the ghost", (Jer. 15:9). Most times *nephesh* is translated *soul.* One other time is it translated *ghost* (Job 11:20). It means:

Breath—Gen. 1:20.

Spirit, that which is life in a body—Lev. 17:11. The place of this vital spirit was supposed to be in the blood.

Soul, mind—Isa. 42:1. This is supposed to be the rational part of man where is the seat of emotions, feelings, affections, etc. This expression may be love, joy, fear, confidence, piety toward God, or desire.

A living soul, a living being—Gen. 2:7. This seems to most fully make man resemble God in whose image he was made.

Myself—Ps. 3:3. Here *nephesh* means a person. In other words, Ghost means an individual; and when that individual gives up the ghost, there is only clay left.

מנח

GIFT: "Many brought gifts unto the Lord to Jerusalem", (II Chron. 32:23). *Monach* means:

To give—Gen. 4:3. Cain and Abel both gave gifts to the Lord, but gifts from both of these brothers were not accepted. It is not only our duty to give to the Lord, but to pray He will accept the gift.

To bestow—Jer. 17:26. The shade of sense here is that of conferring a gift; giving a gift with honor surrounding it.

To divide out. The tithe is a dividing with God what one has.

A present—Gen. 32:13. There is a beautiful practice among people: taking a present to those to be visited. In this word is the idea that when we go to God's house to visit Him, we are to take a gift and present it to the Lord with proper ceremony and with the hope that He will receive it, be pleased with it, and use it.

Tribute—II Sam. 8:2. Here the new subjects of King David brought gifts which seemed to be exacted of them. Since the Lord gives His children everything and they are blessed subjects of His, why should not He expect or demand at least a tithe?

An offering—Lev. 2:1, 4, 5, 6. This means an offering, amounting to a sacrifice, is to be brought to God.

אזר

GIRD: "Thou hast . . . girded me with gladness", (Ps. 30:11). The Hebrew word for *Gird* is *azar*.

It means to surround and bind oneself around as with a garment—Job 30:18. The glad are well clad. He who is clothed in garments sequined with cheerfulness will be welcomed more to more places.

It means to be prepared for battle—Ps. 18:39. God makes this preparation by girding with strength—Ps. 18:32. In fact, those whom God makes glad are pretty well prepared for life's battles.

There is in this word also the idea of being strong and robust. Happy people usually have better health, win more friends, prosper more and thereby collect strength.

נתן

GIVE: "Turn, O backsliding children, saith the Lord . . . And I will give you pastors according to my heart, which shall feed you . . .", (Jer. 3:14, 15). Where translated *give, nathan* is used over 1000 times and means:

To deliver over into the power of another—Lev. 26:25. This is real dedication when it is man giving himself over to God.

To give in custody—Gen. 39:20. This means trust and security.

To place or make a covenant—Gen. 9:13. A promise is given.

To constitute one as something—Gen. 17:4. This is to give one rank, honor or station. This is done by putting this idea, this elegant sense, into the giving act.

To make a thing like something else—I Kings 10:27; Gen. 43:30. Money given to the Lord becomes messengers for Him. Those giving themselves to be the Lord's ministers or missionaries will be speaking in the Lord's stead.

Appointed by the king, Nathan-melech—II Kings 23:11.

Given of God, Nathanael—Num. 1:8. This means one appointed by the Lord. The Lord appoints men and women for His purposes.

יהב

GIVE: "Give unto the Lord . . .", (I Chron. 16:28, 29; Ps. 29:1, 2; 96:7, 8). *Yahab* means:

To give—Ps. 55:22. Here the word is translated *cast,* meaning, of course, *give.* We are to give God our burdens as if they were a burdensome cloak. Then we can perform His work better.

Burden—Ruth 3:15. Here the giving is the transfer of a load.

Trouble—Prov. 30:15. It is not seen readily how the idea of trouble is to be found in the word.

To set—Josh. 18:4. Men were appointed for God. We are to mark ourselves and what we have for God. We are to set them aside for God.

To lay, to put—Ezra 5:16. To lay a foundation is a gift indeed, and to make a gift may lay a foundation. Giving will lay the foundation for kingdom building.

גיל

GLAD: "I will be glad and rejoice in thy mercy", (Ps. 31:7). *Gul* means:

To move in a circle, to dance and leap for joy—Isa. 65:18.

To rejoice in a person—Isa. 29:19. In this case it is to be glad in the Lord, and not in things, people, circumstances which may be swept away.

To tremble, to fear—Job 37:1. This trembling is caused by the palpitation of the heart. Fear of God excited the heart.

Circuit, generation—Dan. 1:10. This means men of a certain age.

Shouting and rejoicing—Isa. 35:2. Here is gladness manifest.

כבד

GLORIFY: "All nations . . . shall glorify thy name . . . I will glorify thy name forevermore", (Ps. 86:9, 12). *Kabed* means:

To be heavy—Job 6:3. Glory is a gem of heavy karat in the casket of characteristics about our God.

To be honored—Job 14:21. Honor is a weighty quality of character.

To be great, abundant, vehement—Judg. 20:34. It would take something strong, and much of it, to begin to describe the glory of God.

To be rich—Gen. 13:2. Like fountains abounding with water would we have the opulence of earth exhibit the name of our Lord.

Magnificent—Ps. 45:13. Just another trace of the significance of this word. It is used about 500 times in the Bible, and in most cases in connection with the Lord of Glory.

הלך

GO: "And . . . Moses . . . said, Be strong and of a good courage: for thou must go . . . and the Lord, He it is that doth go before thee, He will be with thee, He will not fail thee, neither forsake thee: fear not, neither be dismayed", (Deut. 31:7, 8). Go is used about 3,000 times in the Bible. In verse 7, *Bo* is used and its primary meaning is *enter.* This is most proper since the people are to enter the promised land. (For its meaning see *enter.*) In verses 6 and 8 *halak* is used which means:

To go forth—Gen. 7:18. It may be a ship that is going forth, or it may be a boundary that is going on and on to extend one's holdings. How we wish to extend King Emmanuel's territory—Josh. 16:8.

To go through or over a place—Deut. 1:19. There may be a desert place in one's life, but he is to go through it to a better land, stopping at oases on the way.

To go with anyone—Exod. 10:9. The Lord promises to go with us alway.

To have intercourse with—Prov. 13:20. This is rich for travelers who have the Lord with them. They will have sweet converse.

To go away, to vanish—Job 19:10. The Lord may be provoked into leaving us, or, we may leave the Lord!

To increase, to go on adding—Gen. 26:13. Christians may go on growing.

אֵל

GOD: "God is my salvation . . .", (Isa. 12:2). *El* means:

Mighty One, Hero, Champion—Ezek. 31:11. When one would do good, evil is present—Rom. 7:21, but there is a Champion who gives power and righteousness and therefore victory—Phil. 3:9-11.

Power—Gen. 31:29. God gives "Off Limits" memoranda to Satan, and has power both to enforce the regulations and to overcome him to whom it is given.

Divinity—Exod. 15:11. (One stands with unsandaled feet and searches for language he does not have, when wanting to speak of the One so "glorious in holiness, fearful in praises, doing wonders.")

אֱלוֹהַּ

GOD: "But in his estate shall he honor the God of forces", (Dan. 11:38). *Eloah* means One God, the True God, the God of Israel—Exod. 5:1.

אֱלֹהִים

GOD: "In the beginning God . . .", (Gen. 1:1). *Elohim* is plural here and means:

A God having several persons in Himself, like many teachers believe that here in Gen. 1:1 is meant the Trinity: God the Father, God the Son, and God the Holy Ghost. A God of several powers, many resources, many majesties, much glory.

To God belongs whatever is wonderful, excellent, distinguished, unmatched and unmatchable, unequaled, which in the first place was made by God; e.g. "The river of God"—Ps. 65:9; "The hill of God"—Ps. 68:15.

(This plural form of God's name is used about 2,000 times. God's name is found to be translated *God* about 3,500 times in the Bible.)

113

יצא

GOING (forth): "The glory of the Lord filled the house of the Lord . . . and the Lord said . . . Mark well the entering in of the house, with every going forth of the sanctuary", (Ezek 44:4, 5). *Yatsa* means:

To go forth as to war—Job 39:21. The Christian's life is a warfare. There is no armor for his back. He must always go forth.

Going forth as merchantment—Deut. 33:18. The church must traffic to the ends of the earth merchandising the Gospel.

Going forth of slaves manumitted by their masters—Lev. 25:40, 41. Indeed is it jubilee for him who is free from his sins.

Going forth of posterity—Gen. 17:6. Christians ought to be a cause of other Christians being born into the kingdom of God.

Going forth out of dangers—Ecc. 7:18. Those busy going unto the uttermost parts of the earth with the good tidings will not linger in the valley of schisms.

Going forth like the sun—Ps. 19:6. The church upon the hill must let its light shine, so people can see how to get to God and glorify Him.

Going forth like a plant that blossoms—Job 14:2. This is becoming of Christians and is their duty.

Springing forth like a fountain—Deut. 8:7. Jesus said his followers were to have in them fountains of water springing up.

Going forth as a boundary—Josh. 15:3-11. This is a challenge to those who know Him. They will ever want to extend His kingdom.

Laid out, expended like money in the house of the Lord—II Kings 12:13.

To be promulgated—Isa. 42:3. Right shall be proclaimed to all nations.

בצר

GOLD: "If thou return to the Almighty, thou shalt be built up, . . . then shalt thou lay up gold . . .", (Job 22:23-24). *Betsar* means:

To cut off, to cut off access, to restrain, to prevent, to make

114

inaccessible, spoken of high walls—Deut. 28:52. So is there a perfect defense for him who lays up the Lord's word in his heart, returns to the Lord, and puts away sin from the home. This becomes the man's gold.

Fortification—Jer. 51:53. To be ready for war against the devil is silver and gold without alloy.

Sheep-fold—Mic. 2:12. The greatest riches are his who is in The Shepherd's fold.

Drought—Jer. 17:8. That is, the heavens are restrained and there is no rain. Upon reflection this shade of sense might yield many lessons. (There are other Hebrew words for gold, but *betsar* was selected for its richness in the text above. The others mean *shining*).

טוב

GOOD: "O taste and see that the Lord is good . . .", (Ps. 34:8). For the meaning of *tob* see *Merry*—I Sam. 8:16.

חסד

GOODLINESS: "All the goodliness thereof is as the flower of the field", (Isa. 40:6). *Chesed* means:

To feel and practice kindness and love towards anyone—Gen. 21:23. Indeed this is good-will toward all men.

Mercy, grace—Ps. 5:7. They that are merciful and gracious are the goodliest of all, and God is goodlier than that.

Elegance, beauty—Isa. 40:6. The doing of favors and the bestowing of benefits on others is a beauty deeper than the skin.

טוב

GOODS: "The Lord shall make thee plenteous in goods . . .", (Deut. 28:11). For the meaning of *tob* see *Merry*. There are many words translated goods: *chayil* which means wealth; *melakah* which means business; *nitksin* which means riches; *qinyan* which means acquisitions; *rekush* which means substance; etc; but here where the Lord proposes to make one full of goods, *tob* is the word the Spirit put in the heart and on the pen of the writer. It means to be well with one, to be pleasing, to be cheerful in heart, to do good to others, to be virtuous, beautiful, kind, distinguished, etc.

שרה

GOVERNMENT: "And the government shall be upon His shoulder", (Isa. 9:6). *Sarah* means:

To place in a row, to arrange in order. No one has done as much as a cupful is to an ocean-full to arrange things in order for a person, for the social order, for the world, as did He on Whom the government was placed.

To contend—Gen. 32:29. Jesus waged war with the enemy of souls on behalf of man.

Nobility—Lam. 1:1. As a territory is princess among provinces, so is Jesus the King of Kings. Thus did God wisely place the government of His creation on the shoulder of the Everlasting Prince of Peace.

חנן

GRACE: "Noah found grace in the eyes of the Lord", (Gen. 6:8). *Chanan* means:

To be favorably disposed, to be gracious, to be compassionate—Exod. 33:19. That is grace which is manifested mercy, although it might have been hot displeasure.

To give graciously, to bestow mercifully and kindly—Gen. 33:5. It is not our deserts but God's mercy that dictates how much God shall give to us.

To grieve for, to entreat for—Ps. 102:12-14. God's kindness is not only resident in Him in great measure, but is manifest to the children of men with gracious plentifulness. More than that, God even creates *giving* situations.

A prophet, Hanani—I Kings 16:1. Gracious, is a good name for one to receive, especially if that one possesses virtues suitable to the name. Prophets ought to be gracious.

כוא

GRANT: And Jabez called on the God of Israel, saying, "Oh that thou wouldest bless me indeed, and enlarge my coast, and that thy hand might be with me, and that thou wouldest keep

116

me from evil, that it may not grieve me! And God granted him that which he requested'', (I Chron. 4:10). This is an unusually effective use of the word *bo*. For its meaning see *Enter*.

נתן

GRANTED: "The desire of the righteous shall be granted", (Prov. 10:24). *Nathan* is the Hebrew word used here. For its meaning see *Give*.

קבר

GRAVE: "And Jacob set a pillar upon her grave", (Gen. 35:20). *Qabar* means:

To bury—Gen. 23:5.

Sepulchre—Gen. 23:20.

שׁאוֹל

GRAVE: "I will ransom them from the power of the grave; I will redeem them from death: O, death, I will be thy plagues; O grave, I will be thy destruction . . .", (Hos. 13:14). *Sheol* means:

Underworld, subterranean place—Job 10:21, 22. This vast expanse so filled with thick darkness, where the only light is more darkness, is described by both genders—Isa. 5:14; Job 26:6.

In it are shadows of death, gates—Isa. 38:10. It is a hungry cavity—Ezek. 32:21.

(This word may be related to the root *Shaah* which means: noise, uproar, tumult, desolation, etc. Some hold it comes from the root *Shaal* which means: to ask, to demand for oneself. This is grounds for giving the grave the title: *Orcus Rapax,* or, Rapacious Cavity).

חלה

GRIEF: "Surely He hath borne our griefs and carried our sorrows", (Isa. 53:4). *Chalah* means:

To be rubbed, to be polished. When trinkets, necklaces and other female ornaments were so done, they became smooth, sweet, and pleasant. Striking and smiting of our Saviour caused Him to become sweet to those who wear Him in their hearts.

117

To be worn down in strength, to be weak—Judg. 16:7. No wonder our Lord gave way under the load He was bearing up Golgotha. He was carrying our griefs.

To be sick, to be diseased—Gen. 48:1. The Lord was sick from wounds—II Kings 1:2. He might have been sick from love—Song of Sol. 2:5, 5:8.

יעץ

GUIDE: "I will guide thee with mine eye", (Ps. 32:8). For the meaning of *yaats* see *Counsel*.

נחה

GUIDE: "The Lord shall guide thee continually", (Isa. 58:11). *Nachah* means:

To lead, to conduct—Exod. 32:34. Moses is not only to conduct God's people toward the promised land but he will also have their welfare in his heart. It is comforting to know God will lead us and also provide for us along the way and at the end of the way, all the while having our welfare in His heart.

To transfer, to gather—I Kings 10:26. The Lord gathers us up into the church above to be the bride for the Bridegroom. The Lord so leads that the predestinated are called, justified, and glorified.

אשם

GUILTY: "And the Lord spake unto Moses, saying, Speak unto the children of Israel, when a man or a woman shall commit any sin that men commit, to do a trespass against the Lord, and that person be guilty . . .", (Num. 5:5-6). *Asham* means:

To fail in duty to transgress—Num. 5:7. When a person fails in duty toward another, that person becomes guilty. It is easy to conclude that men who commit sins of omission towards God are indeed guilty.

To be laid waste, to be destroyed—Ezek. 6:6. What desolations follow and even accompany sinners.

To be punished—Ps. 34:21. They that sow to sin shall reap corruption.

Fault, blame, guilt—Gen. 26:10; Jer. 51:5. How many faults can be crowded into the strata of society and of a man's hear.

קָדַשׁ

HALLOW: "And this is the thing that thou shalt do unto them to hallow them, to minister unto me . . .", (Exod. 29:1). For the meaning of *qadash* see *Dedicate*.

הָלַם

HAMMER: "She (Jael) put her hand to the nail and her right hand to the workmen's hammer; and with the hammer she smote Sisera, she smote off his head . . .", (Judg. 5:26). Jael, "blessed among women", smote the leader of those who "came not to the help of the Lord," *Halam,* the Hebrew root for *hammer* has several meanings.

It means to come hither—I Sam. 10:22. The signification is the stomping of a foot to firmly call another to come. Perhaps a type of gavel.

It means to melt—I Sam. 14:16. The report here is that the army disappeared as if by melting in their tracks.

It means to smite—Ps. 141:5. Here the anvil was smitten by workmen much like Jael's operation. We note that *hammer* and *smote* in Judg. 5:26 both derive from the same root, the pronouncing of which sounds like fateful blows of a great hammer: Ha-l-o-me.

יָד

HAND: "And I was strengthened as the hand of the Lord my God was upon me . . .", (Ezra 7:28). *Yad* means:

A hand that is with any one—I Sam. 22:17. This has in it the idea of assistance. (In the U.S. Navy, the phrase "Give a hand" carries with it that signification).

A hand that is against any one—Gen. 37:27. This is tragic, and when it happens in Christian work, it is a tragedy indeed.

A hand that is upon any one for good—Ezra 7:28. This is a providential blessing. For evil—Amos 1:8. This ought cause a person to repent of sin and plead for mercy.

The hand of God on one to make him a prophet—Ezek. 1:3. This fitted Ezekiel for a great ministry.

A hand that is given in submission to the Lord—II Chron. 30:8.

A hand that denotes liberality—I Kings 10:13. A hand that grasps and closes on what it grasps is the opposite of the hand that opens and beautifully gives away that which it has.

אשׁר

HAPPY: "Whoso trusteth in the Lord, happy is he", (Prov. 16:20). The Hebrew word for *happy* in this passage is *ashar* and has several significations.

It means to go straight and to be upright—Prov. 9:6. This is the way of noblest living and issues in gladness but the crooked that wander in the crooked way will be bruised by the law and punished by the Lord.

To turn this word around in another form it means to cause to go straight—Prov. 23:19. He who guides his heart into the straight way honors God, gladdens his parents and has joy in his life—Prov. 23:25.

It also denotes a giver of fortune. In Phoenician mythology the planet Venus was called Astarte and was thought to be a spouse of Baal. Devotees of Astarte assumed that they were given license to give rein to their unregulated urges. This gave them only momentary pleasure. God's children curb their physical urges, trust in the Lord and have spiritual happiness evermore awarded them by the giver of good and perfect gifts.

This Hebrew word is used variously in relative forms and greatly affects pronouns, adverbs and substantives. A study of these indicates that solid joy comes as a result of proper relations with proper persons!

קשׁה

HARDEN: "Harden not your heart, as in the day of provocation . . ."; "He, that being often reproved hardeneth his neck, shall suddenly be destroyed, and that without remedy", (Ps. 95:8; Prov. 29:1). *Qashah* means:

To be harsh—II Sam. 19:43. It seems that harsh words are nearly always the product of a Godless heart. Obstinacy and obtuseness in language may be twins.

To be hard, to be difficult—Deut. 1:17. Difficulties issue from a hardened heart.

To be harshly oppressed—Isa. 8:21. The hardened in heart shall be hungry and otherwise oppressed and will curse God who gave them a heart in the first place.

Labor—Gen. 35:16. Here it is reported that it went hard with a women in a birth, but shall it not mean much harder and fruitless labor to him that steels his heart against God.

Yoke—II Kings 2:12. Here in a good sense, Elisha is taking on the work of Elijah; but, he who is hardened in heart has taken upon himslef, in a bad sense, a yoke very burdensome for time and eternity.

Impudence—Ezek. 2:4. Obstinancy and stiffheartedness may lead one to have the hard face of impudence.

רעע

HARM: "And David said to Abishai, Now shall Sheba . . . do us more harm than did Absalom", (II Sam. 20:6). As to how much more *harm,* a study of the Hebrew root *raa* will help to discover.

It means to grieve as the heart—Deut. 15:10. In God's war on poverty, men were exhorted to let not their hearts be grieved in a generous giving program.

It means to go ill with any one—Ps. 106:32. It went ill with Moses when God's people rebelled. But, there was God's mercy.

It means to be displeased: Abraham—Gen. 21:11; the Lord—Gen. 38:10. This displeasure issued in harm.

It means to tremble—Isa. 15:4. Moab's soldiers cried out destruction and life became grievous (a tremble) to the people.

רפא

HEAL: " . . . And with His stripes we are healed", (Isa. 53:5). *Heal* derives from the Hebrew root *rapha* which is onomatopoeic. Its sound suggests a sewing machine and its significations are several.

It signifies a sewing together. Heaven's machines are set up to mend hearts, homes, churches, nations that have been rent by sin.

121

It signifies curing a wounded person, often done by sewing up the wound—Isa. 19:22.

It signifies forgiveness—Hos. 14:4. Such forgiveness and healing the Lord does only after the people return unto Him—Jer. 3:22; II Chron. 30:18-20.

It signifies comforting the wounded—Job 13:4. In this passage the Hebrew root is strikingly employed to describe ineffective physicians who were empty comforters. The Lord, as a contrast, "healeth the broken in heart, and bindeth up their wounds" Ps. 147:3.

It signifies a rendering wholesome: for example, bad water—II Kings 2:21, 22. When a generation drinks sin-poisoned water only God can purify it; and it may please Him to do so through a Moses' rod.

This Hebrew root *rapha* signifies medicine—Jer. 30:13. There is only *one* medicine and only *one* Medic for the sin-sick world—Jer. 46:11.

It signifies health—Prov. 3:8. This health belongs to those who fear the Lord and depart from evil.

It signifies giants—II Sam. 21:16; Deut. 3:11. This is an exciting derivative of the root. Here were men who carried spears with staffs like weavers' beams and who slept in beds over 13 feet in length. They grew to this stature likely because of good health, good water, effective physicians, wholesome spirits and few, if any, breeches of concord in their relationships. The giants in God's kingdom and in the churches became such, likely because of circumstances of this kind being spiritually interpreted; with the addition of prayer, Bible reading, meditation and other holy exercises.

ענה

HEAR: "Hear me, Oh Lord, hear me . . .", (I Kings 18:37). *Anah* means:

To answer—Song of Sol. 5:6. This seems to be the main idea of the Hebrew root, especially in the famous text given above.

To sing—I Sam. 29:5. Chanting was used to celebrate persons.

To lift the voice in address—Job 3:2. Announcement was to take place and it was expected attention would be given.

To imply—the notion being that one means to say something and the listener will have to help to get the message over. Words are being aimed at a person; hence, the idea of hearing. Jesus used this signification many times.

שמע

HEAR: "Hear the word of the Lord", (Isa. 1:10). *Shamea* means:

To listen—Eccl. 7:5. Not only is the hearing process to get attention, but there is to be pleasure in it.

To hear and obey—Exod. 24:7. This makes the word very comprehensive. Those hearing thus make the best listeners to God's word.

To understand—Gen. 11:7. This gives hearing another fine quality. People are not only to hear God's word, but also to get the sense of it.

To summon—I Kings 15:22. Action is added. God's children do not longer stand like posts with ears, but become active in doing the will of Him that speaketh.

To cause to hear, and that with acceptance—Isa. 58.4. Not only is the minister to speak so as to be heard, but he must also be concerned about results favorable to Him whom he represents.

Rumor—I Kings 10:1. As one after another hears and tells, that which is heard and told becomes a rumor. Thus can the fame of our Lord be spread.

Music, sounds—Ps. 150:5. This is the climax to the meanings of *shamea*. Good things in one's ear are like music.

אזן

HEARKEN: "Hearken unto his, O Job: stand still and consider the wondrous works of God", (Job 37:14). The Hebrew word for *hearken* is *azan* and it has depth of meaning.

It means to put in the ears of anyone—Isa. 22:14. Ancients hold that this not only means to get into the ear but also to lay up in the mind as in Exod. 17:14, where this same root is employed.

It means mountain summits—Josh. 19:34. Tabor's "ears" high in the skies as if to remind that God has ears to hear.

It means to give good heed—Eccl. 12:9. Not only does God incline His ear to hear but He will weigh, ponder and consider—which are ideas in the root.

לבב

HEART: "I will take the stony heart . . . and will give them a heart of flesh"; "Cast away from you all your transgressions . . . and make you a new heart and a new spirit", (Ezek. 11:19; 18:31). *Leb* and *lebab* mean:

Life, vital principle—Ps. 84:2. For this reason the heart is said to live and keep itself alive.

Seat of feelings, affections and emotions: Love—Deut. 6:5. Faith—Prov. 31:11. Contempt—Prov. 5:12. Gladness—Ps. 104:15.

Contrition—Ps. 109:16. Grief—Ps. 73:21. Fear—Isa. 35:4. Security—Ps. 57:8.

Mode of thinking and acting: Purity—Ps. 51:10. Sincere—I Kings 3:6. Upright—I Kings 9:4. Forward—Ps. 101:4. Crafty—Ps. 64:6. Ungodly—Job 36:13.

Seat of will, purpose, determination—I Sam. 14:7.

Seat of intelligence—Isa. 10:7. The heart can know and may be wise.

שמי

HEAVEN: "Thus saith the Lord, The heaven is my throne, and the earth is my footstool: where is the house that ye build unto me? and where is the place of my rest? For all those things hath mine hand made . . .", (Isa. 66:1, 2A). *Shamay,* the Hebrew for *heaven* is an interesting word that stems from *shamah.*

It signifies the firmament which spreads out like an arch above the earth. It seems to be supported by a foundation with columns resting on it—II Sam. 22:8.

This heaven seems to be the house of God with a gate that opens—Gen. 28:17. It is represented as an abode of God—Ps. 2:4; Deut. 33:26.

There is an infiniteness about it—Deut. 10:14. These regions where God reigns go on and on, with ample room for all of God's children!

In fact, God with His angels governs this world—Dan. 4:23. God dwells in the heaven of heavens and governs all heavens of heaven! God is God of heaven *and* earth—Ezra. 5:11, 12.

עבר

HEBREW: "And there came one that had escaped, and told Abram the Hebrew", (Gen. 14:13). The noun *Hebrew* comes from the root *ebar* which has colorful meanings.

It means to pass over or to cross over—Josh. 24:2. The Hebrews were descendants of the "crossed over ones:" the ones whose fathers were on the other side. This would suit the favored nation whom God led. They were one of the Northern Semitic tribes who were hated by the Egyptians and later murmured against by the Grecians—Acts 6:1.

It means to march—Josh. 6:7, 8. They moved forward in a stately manner with the Spirit of Jehovah within them.

It means to enter into a covenant—Deut. 29:12. The context tells of the close relationship between God and His chosen ones and the unbrokenness of it on and on even through the time of "him that is not here with us this day."

It means to overcome—Ps. 124:4. Even as the floods overwhelm so do the hosts of God march on, crossing rivers and seas; felling walls; subduing Satan's hordes; conquering evil; overcoming sin.

The scholars among the ancients considered this root the same as *adah*—Gen. 4:19 which means an ornament. God's people beautifully adorn. It also means congregation—Exod. 12:3. What an honor for the writer and the reader of this to be numbered in that congregation; the family and household of heaven. And further, it means a swarm of bees—Judg., 14:8. The children of God assemble, worship and work, and enjoy exquisite sweetnesses peculiar to their tribe.

שְׁאוֹל

HELL: "The wicked shall be turned into hell and all the nations that forget God", (Ps. 9:17). For the meaning of *sheol* see *Grave*.

עזר

HELP: "God is . . . a very present help in trouble", (Ps. 46:1). *Azar* means:

To assist, to aid. A condescension issuing in victory for man: God helps man.

To surround, to enclose, to protect—Ps. 37:40. Could man have better assistance than that the Lord encamps round about him?

To conquer—I Chron. 5:20. The idea is that when God helps, victory is sure.

A priest—Ezra 7:1. Priests can be a great help. All of God's children are priests—Rev. 1:6. Jesus is the High Priest—Heb. 4:14. All Christians should be a help to all. Jesus is the greatest help of all.

כרוז

HERALD: "Then an herald cried aloud, to you it is commanded, O people, nations, and languages . . . hear . . . fall down and worship . . .", (Dan. 3:4, 5). *Karaz* is a great word on preaching and it means:

To cry out, to make a proclamation in the manner of a herald. The root *karaz* has been used by many lanuguages: German: krieschen; Persian: To cry out; English: To cry; Sanscrit: Krus; Greek: Cherusso. The last is the most common word for *preach* in the New Testament.

The context for the passage given above is a perfect setting for this word. The wicked king has made an image of gold. The sheriffs, rulers, governors, captains, treasurers, etc. were assembled. An herald was caused to proclaim. Changing the king to the King of Kings, and the image to the true God, would it not make perfect setting to have a preacher, a *karoz,* to be caused to proclaim?

נחל

HERITAGE: "Lo, children are an heritage of the Lord", (Ps. 127:3). *Nachal* means:

To receive as a possession, to acquire—Prov. 3:35. It is something to thus acquire wealth, glory, or, as the Israelites, the promised land of Canaan—Exod. 23:30; 32:13.

To inherit—Judg. 11:2. One of life's great moments is to inherit something great—Ps. 119:111.

To distribute—Num. 34:17. God is always distributing to His children, and this becomes a heritage.

A river—Gen. 15:18. Showers of blessings form a river pouring into one's life.

A valley—Gen. 26:19. This variety of signification is rich, as valleys usually are.

Estate, domain—Num. 18:21. God has prepared and promised His own a land flowing with milk and honey.

כחד

HIDE: "O God . . . my sins are not hid from Thee", (Ps. 69:5). *Kachad* means:

To deny, to disown—Isa. 3:9. Although a man cannot do it, he would like to disown or deny his sins.

To destroy, to cut off—Zech. 11:8. Man cannot do that with sin, neither with the serpent that tempts him to sin.

צפם

HIDE: "Neither is their iniquity hid from mine eyes", (Jer. 16:17. *Tsaphan* means:

To conceal—Ps. 27:5. The idea here is to defend one by hiding him. In this passage God is reported hiding His child, but who would dare hide or try to defend his sins?

To keep back, to hold back—Job 17:4. Sin is not to be held back, but confessed and consequently forgiven—I John 1:7, 9.

(Zephaniah, Jehovah hides, or Jehovah protects, is a wonderful name for a man of God—Zeph. 1:1. This is a significant name.)

(Pharaoh gave Joseph the name, Zaphnath-paaneah [Gen. 41:45], which probably means: revealer before the face. At least Joseph was that, and scholars translate this Hebrew into Greek using *sotor* and *aion* meaning· saviour of the ages; i.e. he saved Egypt from starvation.)

עלם

HIDE: "I called upon thy name, O Lord . . . hide not thine ear
. . .", (Lam. 3:55-56). *Alam,* the Hebrew root for *hide,* is used
colorfully.

It is used to tell of hidden sin that must be atoned for—Lev.
4:13. These sins could not be remitted without the shedding of
blood.

It is used to describe neglect where eyes were hid from the
Sabbath—Ezek. 22:26. It surely must please God when His people focus attention of the Sabbath since it so displeases Him when
they do not.

It is used to illustrate unneighborliness—Prov. 28:27. People
do turn eyes away from needy situations.

It is used to report that ears can be hid—Lam. 3:56. There are
cases where man does not hear needs' cries. There are also those
who turn away from any person or thing—Deut. 22:1, 3, 4. Then
there is that serious situation when man does not want God to
hide His ears—Ps. 55:1.

The good Samaritan did not hide his eyes from need. The Lord
exhorts us to look on the fields; that is, not hide our eyes from
the harvest.

על

HIGH: "And my people are bent to backsliding from me;
though they called them to the most High, none at all would exalt him", (Hos. 11:7). *Al* means:

Above—Ps. 50:4. How inspiring and refreshing to connect the
thought of God, the Most High, with things above.

Being over—Ps. 29:3. The voice of God is clear and above the
noise of waters like a candle shining above one's head—Job 29:3.
In I Sam. 25:16 the idea is being over anyone to protect him. This
is a wonderful relationship to have with God.

Surpassing—Ps. 89:7, 8. God surpasses all other beings, and
is terrible in power.

Near—Gen. 16:7. Marvelous is it for God to be both high and
near.

Incline—Isa. 60:14. One of the great characteristics of God is

128

His bending over His children—Ps. 40:1.

Around—Job 26:9. Just as God spreads the clouds around Him, so is He willing to encamp around about them that fear Him.

With, towards—I Sam. 20:8. The motion here is in kindness. God comes towards His own to be with them and that to show His mercy. Indeed is God the most High.

במה

HIGH PLACE: "And Solomon loved the Lord . . . went to Gibeon to sacrifice there; for that was the great high place; a thousand burnt offerings did Solomon offer upon that altar", (I Kings 3:3, 4). *Bamah* is the Hebrew root for *high place,* and it has several meanings.

It means a mountain—Jer. 26:18. Many spiritual experiences reported in Scripture took place on mountains. The ancients supposed that sacred rites done on the hills were more acceptable to God—Ps. 87:1; 121:1, 2; John 4:9.

It means strength—Ps. 18:33. In the heights where God treads (Amos 4:13) is a likely place for pilgrims to get strength—Ps. 121:1, 2.

It means a chapel—II Kings 23:12-15. While in some cases chapels on the hills were prostituted, this but braces the fact they must have been "beautiful for situation" originally. " The Lord came from Sinai . . . He shined forth from mount Paran and He came with ten thousands of His saints"—Deut. 33:2.

It means a sepulchral mound—II Kings 23:16. Josiah moved not the bones of the prophet from the mount and Moses is still on Nebo's heights.

סלל

HIGHWAY: "And an highway shall be there, and a way, and it shall be called The Way of holiness . . . the redeemed of the Lord shall walk there", (Isa. 35:8, 9). *Salal* means:

To cast up, to lift up, to raise up—Jer. 50:26. Christ was lifted up on a cross, and became The Way to God.

Rampart—Ezek. 4:2. This is a mound thrown up around a city, and has on it a defense road. A city is defended well when that city has a way of holiness about it.

Ladder—Gen. 28:12. This shade of sense emphasizes the fact that this highway is for the redeemed who are on the way to heaven. It seems almost incredible that scholars should translate this same word *salal* by both *highway* and *ladder*. And yet, reflection upon it gives rich color and breadth to the conversation of saints.

הר

HILL: "Exalt the Lord our God, and worship at His holy hill; for the Lord our God is holy", (Ps. 99:9). *Har* means:

Mountain, mount—Gen. 14:10. These people fled to the mountains for physical safety, but wise indeed are those who flee to the mountain of God for soul safety. Sinai was the mountain where the law was given—Exod. 19:1,3. God's holy mountain was called Zion—Ps. 2:6. Here was a place of refuge and safety—Isa. 11:9. The Hebrews and some other nations regarded mountains as sacred and the seats of deity.

Altar—Ezek. 43:15. The word translated *altar* here is composed of two parts: *har,* mount; and, *el,* God. So we have *mount of God* which becomes a colorful meaning of *altar* as used by Ezekiel.

אחז

HOLD: "Nevertheless I am continually with thee: Thou hast holden me by my right hand", (Ps. 73:23). *Achaz* means:

To lay hold of, to seize, to take—Judg. 12:6. More surely does the Lord hold His own than the Gileadites did those who could not frame their mouths to pronounce Shibboleth.

Fishing, hunting—Song of Sol. 2:15. This grows out of the idea of *catching.* Jesus wants His disciples fishing and hunting for men.

To hold fast—I Chron. 13:9. Just as man would hold fast the ark that was so sacred to all, and do so with all strength and skill, so will the Lord hold His own with all the strength and skill He has.

To join—Ezek. 41:6. Like beams are joined in a building forever to hold together, even so can man be joined to his Lord.

To become possessor—Gen. 34:10. He who is joined to God by faith becomes a possession of God, and God becomes his.

קדש

HOLY: "Who is like unto thee, O Lord, among the gods? who is like thee, glorious in holiness, fearful in praises, doing wonders?", (Exod. 15:11). For the meaning of *qadash* see *dedicate*.

בית

HOME: "Abide now at home . . .", (II Chron. 25:19). *Bayith* means:

A house—Gen. 19:10. This signification makes it a place to stay overnight.

A temple—I Kings 6:37. Sometimes this means a temple for idols, but, most often, a temple of God.

A sepulchre—Isa. 14:18. This is the home of the dead, and has certain glory about it.

A place—Exod. 26:29. That is, things belong in a certain place and that becomes home for those things—Isa. 3:18.

Family, household—Gen. 7:1. Persons of a family, including wife and children, living together make up a household.

The word *home* or *house* is used in the following combinations:

Beth-El—House of God—Josh. 18:13. And, we can assemble there.

Beth-ezel—House of firm root—Mic. 1:11. Perhaps it will stand.

Beth-aram—House of the height—Josh. 13:27. *Aram* means mountain.

Beth-hanan—House of grace—I Kings 4:9. See *grace* for rich meanings.

Beth-lehem—House of bread—Mic. 5:1. The Bread of Life was born there.

Beth-nimrah—House of limpid and sweet waters—Num. 32:36.

Beth-eden—House of pleasantness—Amos 1:5. It is most desirable.

Beth-zur—Josh. 15:58, House of the rock. A home built on The Rock.

Beth-shean—House of quiet—Josh. 17:11.

Beth-malku—House of the King—Dan. 4:30. Could it be made the house of the King of kings?

Bethan—A great house, a palace—Esth. 1:5.

דבש

HONEY: "With honey out of the rock should I have satisfied thee", (Ps. 81:16). Gesenius translates this: "With honey from the rock will I satify thee." The Hebrew for *honey* is *debish* which has several meanings.

It means yellow, that is honey-colored. This will ever be the color of this safe and satisfying food and is a good symbol of safe and satisfying food for the soul. (This is one of the reasons this word is in the title for this book).

It means honey of bees—Prov. 24:13. The wise man said, "My son, eat honey for it is good". Jonathan said that his eyes were enlightened because he tasted a little honey.

It means honey of grapes—Gen. 43:11. The juice of the vine was usually boiled down to about a third of its volume—making a rich food which was exported from Palestine into Egypt.

It means the hump of a camel—Isa. 30:6. This bunch on a camel's back resembled a bee-hive. This root is thought to also mean a heap which well resembles a swarm of bees. I have discovered in the study of Hebrew roots that they have a heap of meanings—a very full bee-hive of colorful meanings.

On the way to the promised land flowing with milk and honey—Exod. 3:8; 13:5, God's children have His word as a lamp unto their feet and a light unto their path—Ps. 119:105, which word is sweeter than honey and the honeycomb—Ps. 19:10.

כבד

HONOUR: "Honour thy father and thy mother . . .", (Exod. 20:12). For the meaning of *kabad* see *Glorify.*

פאר

HONOUR: "And the Lord hath avouched thee this day to be His peculiar people . . . to make thee high above all nations which He hath made, in praise, in name, in honour . . .", (Deut. 26:18, 19). *Paar* means:

To adorn, to beautify, to glorify—Isa. 60:7. In this passage this sort of honor is to fall upon the sanctuary, while in Ps. 149:4, the Lord is so doing to the meek by giving them salvation. In Isa. 44:23, the Lord most wonderfully glorifies Himself by bestowing favors upon His people.

הדר

HONOUR: "In the multitude of people is the king's honour . . .", (Prov. 14:28). There are several Hebrew words translated *honour. Hadar* means:

To be large, to be ample. To honor the church's King, the crowds must be large to be ample.

To be proud—Isa. 63:1. Only the Lord may be proud. Here the word is used to describe our Lord as bearing Himself proudly. Ample was His humiliation.

To reverence—Lev. 19:32. This is the manner in which honor may be shown a king by the subjects.

To favor—Exod. 23:3. This has as its main idea to honor a person by favoring his cause. Here is room for Christians to busy themselves.

Ornament, decoration—Ps. 45:3. Crowds assembled for worship make a very imposing ornament for the Master.

Apparel—Ps. 29:1, 2. Glory, splendor and majesty are the honor the Lord proudly and justly wears.

קוה

HOPE: "Thou art my hope, O Lord God . . .", (Ps. 71:5). *Qavah* means:

To be strong—i.e., God is my strength, and, as is His strength, so is my hope.

To wait for—Ps. 37:9. Here is the notion of enduring, of holding out. This makes for wonderful security.

To gather together, to be wound together—Jer. 3:17. Since it is the Lord that binds His people to Him, shall they ever be unbound? This is ground for hope.

133

בטח

HOPE: "Blessed is the man that trusteth in the Lord, and whose hope the Lord is", (Jer. 17:7). *Batach* means:

To cast one's cares or oneself upon any one—Ps. 22:8. When one throws himself upon the Lord, hope blossoms.

To be secure—Judg. 18:7. The trust of the righteous leads to security; but the wicked, who fear not God nor His punishments, place their confidence in the things of this world and have no security.

Tranquillity—Job 12:6. One can have peace when he knows his life and his goods are secure both for time and eternity.

קרן

HORN: "the Lord is my rock . . . and the horn of my salvation, and my high tower", (Ps. 18:2). *Qeren,* the Hebrew root for *horn,* is full of interesting meanings.

It means a vessel—I Sam. 16:13. Samuel took a horn of oil to anoint David in the midst of the brethren and the Spirit of the Lord came down upon him.

The horn is used as a music instrument—Josh. 6:5. A musical blast was given on the horn as a signal to shout victory in taking Jericho.

It served as symbol of God increasing one's strength—I Sam. 2:10. Dignity, honor and power were associated with the horn.

It is used in reporting the acquisition of new strength and courage—I Sam. 2:1. Hannah takes courage, gives thanks to God, claimed her horn was exalted in the Lord, rejoices in her salvation and declares there is no god like her God.

It means defence—Ps. 18:2. The bull used his horns for defence and David used the horn (dual is used, meaning two) of the salvation of his God.

The root means a mountain—Isa. 5:1. Even in English we have the names of mountains: Schreckhorn, Wetterhorn, Aarhorn, etc.

It means projecting points like the horns of an altar—Lev. 4:7.

The dual (two) is used for "rays of light or splendour"—Hab. 3:4. The poets used horns to describe the rays of the sun in the morning and called the sun *gazelle*. Our hearts way poetic when we re-picture the rays of the sun of righteousness rising for us over the horizon.

בּית

HOUSE: "For thou . . . God of Israel, hast revealed unto thy servant, saying, I will build thee an house", (II Sam. 7:27). for the meaning of *bayith* see *Home,* and discover that God meant more than a cold building, whether of wood, stone or steel.

כּנע

HUMBLE: "And the word of the Lord came to Elijah the Tishbite, saying, Seest thou how Ahab humbleth himself before me? . . . I will not bring the evil in his days", (I Kings 21:28, 29). *Kana* means:

To bend the knee.

To fold together.

To be low, to be humbled—Ps. 107:12. The context here is very dramatic: People rebelled; God felled them. People helpless, cried; God heard them and saved them.

Packages, bundles, wares—Jer. 10:17. A man who submits himself to the Lord, wholly, may become a package containing that which the Lord pleases, sending it wherever the Lord wills.

Merchants—Isa. 23:8. Those who traffic in wares of the Lord are missionaries indeed.

Canaanites—Judg. 1:1. A people who lived in a land that was low.

בּעל

HUSBAND: "For thy Maker is thine husband . . .", (Isa. 54:5). *Baal* means:

To have dominion over—Isa. 26:13. The life fully surrendered to God is filled with peace and a sense of security.

To marry—Isa. 62:5. God is willing to be the Head of the house, do the providing, afford perfect security and eternal bliss. It is for the church to be the bride, follow Him fully, love Him supremely, serve Him acceptably, and be His eternally.

135

To be lord or possessor—Prov. 3:27. Even if a child should leave its parents, or clay disown the hands that moulded it, yet a child of God should call Him Lord of Lords and be yielded always to Him who created him.

חָנֵף

HYPOCRISY: "For the vile person will speak villany, and his heart will work iniquity, to practise hypocrisy, and to utter error against the Lord . . .", (Isa. 32:6). *Chaneph* means:

To be profane, to be polluted—Ps. 106:38. This makes these undesirable persons more undesirable. They are vain. They are like a puff of wind, but not as beneficial.

To be impious, to be ungodly—Jer. 23:11. More offensive is a profane man than his profane language.

One unclean, a heathen. Surely if hypocrites knew this about themselves, they would soon seek a change.

Abandoned—Job 8:13. This is the doom of the hypocrite. Surely if he knew this would be his lot, he would "seek the Lord while He may be found."

עָצָב

IDOL: "But our God is in the heavens . . . their idols are silver and gold, the work of men's hands", (Ps. 115:3, 4). *Atsab* means:

To work, to fashion—hence carved image or earthen vessel.

To pain, to grieve, or cause to travail—I Chron. 4:10. Every idol is a marker, saying, here God is grieved.

To provoke to anger—Ps. 78:40. If God is provoked to anger, how can the pleasure of an idol ever compensate? No wonder Jesus taught that those loving their own more than they loved Him were not worthy to have Him.

Sorrow—Prov. 10:22. The very word *idol* has in it the idea of sorrow, trouble, labor, etc. God used two commandments out of ten to dispose of idols.

שָׁגַג

IGNORANCE: "And the priest shall make an atonement for the soul that sinneth ignorantly, when he sinneth by ignorance before the Lord, to make an atonement for him, and it shall be forgiven him", (Num. 15:28). For the unusual in a word like *shagag,* or *shagah,* see *err;* where ignorance itself is a sin.

פֶּסֶל

IMAGE: "Thou shalt not make unto thee any graven image", (Exod. 20:4). *Pasal* means:

To carve, to form by cutting—Exod. 34:1. Man labors to make a god when the true God is saying, "Return unto me and I will return unto you"—Mal. 3:7.

Quarries—Judg. 3:19. Some sinners further grieve God by having quarries where they fashion idols to love, instead of loving God with all heart, soul, mind, strength.

דָּלַל

IMPOVERISH: "And Israel was greatly impoverished", (Judg. 6:6). *Dalal,* the Hebrew root for *impoverish,* has meanings both timely and relevant.

It means to hang down like the leg of a lame man—Prov. 26:7. Churches limp, too; thereby becoming poor.

It means to be brought low—Isa. 38:14. Failure disappoints and discourages; leads to doubt and despondency; and, on down to despair.

It means to be slack and languid—Isa. 19:5. In the Church: waters may fail, rivers from heaven may not be flowing, brooks may be empty of spiritual blessings and the Lord's fishermen may be mourning and the Lord's workmen languishing. These things result in spiritual poverty.

חָשַׁב

IMPUTE: "Blessed is the man unto whom the Lord imputeth not iniquity", (Ps. 32:2). *Chashab* means:

To think, to meditate, to purpose—Isa. 10:7. Man ought to be most happy when he learns that God's thoughts towards him are favorable.

To regard, to hold—Gen. 38:15. Man's highest concern should be how God regards him.

To reckon to any one—II Sam. 19:20. God is keeping books on the deeds of man.

To purpose—Prov. 16:9. God has a plan for man—Jonah 1:4.

Girdle, belt—Exod. 29:5. The high preist wore one of various colors wrought in damask. God promises neither that the redness of His anger, nor the blackness of our sins shall be woven into the shroud for repenting sinners to wear; but threads of mercy and pardon will make its warp and woof. The idea of the word is *mingling:* like the mingling of colors.

נטה

INCLINE: "I have inclined mine heart to perform thy statutes always", (Ps. 119:112). *Natab* means:

To stretch out, to extend—Exod. 10:12. Much is accomplished when men's hearts stretch out after God's word. This is a holy appetite.

To expand, to spread out—Isa. 40:22. The Psalmist reports that God spread His ear to pick up the prayer he had uttered—Ps. 40:1. Man's heart needs to expand to take in more of the unredeemed of the world, and love them and pray for them and bring them the Gospel.

To turn—Num. 20:17. Man must turn his heart into the right way and activity.

To seduce—Prov. 7:21. While this is in a bad sense, it shows what a strong idea this word carries. Man must be ingenious and industrious in getting his heart bent after God and the things of God.

רבה

INCREASE: "Of the increase of His government and peace there shall be no end . . .", (Isa. 9:7). For the meaning of *rabah* see *Authority*.

שׁכן

INHABIT: "For thus saith the high and lofty One that inhabiteth eternity, whose name is Holy; I dwell in the high and holy place, with him also that is of a contrite and humble spirit . . .'', (Isa. 57:15). *Shakan,* the Hebrew root for both *inhabit* and *dwell* in this text, is used variously and has several meanings.

It means to settle down like the column of cloud and fire— Num. 9:17; Exod. 24:16. O that the Holy Spirit would settle like a pillar upon God's people again today as at Pentecost.

It means to encamp—Num. 24:2. If Balaam saw God's people abiding in their tents today would he also see their God with them there?

It means to possess—Ps. 37:29. The righteous shall inherit the land the Lord gives them but the evil will be moved out.

It signifies intimacy and familiarity—Prov. 1:11. While this is not in a good sense here the idea is clear. God dwells intimately with him who is of a contrite heart.

This root is used to indicate God putting His name on a place to dwell there—Deut. 12:11. O that God would be pleased to put His name on our church buildings. He has put His name on our foreheads.

This root carries the idea of guarding—Gen. 3:24. Then of course, all of us would want God to dwell with us, now and in eternity.

Shekinah is a Hebrew word, not in the Bible, built on this root signifying that which dwells there. For instance there is an allusion to this in Isa. 60:2 (where God's glory is the dwelling agent).

נחל

INHERIT: "The Lord God of Israel was their inheritance . . .", (Josh. 13:33). *Nachal* means:

To acquire—Prov. 3:35. There is no greater possession than God. All who have God have all. Most often this word is used in connection with land, but here is the greatest use of it. It is said of God He took Israel as His own possession and protected and defended them.

To distribute—Num. 34:17. It is missions to share the knowledge of God with those who do not know Him.

(For other significations of this root see *heritage.)*

ירש

INHERIT: "But the meek shall inherit the earth; and delight themselves in the abundance of peace", (Ps. 37:11). In *yarash,* the Hebrew root for *inherit,* there is abundant assurance. (Comp. Matt. 5:5; Rom. 8:17).

It means to occupy—Num. 33:55. To inherit something does not obviate struggling in laying hands on it.

It means to possess—Ps. 37:9, 29, 22. Occupancy of Palestine and all the remainder of the earth is but emblematic of the better prosperity and happiness of life.

It is used to signify an heir—Jer. 49:1. The weeping prophet predicted a glad day for Israel, v. 2.

It means to dispossess—Judg. 14:15. Should God choose to give our inheritance to another we would become paupers. (Comp. I Sam. 2:7).

It is used to signify possession of sins of youth—Job 13:26. What a blessing belongs to those whose sins are not longer imputed to them.

עול

INIQUITY: "If I have done iniquity, I will do no more", (Job 34:32). *Aval* means:

To turn away, to distort.

To be wrong, to be evil, to be wicked, to turn aside from the right—Ps, 71:4. This can be likened to the house that will not walk in the right row.

To be ungodly—Job 18:21. In other words, to be without God not even know God.

Wickedness that extends to the defiling of God's sanctuary— Ezek. 28:18.

רשע

INIQUITY: "And moreover I saw under the sun . . . the place of righteousness, that iniquity was there", (Eccl. 3:16). *Rasha* means:

To make noise, to cause disturbance—Job 3:17. This signification points up the offensiveness of iniquity. Sinners agitate and aggravate.

To do evil, to be wicked—I Kings 8:47. This says iniquitous persons are not only impious but impudent.

Guilty—Gen. 18:23. The iniquitous shall be liable to the punishment of God. His wickedness may take the form of falsehood—Prov. 8:7.

עון

INIQUITY: "And I will punish the world for their evil, and the wicked for their iniquity . . .", (Isa. 13:11). *Avon* means:

To bend, to curve—From the root *avah*. Attempts will always be made to accommodate fixed laws to one's desires, habits and actions.

To writhe—Isa. 21:3. A distortion of laws will cause a distortion of body.

To be bowed down, to be depressed—Ps. 38:6. Iniquity is a calamity that will cause this condition.

Overturn, overthrow—Isa. 24:1. Man would overthrow right.

עמל

INIQUITY: "Thou art of purer eyes than to behold evil, and canst not look on iniquity . . .", (Hab. 1:13). *Amal* means:

To labor—Ps. 127:1. Here is labor with the idea of effort and exhaustion, and the accessory idea of nothing accomplished after all.

Trouble, sorrow, vexation—Gen. 41:51. Not only is this idea in this word for iniquity, but it is related to the mind and to the soul.

Fault—Num. 23:21. God's perfect eyes search imperfect man for defections.

Misery—Job 3:20. This signification is part and parcel of iniquity, for the sinner is a miserable wretch.

141

נקה

INNOCENT: "Whoever perished, being innocent?", (Job 4:7). For the meaning of *naqah* see *Cleanse.*

חפת, חפה

INNOCENT: "I am innocent; neither is there iniquity in me", (Job 33:9). *Chapha* means:

To cover—II Sam. 15:30. Apparently David was declaring that his sins were covered somehow, rather than that he was clean from sin.

To protect—Isa. 4:5. God provided a defence for Zion. Also, this word is used to describe a nuptial-couch or a bed with a canopy with the idea of protection pictured by the curtained top— Ps. 19:5. The atoning blood is a scarlet canopy over sinners' heads.

נשם

INSPIRATION: "And the inspiration of the Almighty giveth them understanding", (Job 32:8). *Nasham,* the Hebrew word for *inspiration,* has several meanings.

It means to breathe strongly—Isa. 42:14. The man himself will know when he is inspired of God, and others hearing and seeing him will also know.

It means to animate, to impart life—Job 33:4. The Spirit of God both makes man and breathes life into him.

It means to impart words and wisdom—Job 26:4. God does promise wisdom to those who ask of Him.

It means a snuffing, a snorting, a blasting with the breath—Ps. 18:15. Here power is shown in God's breath.

שכל

INSTRUCT: "I will instruct thee and teach thee in the way which thou shalt go", (Ps. 32:8). *Sakal* means:

To look at, to behold, to view. To learn of Him who is Wisdom, one is to behold Him as John the Baptist insisted.

To be prudent, to act wisely—I Sam. 18:30. Learning affects

actions. Noblest learning is that which issues in noble deeds.

To consider, to attend to—Deut. 32:29. This verse shows a great facet of this word.

Upright, godly—Ps. 14:2. That is good learning and better instruction which leads a man to seek God.

To prosper—Josh. 1:7. The child of God is promised prosperity if he learns and does the law of God.

Happiness—Prov. 3:4. Sweet instruction is that which leads a man to have the approval of God and fellowman.

בין

INSTRUCT: "With whom he took counsel, and who instructed him", (Isa. 40:14). For meaning of *bin* see *Consider*. For meaning of *yasad,* translated *instructed* in II Chron. 3:3, see *Foundation.* For meaning of *yasar,* translated *instructed* in Jer. 6:8, see *Chastise.*

תם

INTEGRITY: "Till I die I will not remove mine integrity from me.", (Job 27:5). *Tam* means:

Whole, perfect, upright—Job 1:1. This is in a moral sense only.

Fullness, in full measure—Isa. 47:9. It appears that God's judgment came on Babylon and Chaldea in full measure; such measure as one would desire to have of goodness.

Prosperity—Ps. 41:12. Here a man's prosperity lies in his condition, welfare, and property.

Innocence—Ps. 26:1. David resorts unto God in his integrity; inviting the great Judge to judge him.

Simplicity—II Sam. 15:11. It seems this signification would teach there is transparency of character in a person of integrity.

פגע

INTERCESSION: "But if they be prophets, and if the word of the Lord be with them, let them now make intercession to the Lord", (Jer. 27:18). *Paga* means:

To fall upon, to light upon, to assail—Ruth 1:16. Ruth entreated with moving petitions, like Moses did for Israel and like we should for others.

To meet—Gen. 32:1. When man makes an appointment to meet with God on behalf of another, that is intercession.

To strike up, to make peace with—Isa. 64:4. Here the idea is to strike up a league and be at peace with one another. In other words, God is delighting in the just and upright man—I Cor. 2:9.

To lay upon—Isa. 53:6. Just as God hath laid the iniquity of us all on the Suffering Servant, so should we lay the case of our fellowman before God.

לוּץ

INTERPRETER: "If there be a messenger with him, an interpreter . . . to shew unto the man his uprightness", (Job 33:23). *Luts,* the Hebrew root for *interpreter,* comes to mean this through a series of significations.

Its lowest signification is to mock, to deride, to be frivolously impudent—Isa. 28:22.

It means to scorn—Ps. 1:1. That is, to be able to scoff at, if not set at nought, "the most sacred precepts and duties of religion, piety and morals."

It comes up to mean to stammer and to speak in a foreign tongue—Isa. 28:11. This will seem to ignorant persons to chatter unintelligibly.

Therefore he becomes an interpreter because he knows more than one language.

But, the highest signification is intercession. In the context of the Job 33:23 verse, it is discovered that an angel has come to intercede between God and man.

יִשְׂרָאֵל

ISRAEL: ". . . Thou art my strength, O Israel, in whom I will be glorified", (Isa. 49:3). Israel, God's spiritual people, was important to God. A study of her name will reveal the reasons.

The name is made up of two parts, the first of which is derived from *sarah* which means to strive or to contend—Hos. 12:4. Jacob wept, prayed and prevailed in God's house (Bethel) and it was of this kind of stock God made leaders in His religion. There is in this verb the idea of war and of arranging in order as troops. Figuratively the Church with its members or the Bible class with its learners is lined up in a row to bring up the line on its portion of the Kingdom front.

Sarah also means prince or governor—Isa. 9:6, 7. The government shall be upon the shoulder of Him who began the New Israel.

The second part of Israel's name is *El* which means GOD; Almighty full of strength and power—Ps. 50:1. It means champion—Ezek. 31:10 as of the program of morality for time and eternity; it means hero, Isa. 9:5 and 10:21 as the Victor leading earth's greatest minority. (For more on *government* and *God* see index).

מקנא

JEALOUS: "I the Lord thy God am a jealous God . . .", (Exod. 20:5). For the meaning of *qana* see *Envy*.

סגל

JEWEL: "And they shall be mine, saith the Lord of hosts, in that day when I make up my jewels", (Mal. 3:17).

There are four Hebrew words in the Old Testament which are translated *Jewel:* 1. *Chali* which means an ornament; 2. *Keli* which means vessel or instrument; 3. *Nezem* which means a ring for the ear or nose; 4. *Sagal* which is the word in this passage and here only, and has several rich significations.

One is acquisition. As to how this meaning got into the word we may never know but it is easy to relate this meaning to the word *jewel* in the Malachi passage. The Lord acquired His chosen ones by paying a tremendous price in the sacrifice of His only begotten and therefore claims them and will gather them when He makes up His jewels.

Another is property or wealth which is a private possession—Eccl. 2:8. God is personal and it is further proven and confirmed by the fact that His people, whom He bought with a precious price, are His personal property.

Still another is peculiar treasure—Deut. 26:18. The Lord considers the redeemed, not only precious jewels, but peculiar, rare and unique. To God, it appears from this Malachi passage and the meaning of this special Hebrew word, there are none so dear to Him as the ones He has saved who make themselves a "peculiar people" by loving Him and glorifying Him.

לוה

JOIN: "Come and let us join ourselves to the Lord in a perpetual covenant that shall not be forgotten", (Jer. 50:5). *Lavah,* the Hebrew root for *join* has several meanings.

It means to worship a notion which is brought out in the context of Isa. 56:6. Keeping the Sabbath, loving the Name of the Lord and serving Him are elements of worship reported here where the Lord promises to accept their offerings, bring them to the house of prayer on the holy mountain and give them joy in their hearts.

It carries the idea of belonging. Those joined to the Lord will be His people; the Lord will be in their midst; and they shall be aware of it—Zech. 2:11.

It is associated with the idea of borrowing and lending—Prov. 22:7. A borrower or a lender ought to be joined in very intimate relationship. Can a man be so joined unto the Lord that his requests will be granted? A good man, like his gracious heavenly Father, will show favor and lend—Ps. 112:5.

It means to cleave—Eccl. 8:5. A man's eating, drinking, rejoicing ought to cleave to his labor.

When all of the aspects of *join* are studied, one sees why Jeremiah's union with Jehovah in a perpetual covenant would never be forgotten.—Jer. 50:5.

ספח

JOIN: "For the Lord will have mercy on Jacob, and will yet choose Israel, and set them in their own land; and the strangers shall be joined with them . . .", (Isa 14:1). *Sapha,* the Hebrew root for *join,* has interesting meanings.

It means to add. This seems to be the same idea found in Acts 2:47, where it is reported that the Lord added to the church.

It means to pour out. Unless a person is willing to pour out his life on the altar of the Lord it is doubtful whether he will ever be in the kingdom of that Lord.

It means to anoint—I Sam. 2:36. The signification of the Hebrew root in this passage is that the man wanted to be anointed as a bishop in order to get bread. While this is not good, the idea is clear: To be added to God's company and to get God's blessings, one is to be anointed of the Lord.

It means to gather together—Job: 7. What a spiritual thrill to be added to God's people now and one day be gathered together with them for ever.

נסע

JOURNEY: "And Abram journeyed, going on . . .", (Gen. 12:9). *Nasa,* the Hebrew root for *journey,* has several meanings.

It means to pluck up as a tree—Job 19:10. It hurts to be pulled up by the roots out of the garden of acquaintances.

It means to make go forth like sheep—Ps. 78:52. The Lord was the good Shepherd and Abram was a good sheep. As God moved him he was moved to build altars.

This root is used to describe a wind bringing quails to Israel—Num. 11:31. God moves things as well as people.

This root means to be torn away, e.g., a tent—Isa. 48:12.

It means to pull up as stakes in order to move—Isa. 33:20. But Zion will not be moved as indicated in this passage.

It means to break camp and move—Num. 33:5. Abram was willing to do that even as many fine pastors are willing when God speaks.

גיל

JOY: "Then will I go unto the altar of God, unto God my exceeding joy", (Ps. 43:4). For the meaning of *gil* see *Glad.*

דין

JUDGE: "But the Lord . . . hath prepared His throne for judgment . . . and He shall judge the world in righteousness", (Ps. 9:7, 8). Several Hebrew words are translated *judge. Deen,* used here, is like a honeycomb with its cells full.

It means to rule—Zech. 3:7, with the idea that the ruled will become a subject of the ruler. God judges the people whom He "would that they should come to repentance", because "He would that none should perish" but become children of His kingdom.

It means to judge—Ps. 9:7, 8. This Judge will Himself be refuge for the oppressed if they put their trust in Him. He will not forget them when they cry and will not forsake them.

It means to defend—Dan. 7:22. How blessed are God's children to have their merciful judge to be their successful advocate at the same time.

It means justice—Ps. 140:12, 13; Ezra 7:26. There is justice! The cause of the righteous will be maintained and those who will not do the will of God will have death, banishment, "confiscation of goods", and imprisonment.

שׁפט

JUDGE: "The Lord is our Judge, the Lord is our lawgiver, the Lord is our King, He will save us", (Isa. 33:22). *Shaphat* means:

To set upright, to erect—Job 22:13. This is the primary idea of the word and gives to God's judgment a majestic scope.

To condemn, to punish—Obad. 21. This seems to be the most popular signification in the minds of people.

To do justice, to defend, or to vindicate—Isa. 1:17. While writing this paragraph, I was called to defend a family being evicted from an apartment for non-payment of rent. The Lord will defend His own and provide a home for them.

To govern, to rule—I Sam. 8:20. Certainly the people who will be judged by the Lord will want that Lord to govern them.

מׁשפט

JUDGMENT: "He shall not fail nor be discouraged, till He have set judgment in the earth . . .", (Isa. 42:4). For the meaning of *mishpat* see *Judge*.

צדק

JUST: "Behold, his soul which is lifted up is not upright in him: but the just shall live by faith", (Hab. 2:4). *Tsadaq* means:

To be right, to be straight—Ps. 23:3. Paths of righteousness are always straight and right.

To be just, to be righteous—Ps. 19:9. God is just in dispensing justice.

To have a just cause, to be in the right—Gen. 38:26.

To speak the truth—Job 33:12.

To be good—Job 15:14. Although there is none good, there was One who was all good.

To be vindicated—Dan. 8:14. Only in this way can anyone become righteous.

To pronounce innocent—Job 33:32. Surely the righteous will be innocent, or how can he be righteous.

Happiness—Isa. 32:17. This is the consequence and reward of being justified.

Prosperity—Isa. 45:8. Upon the just, upon the righteous, shall prosperity rain down.

מִשְׁפָּט

JUSTLY: "He hath shewed thee, O man, what is good: and what doth the Lord require of thee, but to do justly, and to love mercy, and to walk humble with thy God?", (Mic. 6:8). For the meaning of *mishpat* see *Judge*.

שָׁמַר

KEEP: "And, behold, I am with thee, and will keep thee in all places whither thou goest . . .", (Gen. 28:15). *Shamar* means:

To watch, to protect—Gen. 2:15. Just like God wanted man to keep the garden, so will God keep man; and He is able to do it.

To retain—Dan. 9:4. Just like God keeps mercy for those that love Him, so will he keep those persons that love Him.

To observe, to watch over—Prov. 2:20. God will keep His own in sight in His watch over them. This is security. God is on watch duty.

To honor, to regard—Prov. 27:18. The keeping becomes sur-

149

er when regard and honor enter into it. In the case of the text, it is the regard and honor of God.

בעט

KICK: "Wherefore kick ye at my sacrifice and at mine offering . . .?", (I Sam. 2:29). The Hebrew for *kick* is *Baat* and is used colorfully.

The chronicler employs it above to mean that evil men have trampled under foot that which is sacred and have come to despise God and therefore reap much ill. Today the first part— the sowing part—seems to be taking place.

Moses uses it in his song (Deut. 32:15) to tell of obstinate Jeshurun who kicked like an ox, forsook God and lightly esteemed the Rock of his salvation. There are Jeshuruns about with coldness and backsliding, kicking like an ox on their way to the fate of fat oxen.

מות

KILL: "The Lord met him and sought to kill him", (Exod. 4:24). For the meaning of *muth* see *Die.*

רצח

KILL: "Thou shalt not kill", (Exod. 20:13). *Ratsach* means:

To break, to dash in pieces. This sort of violence ought to be prohibited.

To slay—Num. 35:6. This, in particular, means slayer of man.

To be a murderer—II Kings 6:32.

Outcry, clamor. Where there is an outbreak of the voice, there may be violence.

נכה

KILL: "He that killeth any man shall surely be put to death", (Lev. 24:17). *Nakah* means:

To smite, to strike—Deut. 25:3. This may be done with rod, staff, etc. It may be done to one's spirit—Isa. 66:2.

To harm, to blast—Jonah 4:8.

To slay, to murder—Jer. 18:21.

דלק

KINDLE: "And the house of Jacob shall be a fire . . . and the house of Esau for stubble, and they shall kindle in them and devour them . . .", (Obad. 18). The Lord said His people live on, but nothing will be left of Satan's stubblefields—Joel 3:20. As to how we may have this fire is signified by *dalaq,* the Hebrew root for *kindle.*

It means love and warm friendship (for the Lord) expressed with burning lips—Prov. 26:23.

It means holy ambition—Ps. 39:3. This kind sets men on fire.

It means ardently working—Gen. 31:36. When saints perspire souls burn with fire.

It means to be inflamed—Isa. 5:11. God's children will be inflamed by that wine unless well refined—Isa. 25:6.

Certainly there will be Pentecostal fire when the people follow the Ancient of days whose throne flames and chariot wheels burn with fire—Dan. 7:9, 10.

חסד

KINDLY: "The Lord deal kindly with you . . .", (Ruth 1:8). For meaning of *chesed* see *Goodliness.*

טוב

KINDLY: "He spake kindly to him . . .", (II Kings 25:28). for meaning of *tob* see *Merry.*

מלך

KING: "Thus saith the Lord, the King of Israel . . .", (Isa. 44:6). *Malak* means:

To reign, to govern, to rule—I Kings 6:1. The Lord has built a great world and He rules it. He is building a greater place and in it will be King of Kings.

151

To consult, to counsel—Neh. 5:7. No wonder that in prophecy (Isa. 9:6) Jesus was called Counsellor.

מֶלֶךְ

KINGDOM: II Chron. 11:17. People and territory under kingly rule make a kingdom. What a kingdom that is which is the empire of the King of Kings.

(Unto Moloch, which is derived from *malak,* the Hebrews sacrified human beings in the valley of Hinnom, Lev. 18:21, 20:2. According to Rabbins and Deodorus, there was a brass statue of Moloch with the members of a human body, but the head of an ox: it was hollow, heated from below, and children to be sacrificed were placed in the hungry arms.) For the meaning of the Hebrew word *malak* turn back to *King.*

גאל

KINSMAN: "And now it is true I am thy near kinsman: howbeit there is a kinsman nearer than I", (Ruth 3:12). *Gaal* means:

To redeem, to ransom—Lev. 25:25. Is it not wonderful to have an Elder Brother, one that "sticketh closer than a brother," to help them who are waxen poor in sin?

To ransom blood—Num. 35:19. The revenger of blood slays the murderer. This is interesting to apply to the program of redemption of man.

Blood-relative—Num. 5:8. The ransomed become kin of the Redeemer. The sons of God are bought with a price.

(When a man died, the Mosaic law made it the duty of the next of kin to marry the widow and raise up children in his name, e.g.—Ruth 3:13. Jesus becomes the Kinsman of the sons of God. He is the "ransomed-price paid"—in order that there may be children of God.)

נשק

KISS: "Kiss the Son, lest He be angry, and ye perish from the way . . . Blessed are all they that put their trust in him", (Ps. 2:12). *Nashaq,* the Hebrew root for *kiss,* has very colorful meanings.

It means to be disposed or adjusted—Gen. 41:40. When one has the feeling of confidence and is rightly positioned in relation to the Son, he then will not perish but have everlasting life.

It means to pledge homage and fidelity—Ps. 2:12. Though false, this must have entered into the ceremony as far as some were concerned when Judas planted the betrayal kiss.

Righteousness and peace show love for one another but if a person does wrong and evil he will not have peace and will not be able to sleep because of the clanging of his conscience—Ps. 85:10.

בָּרַךְ

KNEEL: "Solomon . . . kneeled down upon his knees before all the congregation of Israel, and spread forth his hands toward heaven", (II Chron. 6:13). The Hebrew for *kneel, Barak,* is full of meaning.

It means to break down, to humbly bow—Ps. 95:6. Contriteness and child-likeness make kneeling pads.

It means to bless—Josh. 24:10. Kneeling—best posture for invoking God.

It means to celebrate—II Chron. 6:13. Two of the best celebrations of goal achievement were done by the pilgrims in 1620 who knelt on the new land and praised God, and by Solomon, in this verse.

It means to salute—I Sam. 13:10. A kneeler with bowed head exhibits harmlessness and submissiveness—excellent approach to the Lord and to one another.

It means to bid peace and prosperity—Gen. 24:60. Relatives did this as Rebekah rode away by camel to join Isaac in the field at eventime.

יָדַע

KNOW: "They that know Thy Name will put their trust in Thee . . .", (Ps. 9:10). *Yada* means:

To perceive, to discern, to be aware of, to understand—Judg. 13:21. This word corresponds to the Greek *oida.*

To come to know, to discover, to learn—Hos. 9:7. Israel shall learn by experience, Hosea foretells.

To become acquainted with—Deut. 9:24. When a person has

153

an experience of grace, he really becomes acquainted with the Lord.

To regard, to see after, to care for—Gen. 39:6. In this light, how wonderful to think that the Lord knows His own as a shepherd knows his sheep—Ps. 144:3. Over against this, consider I Sam. 2:12.

To be wise—Isa. 32:4. This is knowledge that leads to blessedness.

To cause to know—Job 38:12. This signification may point up the greatest responsibility of the Christian.

עמל

LABOUR: "Except the Lord build the house, they labour in vain that build it . . .", (Ps. 127:1). For the meaning of *amal* see *Iniquity*.

עשׂה

LABOUR: "So we laboured in the work . . .", (Neh. 4:21). For the meaning of *asah* see *Accomplish*.

יגע

LABOUR: "Labour not to be rich: cease from thine own wisdom", (Prov. 23:4). *Yaga* is the most intensive word for *labour* and means:

To toil—Isa. 49:4. This is to work with wearisome and painful effort.

To become wearied, to become exhausted—Deut. 25:18. Certainly no man ought to so dissipate his strength in order to make money-but men do.

חסר

LACK: "Yea, forty years didst thou sustain them in the desert, so that they lacked nothing . . .", (Neh. 9:21). *Chaser* means:

To want, to be without—Deut. 2:7. The Lord provided.

To suffer need—Ps. 23:1. The Lord's lambs lack not.

To be diminished, to fail—Gen. 8:3. The barrel of meal does

not fail for the child of God. Always is there oil.

Poverty—Prov. 28:22. But children of God are rich.

תּוֹרָה

LAW: "Come ye, let us go up . . . to the house of the God of Jacob; and He will teach us of His ways, . . . for out of Zion shall go forth the law . . .", (Isa. 2:3). *Torah* means:

To lead one about, especially in order to show him the way in places where he is unacquainted.

A row, a string—Song of Sol. 1:10. The elements of God's law are like pearls on a string.

Direction. Anyone taking seriously the law of the Lord will receive direction.

Instruction, precepts—Isa. 8:16. Good instruction it is that leads one to God.

מִשְׁפָּט

LAW: "For this was a statute for Israel, and a law of the God of Jacob", (Ps. 81:4). For the meaning of *misphat* see *judge.*

נוּחַ

LAY UP: "Therefore shall ye lay up these my words in your heart and in your soul . . .", (Deut. 11:18). The Hebrew word for *lay up* is *nuach* which has several denotements. It denotes quiet, as the ark of the Covenant placed in its temple location. It denotes depositing, as God's word in the heart so that sin will not be committed.

For more on this root turn to *rest.*

הָלַךְ

LEAD: "Who led thee through that great and terrible wilderness. . .", (Deut. 8:15). There are several words translated *lead,* but *halak* is both quite frequent and very colorful. It means:

To bear, to bring forth—Gen. 4:1. God leads along His children that He caused to be born into His kingdom.

To create—Job 38:28. God created the storehouses of dew and

155

the dew falls (or rises) where He wills. God leads His willing people to be a softening, refreshing dew to the places parched by sin.

נהל

LEAD: "He leadeth me beside the still waters . . .", (Ps. 23:2).
Nahal means:

To conduct—Ps. 31:3. A conductor is needed for every tour.

To protect—II Chron. 32:22. God can so guide one that he will
be protected.

To provide for, to sustain—Gen. 47:17. God furnishes fowls
for flesh and sweet water to drink, when He leads the people.

נהג

LEAD: "Thou that leadest Joseph like a flock . . .", (Ps. 80:1).
Nahag means:

To pant—that is, be exhausted from running or from being
made to run.

To urge on, to drive—Gen. 31:18. There are times when providence prescribes the course.

To bring, to bring up to—Exod. 10:13. The Lord purposefully
brings creatures down certain ways and to certain places.

נחה

LEAD: "Lead me, O Lord, in thy righteousness . . .", (Ps. 5:8).
For the meaning of *nachah* see *Guide.*

דרך

LEAD: "Lead me in Thy truth and teach me: for Thou are the
God of my salvation", (Ps. 25:5). For the meaning of *darak* see
Conversation.

בוא

LEAD: "But, the Lord liveth . . . which led the seed of the
house of Israel", (Jer. 23:8). For the meaning of *Bo* see *Enter.*

לָמַד

LEARN: "That thou mayest learn to fear the Lord thy God always", (Deut. 14:23). For the meaning of *lamad* see *Disciple*.

נָחַשׁ

LEARN: "I have learned by experience that the Lord hath blessed me . . .", (Gen. 30:27). *Nachash* means:

To augur, to forebode, to divine—Gen. 44:15. This signification has in it the idea of presentiment.

יָדַע

LEARN: "And the vision of all is become unto you as the words of a book that is sealed, which men deliver to one that is learned . . .", (Isa. 29:11). For the meaning of *yada* see *Know*.

עָזַב

LEAVE: "The Lord our God be with us, as He was with our fathers; let Him not leave us, nor forsake us", (I Kings 8:57). *Azab* is also used in such passages as Ruth 1:16 and Ps. 16:10. For its meaning see *Forsake*.

אָגַר

LETTER: "Then I came to governors beyond the river, and gave them the king's letters", (Neh. 2:9). In the New Testament men were called epistles, read of all. In the Hebrew root *agar* are several meanings that would enhance further this attractive metaphor.

It means to gather or collect—Deut. 28:39. Man is a granary for the harvest of good things or bad.

It means a fist—Exod. 21:18. A knot of men, good or bad, can make quite an impact on society.

It means a charger—Ezra 1:9. A man whose life and heart are filled with good things would be considered a charger full of silver and gold by those with whom he shared his life. Some believe that this root signifies a fruit-basket.

It means a courier—Neh. 2. In this context and others, the bearer of the letter and the letter seem to be identified. Ancients hold that there is a form of this root that denotes one hired to carry the letters. Then the New Testament idea of men being letters takes on still more strength.

כזב

LIAR: "I believed, therefore have I spoken: I was greatly afflicted: I said in my haste, All men are liars", (Ps. 116:10, 11). *Kazab,* the Hebrew root for *liar,* has several ugly facets.

It means to lie—Job 6:28. A lie is evident or will become so. It means to break one's word—Job 24:25. This is, e.g., marriage vows are "nothing worth", if not kept.

It means to fail—Isa. 58:11. How beautiful to have a well-watered garden supplied by a spring that fails not.

It means deceitful—Jer. 15:18. Waters that fail are liars for they deceive the hope of pilgrims that come by.

It means fallacious—Job 41:9. When hope in another is vain the sight of him offends.

This root is used to build a name (appropriate) for a place (I Chron. 4:22) of men who had dominion in Moab.

It is used to build a name of a godless woman in Midian—Num. 25:18.

דרור

LIBERTY: "The Spirit of the Lord God is upon me; because the Lord hath annointed me . . . to proclaim liberty to the captives . . .", (Isa. 61:1). *Daror* is from *Darar* which means:

To sparkle, to radiate—Eccl. 1:6. The idea is that the South is a sunny region that sparkles, radiates. This is opposite to *tsaphon* which signifies a region of darkness. From this it is easy to see what Jesus had in mind when He wanted His followers who were to be free from sin to circulate among people, shining like a light upon a hill so God may get glory.

To flow—Exod. 30:23. Such flowing is to be spontaneous and free, hence there is liberty, freedom and a letting go free. These kind of Christians, radiantly heralding the gospel around the world, will be bringing in God's kingdom. (In the verse in Exod. this word is translated *pure,* meaning a myrrh that flows spontaneously, or that its sweet-smelling odor flows freely.)

כחש

LIE: "Ye shall not . . . lie to one another", (Lev. 19:11). Varied are the meanings of *kachash*, the Hebrew root for *lie*.

It means to fail—Ps. 109:24. Lies fail the one from whom they issue as well as the rest of society.

It means to deny—Gen. 18:15. If Sarah laughed and then said she did not, she lied.

It means to disappoint—Hab. 3:17. It was meant for the olive tree to bear and when it did not, hope was disappointed.

It means to feign—Ps. 81:15, 16. The vanquished play hypocrites when they profess devotion to their victors.

It means leanness—Job 16:8. When the body fails in leanness it is not truthfully serving its purpose. When a man lies he is misrepresenting mankind.

חיה

LIFE: "And the Lord formed man of the dust of the ground, and breathed into his nostrils the breath of life; and man became a living soul", (Gen. 2:7). *Chayah* means:

To live, to remain alive—Josh. 6:17. This is just not to die.

To live again, to be revived—Ezek. 37:5. Therefore it is believed the Lord can revive a church which seems to be dead.

To become well, to recover from sickness—II Kings 1:2. The human body and the church are subject to many ills but the Lord can heal them all.

Lively, vigorous, strong—II Sam. 23:20. Such vigor and strength used for the Lord would cause wonders.

Flourishing, prosperous—I Sam. 25:6. This kind of life can grandly advance the Kingdom.

Fresh—Gen. 26:19. This is opposite to flat, dead, putrid or stagnant. Another word for *life* or *soul* is *nephesh* which means vital spirit, animus, to which is ascribed hunger, thirst, loathing, etc.

נשא

LIFT: "Save thine people and bless thine inheritance: feed them also, and lift them up for ever", (Ps. 28:9). For the meaning of *nasa* see *bear*.

אוֹר

LIGHT: "Arise, shine, for thy light is come and the glory of the Lord is risen upon thee", (Isa. 60:1). He who glorifies his God by letting his light shine before men is surrounded wonderfully and is resplendent. This word *or* means:

To illuminate—Ps. 77:18.

To refresh, to gladden by opening the eyes of one in the dark—Ps. 19:8. Those are happy who are converted by the perfect law of the Lord.

To cause one's face to shine, to enliven, to cheer—Eccl. 8:1. "Ignorance of the law excuses no one", but it droops the countenance.

To kindle, to set on fire—Mal. 1:10. Build a fire in the pulpits and in the pews and thereby become a flame for God.

To typify welfare, prosperity, happiness—Job 22:28.

Revelation, Urim—Num. 27:21. Urim was likely a small sapphire image inserted between the double folds of the robe of the priest serving in the temple. This gem represented light and revelation. Christians wear the Pearl of great price in the folds of their heart and soul and life. To them He is the Light of the world.

Greens, herbs—II Kings 4:39. The idea of brightness, is in the Semitic languages (Arabic, Hebrew, Syriac, etc.), often expressed in verdure and in flowers.

Uriel, flame of God—I Chron. 6:9; 15:5, 21.

Urijah, flame of Jehovah, prophet—Jer. 26:20. How wonderful to have a prophet who is a flame of God.

בּרק

LIGHTNING: "Thou art the God that doest wonders . . . the lightnings lightened the world", (Ps. 77:14, 18). *Baraq,* the Hebrew for *lightning,* is interestingly used.

It is used to describe an article in God's arsenal—Ps. 144:6.

It is used to build the name for God's warrior—Judg. 4:6. Barak

160

was a bolt of lightning from God to defend Israel—but Barak was one victorious leader who was not to get the credit, (see verse 9). So, it is predicted, "It is yet to be seen what God can do with a surrendered life that does not care who gets the credit".

It is used to signify lightening—Ps. 77:18. God sends rays of light through his ministers to the nations which become sort of a holy radium active in generations following.

It is used to signify a glittering and sparkling gem, the carbuncle—Ezek. 28:13. Talk of glamour, our missionaries are gems, emitting light "that lighteth every man" whose source is the Light of the world.

שׁמע

LISTEN: "Listen, O isles, unto Me . . .", (Isa. 49:1). For the meaning of *shamea* see *hear.*

קטן

LITTLE: "And Solomon said . . . And I am but a little child: I know not how to go out or to come in", (I Kings 3:7). Solomon, the great king, called himself a little child and this pleased the Lord. It will pay us to look into the significations of *qaton,* the Hebrew root for *little.*

It signifies smallness—Exod. 18:22, 26. Great men think themselves small while others consider them great; but, men who think themselves great are known to be small by others.

It signifies unimportance—Isa. 31:9. Important persons do not feel important, neither do they need to advertise their importance.

It means lesser, as of two—Gen. 1:16. Solomon plainly shows in I Kings 3 that David was greater than he. This is a mark of greatness.

It means of no account and unworthy—Gen. 32:10. Jacob was telling God of his unworthiness Who ordained him to greatness. In Ezek. 21:26 we read, "Exalt him that is low, and abase him that is high".

It means to make small—Amos 8:5. Those who esteem themselves small as a little child like the wisest of men did may be made great like he was.

161

חוה

LIVE: "And Adam called his wife's name Eve; because she was the mother of all living", (Gen. 3:20). *Chavah,* the Hebrew verb for *live* has several meanings.

In the above verse it is used in building a name for the first woman and also to signify *living.*

It means to breathe. This signification is obvious in the first chapters of Genesis. When God breathed there was life.

It means a village—Num. 32:41. This was a town of live people.

It means to show by breathing out that to be shown—Ps. 19:2 and Job 32:6. Knowledge is shown on night's screen and the glory of God is flashed across the heavens. In the second passage Elihu has an opinion to declare but dares not. So, putting all of these together, we would have a community of lively people sharing their divine culture.

חי

LIVE: "How long have I to live . . .", (II Sam. 19:34). For the meaning of *chai* see *life.*

פנה

LOOK: "Look unto me and be ye saved, ye ends of the earth", (Isa. 45:22). *Panah* means:

To turn oneself, to turn the back. This is repentance when one turns himself to God.

To turn to or towards—I Sam. 13:17; Isa. 53:6. To betake oneself after Christ is christianity.

To put in order, to prepare—Gen. 24:31. The heart is to be made ready for the Lord's coming.

Face, countenance—Gen. 50:1.

יהוה

LORD: "And the Lord God formed man of the dust of the ground, and breathed into his nostrils the breath of life; and man became a living soul", (Gen. 2:7). The Hebrew for *Lord* is *Jehovah,* signifying the supreme deity of the devout Hebrews. But, because they were conscientious objectors to pronouncing *Jehovah* on the ground that it was too sacred, they used *Adonai* (Lord) instead.

Jehovah is derived from the verb *havah* (to be). That is, God is the great I AM. He "who will never be other than the same", is for ever Lord. "The Lord Jehovah is His memorial", Hos. 12:5.

אָדוֹן

LORD: "O Lord, our Lord, how excellent is thy name in all the earth", (Ps. 8:1). *Adon* means:

Master.

Owner—Gen. 24:14. The Lord has the right to own man because of creation and redemption. All of creation is His.

Governor—Josh. 3:13. God guides the affairs of His people.

(The Jews had a conviction they should never pronounce the name Jehovah, so when they came to it in sacred writings they substituted *Adonai,* thereby wishing the more to reverence God, Dan. 9:7, 8, 16).

אָבַד

LOST: "I will seek that which was lost . . .", (Ezek. 34:16). For the meaning of *abad* see *Destroy.* See passage in Luke 19:10.

אָהֵב

LOVE: "His banner over me was love", (Song of Sol. 2:4). "He will save, He will rejoice over thee with joy; He will rest in His love . . .", (Zeph. 3:17). For the meaning of *ahabah* see *Beloved.*

חָשַׁק

LOVE: "Thou hast in love to my soul delivered it from the pit of corruption", (Isa. 38:17). *Chasaq* means:

To join or fasten together—Exod. 38:28.

To be attached, to cleave—Deut. 10:15. This is to love with warm affection and to stick fast to any one.

To delight in doing, to please—II Chron. 8:6. Love is always building up something; e.g. a church or the kingdom of God.

163

Spokes—I Kings 7:33. These spokes connect the rim with the nave or hub. The Lord is the center of all and all that are attached to Him fan out from Him as missionaries.

שׁפל

LOW: "Thus saith the Lord God . . . exalt him that is low, and abase him that is high", (Ezek. 21:26). This sounds so much like the New Testament. *Shaphal* means:

To be cast down, to be made low—Isa. 10:33. This speaks of trees but it might be spoken of haughty men.

To humble—Ps. 18:27. The Lord will humble those with high looks, and will set on high those that are low—Job 5:11.

Low country, plain—Josh. 11:16. The lowlands benefit most from the rains of heaven and likewise those persons who are low will benefit most from the showers spiritual.

Slothfulness, idleness—Eccl. 10:18. This comes out of the root that means a letting down, i.e. of the hands. Perhaps God wants us at times to let down our hands, relax in His presence and let Him move us by His spirit.

אוה

LUST: "The mixed multitude . . . fell a lusting", (Num. 11:4). *Avah* means:

To bend, to inflect.

To have a bent, to desire, to long for, to wish—Prov. 21:10. This stir or gnawing takes place principally in the soul.

To howl. This is like the jackal, dog or wolf.

Pleasure, will, desire—I Sam. 23:20 and Hos. 10:10.

שׁקר

LYING: "Lying lips are abomination to the Lord: but they that deal truly are His delight", (Prov. 12:22). *Sheqer* means:

To deceive—Gen. 21:23. The primary idea is that of painting and coloring. In fact this word could be translated paint.

A little bit of powder, a little bit of paint, Makes someone look like what he ain't.

Infidelity—Ps. 89:33. Breaking a promise is telling a lie.

Disappointment, vain—Ps. 33:17. The cavalry cannot bring victory.

הלל

MAD: "He . . . feigned himself mad in their hands", (I Sam. 21:13). *Halal* means:

To be foolish, hence to be mad—Jer. 51:7. In Jer. 50:38 it is reported that they madly trust in idols.

For other meanings of this root see *Boast.*

שׁגע

MAD: "The spiritual man is mad . . . ", (Hos. 9:7).

To be vigorous, brave, fierce. The idea seems to be that of impetuous excitement. This is most becoming a prophet of God. Perhaps he could be said to be on fire.

Raving, frenzied, furious—This could well be spoken of true prophets of God.

Insane—I Sam. 2:15. A true prophet would have to speak out of his mind. If he spoke his own mind he would not be speaking the mind of God.

עשׂה

MADE: "By the word of the Lord were the heavens made", (Ps. 33:6). For the meaning of *asah* see *Accomplish.*

גדל

MAGNIFY: "Let such as love thy salvation say continually, The Lord be magnified", (Ps. 40:16). *Gadal* means:

To grow—Exod. 2:10. This must be that we should grow in knowledge and in capacity for glorifying the Lord.

To be great—Gen. 24:35. We would like for our Master to have flocks, gold, servants or anything that would indicate His greatness.

To be greatly valued, highly prized—Ps. 35:27. The Lord is so highly valued that His Name shall be extolled.

To increase—Gen. 19:19. The Lord's mercy increases towards us; or, at least, we discover Him more merciful with time. Perhaps this word could be used to speak of increasing His kingdom.

אדם

MAN: "Let us make man in our image", (Gen. 1:26). *Adam* means:

To be red, ruddy, beautiful—Lam. 4:7. All of God's creations were good in His sight.

A man—Gen. 6:1. This means male and female.

Adam—Gen. 2:7. This seems to be a name given this distinctive creature to distinguish him from all other creatures.

Ruby—Ezek. 28:13. Likely a gem of a red color is signified here.

The earth—Gen. 47:19. Man seems to be ground, land. Why not since he came from the ground and to the ground must return?

A country—Gen. 28:15. Man can be a country where dwelleth Jehovah for is not his body to be a temple?

איש

MAN: ". . . Moses, the man of God . . .", (Deut. 33:1). The Hebrew for *man* in this verse is *ish*. While *adam* is used in about four hundred passages, *ish* is used in about twice as many and has several denotements.

It denotes a noble one of high rank. The men whom God uses are like that.

It denotes one opposite to a female—I Sam. 11:11. This is one who has vigor and manly age with warlike valor who is to be a husband as opposite to a wife—Ruth 1:11.

It denotes a citizen of Zion by virtue of the sonship of God. If he is not God's son, he is not a citizen of God's country.

It denotes great build, intelligence and fame—Gen. 6:4. God wants His sons to become great men. No wonder a sacred writer milleniums later exhorted, "Quit you like men . . .".

A derivative of this root means manikin or little men. How despicable in the eyes of God and man is a little man—little in spirit and in heart. What a contrast is he to him described above.

166

בעל

MAN: "A furious man aboundeth in transgression", (Prov. 29:22). For the meaning of *Baal* see *Husband*.

גבר

MAN: "There is a man in thy kingdom . . .", (Dan. 5:11). *Gibar* means:

To be mighty, strong.

To prevail.

An archangel, Gabriel—Dan. 8:16. This name means a mighty man of God. Comp. Luke 1:19. God made man for Himself and meant for man to be in His presence and not run off to his own way.

(Note: The English word *man* is found about 2,500 times in the Bible; about 1,800 times being in the Old Testament.)

אנוש

MAN: "What is man that thou art mindful of Him?", (Ps. 8:4). *Enosh* is from the root *Anash* which means:

Man—Dan. 4:32. The word is plural here and in all other places where used. Man was spoken of as a group.

Son of man—Dan. 7:13. This seems to be the origin of the title: Messiah, used so much of our Saviour in the New Testament and in apocryphal literature.

Mortal—II Sam. 12:15. How many ills befall the human race. Although scholars attempt to take this meaning out of this word and make another with it, it seems that *mortal* and *man* are so very closely related that reference to one reminds one of the other. Both meanings come from the three Hebrew characters: *anash*.

ברר

MANIFEST: "I said in mine heart concerning the estate of the sons of men, that God might manifest them, and that they might see that they themselves are beasts", (Eccl. 3:18). *Barar* means:

To separate—Ezek. 20:38. Here we are told the rebels that transgress against the Lord will the Lord sever or purge out from among His people. The Lord will separate the sheep from the goats. The Lord, not man will pull the thorns and thistles from among the good grain.

To select, to choose out—I Chron. 9:22. A great selecting and a great choosing will take place. This supports the belief God has a chosen people.

To examine, to prove—Eccl. 9:1. Here a matter is declared because it has been examined and proved. This is clear that the righteous and their works are in the hands of God.

To clean, to purify, to reform—Dan. 12:10. Yes, many shall be purified, "and made white and tried; but the wicked shall do wickedly . . ." Although the word "manifest" is found only once in the Bible, the word *Barar* is found many times in the Hebrew Bible and has some very rich meanings.

To be upright, just and pure—Ps. 18:26. It is said God will show Himself upright, pure and just with the pure, just and upright. The same word, *barar,* is used of God and of man. This is a great word.

שׁפט

MANNER: ". . . And let him teach them the manner of the God of the land", (II Kings 17:27). *Shapat* means:

Judgment, to judge, to govern, to rule, etc. For a full treatment see *judge*. This is a key word. *Manner* may not carry much of the meaning to the average mind in the English. So much hinges on its meaning in this passage in particular. The people in this land herein mentiond did not know the rules of God and a remedy was outlined: A priest should be sent to them to teach them the judgment of God. If they do not learn lions will be sent in to slay the people. It is learning time for them lest they perish.

אדר

MANTLE: "Elijah passed by him and cast his mantle upon him", (I Kings 19:19). For the meaning of *adar* see *Excellent.*

הלךְ

MARCH: "They shall march everyone on his ways, and they

168

shall not break the ranks", (Joel 2:7). For the meaning of *yalak,* (same as *halak*), see *Go.*

צער

MARCH: "O God, when thou wentest forth before thy people, when thou didst march through the wilderness; Selah", (Ps. 68:7). *Tsaad* means:

To step forward—II Sam. 6:13. This was done slowly and in a regular and stately manner since it was a very solemn procession.

To mount—Gen. 49:22. This action was a slow gait like a vine growing over a wall. Sin and sinners may get into society or into individuals at such a gait but Christianity can march around the world although it may be at a snail's pace.

Step-chains—Isa. 3:20. These ornaments for the legs were short chains which oriental females wore attached to the ankles to make them take short and mincing steps.

בעל

MARRY: "For as a young man marricth a virgin", (Isa. 62:5). For the meaning of *baal,* the Hebrew word for *marry,* see *husband.*

פלא

MARVELOUS: "This is the Lord's doing: it is marvelous in our eyes", (Ps. 118:23). *Pala,* the Hebrew word for *marvelous,* has several meanings.

It means to be distinguished, extraordinary—II Sam. 1:26. The love between David and Jonathan passed that of women.

It means to be great, to be hard, to be difficult—Zech. 8:6. Certainly arduousness only will produce the marvelous.

It means to separate, to consecrate—Lev. 22:21. Marvelous is it when a vow is kept at great sacrifice.

It means admirable—Isa. 28:29. Counsel that cometh from the Lord is both admirable and marvelous.

It means miracle, wonder—Exod. 15:11. There is no one among the gods like the Lord who does wonders.

169

מדד

MEASURE: "Your iniquities . . . saith the Lord, . . . will I measure . . . ", (Isa. 65:7). *Maded* means:

God will extend a measuring line on all sinners, even upon those who have blasphemed Him upon the hills and will mete out to them just retribution!

Also there is here the idea that God will mete out "the valley of Succoth," Ps. 60:6, or as for that the possessions any have, to God's victorious troops who shall settle there permanently as inhabitants.

שׁוּח

MEDITATE: "Isaac went out to meditate in the field at eventide", (Gen. 24:63). The primary idea of *suach* seems to be that of bowing down and musing—Ps. 119:15. There is also the idea of a pilgrimage in this root perhaps coming from the notion of pious meditation, chanting and walking. Of course one could do this pilgrimage with God or into his word.

הגה

MEDITATE: "In his law doth he meditate day and night", (Ps. 1:2). *Hagah* means:

To speak with oneself in a low voice, to think out loud on someting—Josh. 1:8. This is done in order to keep the mind on what would be a proper word or answer.

To be separated—Prov. 25:4. Like the dross is separated from the silver so must man separate himself from the crowd in order to be able to help the crowd.

ענו

MEEK: "The meek shall inherit the earth . . .", (Ps. 37:11). *Anav,* which comes from the root *anah* means:

Humble—Ps. 10:12. These the Lord will not forget.

Afflicted—Ps. 18:27. The Lord will lift up the humble who are miserable, distressed, needy because of sin in their lives but will bring down those with high looks.

170

Oppressed—Isa. 53:4. Jesus, before us, was oppressed, afflicted and humbled but we know also that He came to be lifted up and draws all men unto Himself and is glorified by those that come unto Him.

Gentleness, mildness, clemency—Ps. 18:35. All of those that suffer with the Lord—are meek and lowly and afflicted—will also with Him be glorified.

קרא

MEET: "And Moses brought the people out of the camp to meet with God", (Exod. 19:17). The people and Moses were out to propose an alliance with God. For the meaning of *qara* see *call.*

יעד

MEET: "And there I (God) will *meet* with thee, and I will commune with thee from above . . .", (Exod. 25:22) *yaad.*

This Hebrew word means to betroth which is so close to the New Testament idea of Christ-the-bridegroom and The-Church-the-bride. It is akin to the beautiful Arabic word that says "to point out before hand for good."

Also there is here the signification of meeting together at an appointed time and place like assembling in God's house for protection—Neh. 6:10; and being summoned to court—Job 9:19. The judgment day will be a scene of both of these events.

זכר

MEMORY: "The memory of the just is blessed . . .", (Prov. 10:7). *Zakar* means:

To recollect—Gen. 8:1. This is early in the Bible to let man know that God will be calling to mind everything about man.

To reflect, to consider—Deut. 5:15. Man is to let bear in and on his mind facts concerning his past, his present and his future. This calls for meditation which is another shade of meaning in this root.

To renew one's care for anyone—Gen. 19.29. This is wonderful to be stored in one's memory: that care for one was renewed with the accessory idea of kindness—most especially if God is the One doing the caring.

A name as a memorial—Exod. 3:15. God instructed Moses to teach the people that His Name was to be a memorial across the unfolding generations.

חסד

MERCY: "The Lord is longsuffering, and of great mercy . . .", (Num. 14:18). For the meaning of *chased* see *Goodliness.*

חנן

MERCY: "Have mercy upon me and hear my prayer", (Ps. 4:1). For the meaning of *chanan* see *Grace.*

רחם

MERCY: "O Lord, revive thy work . . . in wrath remember mercy" (Hab. 3:2). For the meaning of *racham* see *Compassion.*

כפר

MERCY SEAT: "I will appear in the cloud upon the mercy seat", (Lev. 16:2).

Here it means a lid, place of covering but the spiritual significance is brought out under *Atonement.*

See: *Atonement.*

טוב

MERRY: "He that is of a merry heart hath a continual feast", (Prov. 15:15). This Hebrew word *tob* has much color and instruction in it. It means:

To be well—I Sam. 16:16.

To ge good—Deut. 5:29.

To be goodly, fair, pleasing—Num. 24:5; Song of Sol. 4:10.

To act well. "And the Lord said unto David . . . Whereas it was in thine heart to build a house unto my Name, thou didst well that it was in thine heart"—I Kings 8:18.

To do good to others—Exod. 36:11.

To be virtuous, upright—Isa. 5:20.

To be kind—Lam. 3:25—and to be of a kind eye—Prov. 22:9.

To be fair, goodly—Exod. 2:2; to be beautiful—Esther 1:11.

To be pleasant, sweet—Song of Sol. 4:10.

This word *tob* is used to describe cane that is sweet—Jer. 6:20. Christians, virtuous, kind, beneficent and pleasant make a church like a patch of sweet cane.

Happy man—Lam. 3:26.

Pleasing to Jehovah—Zech. 6:14. When we please the Lord we have grounds for being shouting happy.

שמח

MERRY: " A merry heart doeth good like a medicine", (Prov. 17:22). Here the word *samach* means:

To be cheerful, joyful—Prov. 13:9. The primary idea here in the Hebrew word is to be clement, lenient, liberal. This verse could be translated: "The candle of the righteous shineth cheerfully"—there is no harm in the light of a candle but rather it tendeth to cheer.

To rejoice in the Lord—Ps. 9:2. To rejoice in the Lord by bringing offerings into the courts of the sanctuary—Lev. 23:40; Deut. 14:25, 26. These people of God are at once medicine and medics to the world.

דבר

MESSAGE: "So I have a message from God", (Judg. 3:20). *dabar.*

Another Hebrew word, *basar* is also translated *message* and for its full meaning see *Tidings*. In Hag. 1:13 both *message* and *messenger* come from this same root, thus identifying God's spokesman with God's speech. See: *Commandment.*

מלאך

MESSENGER: "Behold, I will send my messenger, and he shall prepare the way before me: and the Lord, whom ye seek, shall suddenly come to his temple, even the messenger of the covenant . . .", (Mal. 3:1). *Malak* is from *laak* which means: to send, to minister, to wait upon. A great meaning of *malak* is brought out in Exod. 23:20 where it is translated angel. It means a prophet in Hagg. 1:13 and priest in Mal. 2:7. Once, Isa. 42:9, it speaks of Israel as sent from God to teach the nations.

The Hebrew word for *messenger* in "Then spake Haggai the Lord's messenger in the Lord's message unto the people . . ."— Hag. 1:13, is *basar:* the same as that for *message,* thus identifying the preacher with that preached and both as belonging to the Lord. The prophet delivered not his but the Lord's good news unto the people namely, "I am with you, saith the Lord." For a fuller meaning of *basar* see *Tidings.*

מָשִׁיחַ

MESSIAH: "From the going forth of the commandment to restore and to build Jerusalem unto the Messiah the Prince . . .", (Dan. 9:25). *Messiah* means:

Anointed—II Sam. 1:21. This is spoken in connection with Saul and may be referring to a shield. Jesus is the believer's shield.

Anointed high priest—Lev. 4:3, 5, 16. Jesus is the High Priest.

Honor, consecration, holiness—I Sam. 2:10; II Sam. 1:14; Ps. 2:2. These meanings help to set apart and above all others, the Anointed of Jehovah.

"The Lord hath *anointed* me . . ."—Isa 61:1.

This means the Lord made Him *The Messiah,* the one consecrated by unction to office or priest—Exod. 28:41; to office of prophet—I Kings 19:16; to office of king—I Sam. 10:1. Many hold that Ps. 2:2 speaks of the Messiah to come.

This same root is treated under *Anoint.* It also is the name for Moses—I Chron. 6:3, meaning to draw out, to deliver, to preserve, to save.

גְּבוּרָה

MIGHT: "O Lord God, thou hast begun to shew thy servant thy greatness, and thy mighty hand: for what God is there in heaven and in earth, that can do according to thy works, and according to thy might?", (Deut. 3:24). *Geburah* means:

Strength—Ps. 90:10. Here strength has to do with life and the prolonging of it.

Valor—Isa. 36:5. This is to have strength for war.

Power—Isa. 30:15. God says in quietness and in confidence shall one have power.

To bind—Exod. 17:11. This is, to bind up something that is broken, to confirm it and give it strength.

To prevail—Ps. 12:4. This is done by exercising strength which may be hidden.

"Not by might . . ."—Zech. 4:6, has the Hebrew *chayil* for the meaning of which see *Able*.

אוּל

MIGHTY: "The *mighty* of the land, those carried he into captivity from Jerusalem to Babylon", (II Kings 24:15). The king, his mother and his officers were carried into Babylon; but to most affect God's people the *mighty* must be taken. The Hebrew root, *ul,* from which *mighty* is derived has several significations.

It means the powerful, or the chief because of strength as in the text above. Babylon's chiefs were after the chiefs in God's army.

It means to twist or to roll like a ram's horn and signify strength.

It means posts—Ezek. 41:1. Often have the best men been called the pillars of the church or the columns on which the world is supported—I Sam. 2:8.

A beautiful use is made of a derivative of this root in the inscription to Psalm 22: "Aijeleth"—the hind of the morning. Psalm 22 gives details of the crucifixion of Jesus who became the hind (ram) for the world's new morning.

לֵב

MIND: "Was joined . . . for the people had a *mind* to work", (Neh. 4:6.) *leb.*

The Hebrew word here translated *mind* is in most passages translated *heart* and means:

1. Life—Ps. 84:2;

2. The Seat of feelings, affections and emotions—Deut. 6:5,6;

3. A mode of thinking and acting—Ps. 51:10. God gave David a new heart which precipitated into glorious activity.

4. Seat of will, purpose, determination—I Sam. 14:7.

5. Understanding—Job 12:3.

It appears then when the mind was made up that man's whole soul entered in and the heart was stirred to complement and confirm the mind's action.

שׁרת

MINISTER: "Let the priests, the ministers of the Lord, weep between the porch and the altar, and let them say, Spare thy people, O Lord, and give not thine heritage to reproach, that the heathen should rule over them . . .", (Joel 2:17). *Sharath* means:

To wait upon—Gen. 39:4. To serve is the sign of the servant of the Lord.

To minister unto the Lord—I Sam. 3:1. One side of this word means to serve the people while the other means to serve the Lord.

Attendant—Josh. 1:1. The minister of the Lord is always to be standing by ready for a call from the Lord some work to do. He is to be an attendant in God's service station on the road of lives. The idea of sacrifice is connected with this office. It grows out of another meaning of this word. Rams shall minister by being presented for sacrifice on the Lord's altar—Isa. 60:7.

(Another word, translated *ministry* in II Chron. 7:6 and in Hos. 12:10, is *yad* and it means hand. For its meaning, see *hand*. The Navy has an expression, "Give me a hand . . ." meaning, Come over and help me).

אות

MIRACLE: "Because all those men which have seen my glory and my miracles which I did in Egypt and in the wilderness . . .", (Num. 14:22). *Oth* means:

A sign—Exod. 12:13. The blood was a miraculous sign on the door posts.

A flag—Num. 2:2. A banner for a Christian or a standard for a military man has a miraculous power about it.

A memorial—Exod. 13:9. A sign of something past has an invisible power about it for the heart—especially as here, when a great deliverance is remembered.

A portent—Isa. 20:3. When something future is set out in front of a person he thinks it almost incredible or miraculous.

A wonder, a prodigy, a miracle—Deut. 6:22. It is no wonder that Egypt, Pharaoh and Israel were moved by God's wonders.

חטא

MISS: "There were seven hundred chosen men lefthanded; everyone could sling stones at an hair breadth and not miss", (Judg. 20:16). *Chata* means:

Not to hit the mark—Judg. 20:16. While these men did hit the mark there are men who miss living a life pleasing to God, and that is sin.

To make a false step, miss with the foot—Prov. 19:2. The soul that is without knowledge of the way may stumble and fall.

To harm—Prov. 8:35-36. He that finds wisdom as it is in the Lord will find favor of the Lord but he that misseth that wisdom does his soul irreparable and eternal harm.

To sin—Gen. 20:6. This is to err from the path of right and duty.

To forfeit—Hab. 2:10. This is some sin: a man misses the mark, the blessing of God, the high goal of great living because he sins.

Guilty—Isa. 29:21. A man who misses the mark in the soul's realm is pronounced an offender.

Punishment—Zech. 14:19. Missing the mark brings its own punishment.

Calamity, misfortune—Isa. 40:2. Missing the mark is sin and calamity.

לעג

MOCK: "Whoso mocketh the poor reproacheth his Maker: and he that is glad at calamities shall not go unpunished", (Prov. 17:5). *Laag*, the Hebrew root for *mock*, has several severe significations.

It means to stammer, pointing the fact that mockers usually stutter nonsense.

It means to be unintelligible, adding the fact that mockers are usually not understood as they sputter vainly.

It means to deride—Ps. 2:4. But as in this case, it may be Lord who laughs.

It means to scorn—Prov. 1:22. How foolish to scorn things good and noble.

It means to speak as in a barbarous or foreign tongue—Isa. 28:11. Mockery is barbaric and certainly its language is foreign to the Christian.

This root is used to signify a buffoon—Ps. 16. At the table of the rich, the jester was a welcome parasite because he could make his moping master laugh, although, according to this scripture, there was hypocrisy in it all.

This root is used in Ps. 1:1, "Blessed is the man that . . . sitteth not in the seat of the scornful".

הגג

MUSE: "While I mused, the fire burned within me; then my tongue spake . . .", (Ps. 39:3). The Hebrew for *muse* is *hagag* and means a focusing as the rays of the sun through glass. When the rays of God's love and power focus on a man's heart a fire starts and his tongue begins. For more on this root see *Meditate*.

יתד

NAIL: "Out of him came the corner, out of him the nail, out of him the battle bow . . .", (Zech. 10:4). Depressed Judah, deprived of her Davidic monarchy, is oppressed by bad shepherds but will become a victorious people. The manner in which Jehovah will do this is signified in *yathed,* the Hebrew root for *nail.*

It signifies a pin—Exod. 38:31. These pins were used to peg a tent securely to the ground. Judah needed such men.

It signifies a nail used as a weapon—Judg. 4:21, 22. Men, tough as nails, as straight and as dispensable would be used to bring Judah victory.

In Isa. 22:23 this root is used to describe a solid dwelling to these wanderers. Gibbon said in the eighteenth century that one of the reasons for the fall of the Roman Empire was the undermining of the dignity and sanctity of the home.

This root signifies a prince on whom the care and the welfare of the government depends—Zech. 10:4. The walls of houses in those days were provided with plugs or pegs on the walls for hanging many things. The Lord chose upholders of the political constitution of His people.

שֵׁם

NAME: "Help us, O God of our salvation, for the glory of thy name: and deliver us and purge our sins, for Thy name's sake", (Ps. 79:9). *Shem* means:

A sign, a mark which one receives. The name of Jehovah was set by divine authority—Jer. 11:21; 26:9.

Renown—Gen. 11:4. While here the attempt at renown was foiled and properly so, God's renown is everywhere hailed and justified.

Praise and fame—Zeph. 3:19. This Hebrew word is so used here as to carry the idea of fame and praise. This is good use of it in connection with God.

Monument—Isa. 55:13. An impressive and glorious color is seen in the word as used in this passage. This is due God and much more.

נָגַשׁ

NEAR: "Assemble yourselves and come; draw near together . . .", (Isa. 45:20). In the context here there is the appeal of the God of eternity. He wants the people to leave gods that cannot save. He declares there is no God beside Himself and that He would be their Saviour. He wants the people to draw near unto Him. *Nagash,* the Hebrew root for *near,* is a moving verb.

The first action signified by it is to approach as to the holy of holies—Num. 4:19; and, as His altar—Exod. 30:20. This makes a strong case in favor of public worship in the Spirit; if not a command to do so.

The next action in this root is to pray—Jer. 30:21, 22. The Lord will cause him to draw near who engages in so warm an exercise and more, He will be his God and he will be God's son.

Another action is to recede, to near away—Isa. 49:20. The idea is the place is too hard and there must be a moving near to some other place—hence recede. This is like backsliding.

Another action is to stand back—Gen. 19:9. If a person does not draw near to God he stands back in the first step of backsliding.

Still another action is to offer or to present—Amos 5:25. The worshiper draws near to God with a gift so that the drawing near becomes so significant that the object may be omitted to give more emphasis to the nearness.

רע

NEIGHBOUR: "Thou shalt not bear false witness against thy neighbour", (Exod. 20:17). *Rea* means:

Friend—Prov. 25:17. A neighbour ought be a friend; only positive witness of good should be borne to him and over-familiarity and overstaying in his house ought be guarded against lest the friend be lost. "Company after three days becomes stale."

Lover—Song of Sol. 5:16. The Lord wants His children to love one another as he loved them and this other is any member of the human family.

עמם

NEIGHBOUR: "In righteousness shall thou judge thy neighbour", (Lev. 19:15). *Amah* and *amam* mean:

Communion—Exod. 28:27. Just as rings of gold were to be placed on each side of the ephod for balance and symmetry, each helping the other to improve the whole so is the idea of companionship and society found in this word and is applied to people.

Equally with—I Chron. 24:31. Neighbour carries with it the idea of equality, e.g., in privileges and facilities.

To congregate—Isa. 7:14; 8:8. Butter and honey go together, God and His people are together in Immanuel and the people ought be brothers and sisters in the Lord. The meaning of this word is so deep that one would scarce believe it can be used outside of Christianity.

חדש

NEW: "A new heart also will I give you, and a new spirit will I put within you . . .", (Ezek. 36:26). *Chadash* means:

Primarily the notion of cutting, scraping, polishing. No wonder becoming a new creature in the Lord is a moving work of the Holy Spirit.

To renew or make anew—Ps. 51:10. Note must be made of the fact that the renewing takes place in the realm of the spirit.

To repair, rebuild—Isa. 61:4. A life wrecked by sin must be rebuilt by the Lord from within and may call for cutting, etc.

Unheard of—Eccl. 1:9. A Christian finds a new King, a new song, a new Name, but these have always existed, only the discovery of them is new to those who have had a new heart and a new spirit created within them. To others these things are unheard of.

ליל

NIGHT: "Watchman, what of the night?", (Isa. 21:11). *Layil,* the Hebrew root for *night,* has terrible denotements.

It denotes darkness at noonday—Isa. 16:3. The proud are condemned and judgment is pronounced. The people shall not have vision; shall not have seer capacity; the sun shall go down on their prophets—Mic. 3:6.

It denotes misery sent by the Lord—Lam. 2:19. As a result their tears will run down and they will not be able to see.

It denotes a burden—Isa. 21:11. A calamitous adversity will bear down on them.

Some ancient Rabbins held that this root was used to build the name for a night-spectre (a ghost) which had the form of a female monster, appealingly clad, who laid in wait for children by night and who dwelled in desert places to attract men and tear them in pieces—Isa. 13:22.

מנה

NUMBER: "This is the interpretation of the thing: MENE: God hath numbered thy kingdom, and finished it", (Dan. 5:26). *Manah,* the Hebrew root for *number,* means much more than counting heads. It has several exhortative significations.

It means to make ready as an army—I Kings 20:25. This army was to be divided into parts and the parts arranged so as to be most effective. God's army is numerous, scattered in parts (churches) and effective.

It means to allot—Isa. 65:12. God determines the people's lot—Jer. 13:25.

It means to constitute—Jonah 4:6. God prepared a gourd, a worm, an east wind and a preacher. Jonah was taught to know mercy.

It means to review—Dan. 5:25. The counted were brought to a reckoning.

It means to ordain—Dan. 2:24. When God numbers his children He gives them work assignments; sending one here and others yonder in His great vineyard.

שמע

OBEDIENT: "That all the congregation . . . may be obedient", (Num. 27:20) *shama.*

See *Hear* for a fuller treatment of this word which means to listen, to understand distinctly.

נשג

OBTAIN: "Therefore the redeemed of the Lord shall return . . . they shall obtain gladness and joy", (Isa. 51:11). *Nasag,* the Hebrew root for *obtain,* has varied meanings.

It means to overtake—Deut. 28:2, 15. That is, blessings or curses will overtake God's child depending on whether he is obedient.

It means to take hold of—Ps. 40:12. That is, evil, like a habit may take hold of one. Or, the wrath of God may seize upon one—Ps. 69:24.

It means to reach forth towards—I Sam. 14:26. In this passage the Hebrew root is employed to report the reaching out to gather honey that was on the ground. This is a primary meaning of the verb.

A very varied meaning is to recede or cause to recede—Job 24:2. Blessings which may recede from one may be obtained by another and God may cause this.

אשם

OFFEND. "Whereas we have offended against the Lord", (II Chron. 28:13) *ashem.*

This Hebrew word is treated under *Guilty* which signifies that the Lord considers at once guilty those that offend.

עלה

OFFER: "*alah.* "I will go into thy house . . . I will offer unto thee . . .", (Ps. 66:13, 15).

He will cause to go up, he will bring up the offering upon the altar as he would put lamps upon the candlesticks. For further treatment of *alah* see *Ascend.*

But another word translated *offer* is *qarab* and means:

To cause to come near or to cause to approach, a sacrifice, one's self or an offering to the Lord. "Ye shall offer at your own will"—Lev. 22:18, 19; for instance, a freewill offering.

פקה

OPEN: "For God doth know that in the day ye eat thereof, then your eyes shall be opened, and ye shall be as gods, knowing good and evil", (Gen. 3:5). The word *open* in Mal. 3:10 derives from the root *pathach* but here *open* derives from *paqah* which is usually used with eyes to mean understand or possess knowledge. It is a colorful root and has several meanings.

It means to open the eyes upon any one—Job 14:3. The idea is to observe that one closely.

It means to look after or to care for any one—Zech. 12:4. God puts His eyes upon Judah in order to restore her victoriously.

It means to be diligent—Prov. 20:13. One will have his eyes opened; be wakeful; which will be opposite to sleepy or slothful.

It means to give sight to the blind—Isa. 42:7. This is done by opening their eyes. Those blinded by sin may see spiritually if they have the gospel preached unto them.

It means to be enabled to see what is hid from others—Gen. 21:19. God opened the eyes of Hagar so she could see a well of water.

It means open-eyed as opposed to blind—Exod. 4:11.

This root is used to build the name for Pekahiah, king of Samaria, whose eyes the Lord opened and who served in the time of the great Isaiah. We need churches named Pekah, and members who deserve the name Pekahiah—II Kings 15:22-26, Jehovah has opened his eyes.

It means deliverance—Isa. 61:1. That is, the Spirit of the Lord hath anointed His called to open the prison of sin where men are bound.

פתח

OPEN: " . . . If I will not open the windows of heaven and pour . . .", (Mal. 3:10). For the meaning of *pathach* see *Door.*

לחץ

OPPRESS: " . . . Behold, the cry of the children of Israel is come unto me: and I have also seen the oppression wherewith the Egyptians oppress them", (Exod. 3:9). The Lord heard His children, He saw their oppression and promptly relieved them. *Lachats,* the Hebrew root for *oppress,* is colorfully and dramatically used.

Balaam's ass saw the angel of the Lord, then thrust herself against the wall, crushing Balaam's foot against the wall and put Balaam in a considerable bind. There are many ways in which the Lord's people may be afflicted or put in a bind and thereby be made to bow down the head—Num. 22:25. *Lachats* is twice used in verse 25.

It has an exciting use in II Kings 6:32 where the wicked king sent a murderer to slay the prophet of the Lord. Elisha sat in his house, gave orders to the elders to hold fast the murderer at the door thereby putting him in a bind causing him to fail on his nefarious mission. God takes care of His Elishan family.

This root is translated affliction in I Kings 22:26. A prisoner was to be fed the bread and water of affliction. God's prophet may be afflicted like Job but there will be prosperity and happiness by and by as there was for the poet.

It means to be in straits, Job 36:15, but the Lord will deliver. How many scriptures tell of God delivering saints and sinners from tight places and from hell, from death and from the grave.

עָשַׁק

OPPRESS: "O Lord, I am oppressed; undertake for me", (Isa. 38:14). Aged king Hezekiah had been so sick that now, although well, he was depressed and felt this would be the end of him. *Ashaq,* the Hebrew root for *oppress,* has intensive significations.

It means to be so burdened as to lose blood—Prov. 28:17.

It means to wrest—Mic. 2:2. A man is robbed of his field and his house; and he and his family are oppressed.

It means to be proud and insolent—Job 40:23. The oppressor is like a river out of its banks.

It means to violate, as a virgin—Isa. 23:12. A city was ravaged by its captors.

It means injury—Ezek. 22:12. Violence and injury attended the act of extortion.

With all of these meanings in the root used to describe the condition of the king's soul, it is easy to believe he was distressed.

נָתַן

ORDAIN: *Nathan.* "Before I formed thee in the belly I knew thee; and before thou camest forth out of the womb I sanctified thee, and I ordained thee a prophet unto the nations", (Jer. 1:5).

This is ground for believing in God's call to the ministry. Here we have God giving Jeremiah to the work of a prophet to the nations and that before he was born. For more on the word *nathan* see *Give.*

Another word, *amad,* is translated *ordain* in II Chron. 11:15. "He ordained him priest for the high places." It means to cause to arise, to stand up, to stand firm, to persist, to endure. A man really called of God and ordained of God for His service will bear up under cold—Ps. 147:17; will bear up even under judgment—Ps. 130:3; will try standing up even in the presence of an angry God—Ps. 76:7. This ordained one will be destined of God—II Chron. 33:8.

נדח

OUTCAST: "I will heal thee of thy wounds, saith the Lord; because they called thee an Outcast . . .", (Jer. 30:17). *Nadach,* the Hebrew root for *outcast* has several significations.

It means to thrust forth as an axe—Deut. 19:5.

It means to expel—I Sam. 14:14. God devises means by which the banished shall not be expelled from Him. This illustrates the whole redemptive program.

It means to be chased—Isa. 13:14. The wicked Babylonians shall be chased and destroyed.

It means to be seduced—Prov. 7:21; enticed, driven—Deut. 4:19. Being lured into immorality is at the same time being thrust out of the path of righteousness. Being enticed to worship sun, moon and stars is to be expelled from God's sanctuary.

It means to be dispersed as a flock—Ezek. 34:4, 16. Man as a shepherd has not brought again that which was driven away but God will seek that which was lost and bring again that which was driven away.

יכל

OVERCOME: "Let us go up at once and possess it; for we are well able to overcome it", (Num. 13:30). The Hebrew word for *overcome* is *yakol* which has several denotements.

It denotes faith in God's ability to overcome—Job 42:2. Because Caleb had faith in God, God was able to make his life one of victories.

It denotes having prevailing power—Hos. 12:3-5, because one has God through trusting.

This Hebrew word denotes also the capacity for holding on until the contest is won—Gen. 32:26. This capacity was given to Jacob by the Lord who preserved his life and changed it completely.

It denotes assignment in a situation which becomes a stage where God makes His powerful appearance—Ps. 139:5-7.

כפר

PARDON: *kaphar.* "But Hezekiah prayed for them, saying,

The good Lord pardon every one'', (II Chron. 30:18).

This Hebrew word means to pacify, to cover as if with the blood of Jesus. For more on *Kaphar* see *Atonement.*

Another Hebrew word translated *pardon* is *salach* which means to forgive, to pass over.

"But thou art a God ready to *pardon* (full of pardons), gracious and merciful, slow to anger, and of great kindness, and forsookest them not"—Neh. 9:17; "To our God for He will abundantly *pardon*"—Isa. 55:7. In this word the primary idea seems to be that of lightness and of being lifted up. The sinner who is burdened with the load of sin would rejoice in discovering this about his loving God.

רעה

PASTOR: *raah.* "And I will give you pastors according to mine heart, which shall feed you with knowledge and understanding", (Jer. 3:15). The word *pastor* is found in the New Testament only once—Eph. 4:11 and eight times in the Old Testament where its primary meaning is that of feeding. For more see *Feed.*

שלם

PAY: *shalam.* "Vow and *pay* unto the Lord your God: let all . . . bring presents unto Him . . .", (Ps. 76:11)..

This Hebrew word *shalam* means to make complete and to have peace. Happy and content are the tithers and the "heavy givers" unto the Lord. For a treatment of *shalam* see *Peace.*

שלם

PEACE: "Thou shalt keep him in perfect peace, whose mind is stayed on thee . . .", (Isa. 26:3). *Shalam* means:

To be whole, to be sound, to be safe—Job 22:21. One who is set against God or one who does not know God does not remain in safety.

To be completed, to be finished, to be ended—I Kings 7:51. This passage uses the word *shalam* to mean that a building was completed. When an important assignment from the Lord is ended one has tranquility.

To be as peace, to be in friendship with—Ps. 41:9. It is good

187

for peace for one to have a familiar and intimate friend. This multiplies beyond count when that One is the One that sticketh closer than a brother.

To be made secure—Job 8:6. Job's habitation was prosperous. He had a sense of security which God gave him when he lost all and faced the stormy accusations of his friendless friends.

To repay—Ps. 37:21. One derives peace from knowing his debts are paid—especially those to God.

To impart—Isa. 57:18. Here to impart comfort to mourners brings the imparter peace.

Prosperity—Dan. 4:1. This signification of peace is closely associated with peace.

עַם

PEOPLE: "Then rose up certain of the elders of the land and spake to all the assembly of the people", (Jer. 26:17).

People, people, people everywhere. In this text "certain" (called of God) elders preached to the people. This word *am* means a common people, a holy people and is used most often to indicate them who are God's own possession. In Judg. 5:18, we have tribe; in Lev. 21:1, 4, we have a family of relatives and as a church of brothers and sisters we have very much the same or better. In Ps. 18:28, we have an afflicted and wretched people, perhaps out of the Lord whereas a righteous people is catalogued in Gen. 20:4. In Judg. 5:2, we have soldiers and also some were attendants and formed a princely retinue such as people ought be for the "Prince of God." So troops, flocks, Prov. 30:25, Ps. 74:14 move across history. People, people. This word is found in the Bible about 1900 times and people are in great numbers in many places so that we might say with Solomon, "There is no end of all the people," and feel with the One greater than Solomon as reflected in Matt. 9:36.

תָּמַם

PERFECT: "There was a man in the land of Uz, whose name was Job; and that man was perfect . . .", (Job 1:1). *Tamam,* the root for *perfect,* has several meanings.

It means consumed—Josh. 8:24. Job was exhausted and well nigh spent when he lost possessions, friends, family and health.

Yet, for all of that he trusted God unwaveringly.

It means to be upright—Ps. 19:13. The psalmist declared God's law perfect and he himself wanted to be kept back from sins and be upright.

It means to finish—I Kings 7:22. In order to be a perfect job the lily work was to be done on top of the pillars. Man, who may be a pillar in the church, must get everything in order in his life and see that the job of building a good man is perfectly done.

It means to complete—Ezek. 24:10. The Lord said, "Heap on wood, kindle the fire, consume the flesh, and spice it well, and let the bones be burned." All of these and other details were to take place in the parable of the pot. Even so there are many details in man's life that must have attention if he would be perfect as God commanded—Deut. 18:13.

It means to pay out (in full)—II Kings 22:4. Man, in order to be perfect, must be fully ransomed (paid out in full).

It means a way of life—Job 22:3. For the perfect man, righteousness will be habitual and every day. For him it will never be right to do wrong.

It means to be without blemish—Exod. 12:5. There shall not be a fault in the perfect man, discoverable to the people. He shall be sound.

It means blameless with God—Ps. 18:21. This is the top rung of the perfect man's ladder.

תֹם

PERFECT: "And the Lord said . . . Job . . . a *perfect* and an upright man, one that feareth God and escheweth evil", (Job 2:3). For the meaning of *tam* see *Integrity.*

"Nevertheless Asa's heart was *perfect* with the Lord all his days"—I Kings 15:14. Here the Hebrew word is *shalam* and for its meaning see *Peace..* Is it not easy to see that he whose heart is right with the Lord has peace with the Lord?

אָבַד

PERISH: "I call heaven and earth to witness against you this day that ye shall soon utterly *perish"*, (Deut. 4:26).

189

No wonder this people were to be destroyed. They corrupted themselves and made a graven image and did evil in the sight of the Lord. For more on *abad* see *Destroy*. This word means to be lost and is translated *perish* in the Old Testament about 100 times.

לוּז

PERVERSENESS: " . . . Thus saith the Holy One . . . Because ye despise this word, and trust in oppression and perverseness . . .", (Isa. 30:12).

Perverseness is consummate wickedness. *Luz,* the Hebrew root for it, unfolds this meaning.

It means to bend or to incline aside. When one does not walk uprightly he disappoints heaven.

It means to depart—Prov. 3:21. The Lord does not want His child to turn away from wisdom which is life to the soul and grace to the neck. The prodigal son was perverse.

It means to be froward—Prov. 3:32. One who becomes froward is one who bends his neck and goes away from the high and holy. The secret of the Lord is with the righteous but frowardness is an abomination to Him.

כּוּר

PIERCE: "For dogs have compassed me: the assembly of the wicked have enclosed me: they pierced my hands and my feet", (Ps. 22:16). That this psalm is applied to the Messiah is supposed by most interpreters, especially those acquainted with the New Testament. That the dogs and the assembled wicked apply to those hunting and destroying the Christ is agreed upon by a large segment of if not all of Christendom. *Kur,* the Hebrew root for *pierce,* has several colorful meanings.

It means to dig or to bore through. The crude nails of Jesus' day would likely have to be drilled through.

It means to bind. This piercing bound Him to the cross as well as killed Him.

It means to disfigure. Those assembled wicked made history when they defaced the most benign face of history.

בּוֹר

PIT: "He brought me up also out of an horrible *pit,* out of the miry clay, and set my feet upon a rock and established my goings. And hath put a new song in my mouth . . .", (Ps. 40:2, 3).

Bor means a cistern—Gen. 37:20. When without water these were used for prisons and probably had mud in them. David used vivid and powerful language to describe his condition as a sinner and of being cleansed from sin.

Bor also means a sepulchre or a grave—Ps. 30:3. One dead in his trespasses might as well be placed in a grave to continue the figure.

חמל

PITY: *chamal.* "In His love and in His *pity* He redeemed them", (Isa. 63:9).

Pity runs along by the side of love which shows how important it is in God's treasure chest of virtues. It tells that God is mild, gentle and clement. It reveals His sympathy and compassion—I Sam. 23:21. It advises us the Lord will not destroy us but spare us—I Sam. 15:15.

With Jeremiah we may ask, "Who shall have pity upon thee, O Jerusalem?"—Jer. 15:5.

Or, as for that, upon our city? The answer comes from Isaiah, saying that God in His love and in His pity will redeem.

נטע

PLANT: "For the Lord of hosts, that planteth thee . . .", (Jer. 11:17). "Yet I had planted thee a noble vine", (Jer. 2:21).

Nata means to plant, as a tree or garden. Gardens yield beauty and fruit. O that men would give themselves to the Great Husbandman to be used in spiritually landscaping the world. Trees are beneficial to man, beast and birds. O that men would give themselves to the Heavenly Arboriculturist to be planted by the roadsides around the world.

This word means also to fix or fasten as a nail. God uses Abrahams, Davids and Isaiahs, Johns and Pauls, Lydias and Marys, Luthers and Calvins, Spurgeons and Truetts to nail this old world together to keep it from coming apart morally and spiritually.

Nata means also to pitch as a tent. Preachers, missionaries, and Bible teachers shed holy influences which are like sheltering canopies in their communities. The story of Sodom would have ended differently had holy men been planted there—Gen. 18. Sinning America may obtain pardon if we run to and fro in her streets, find saints and sow them where streams of humanity are flowing—Jer. 5:1.

ריב

PLEAD: "Wherefore I will yet plead with you, saith the Lord, and with your children's children will I plead", (Jer. 2:9). *Rib* means:

To seize by the hair and pull and pluck. Judah had changed God for gods that were not gods. They had changed their "glory for that which doth not profit" and their apostasy precipitated a remonstrance. Their wickedness had caused serious misfortune and now God was contending with them, even striving and quarrelling with them to save them. So, we may be saved by the hairs of our heads and by the skin of our teeth.

To contend in words before a judge for a certain and important cause—Ps. 43:1. Man's helplessness will be helped if that man retains the Judge of all to plead for him. This is where Jesus comes in. Man desperately needs Him to be the "Advocate with the Father."

שפר

PLEASANT: "The lines are fallen unto me in pleasant places . . .", (Ps. 16:6). *Shaphar,* the Hebrew root for *pleasant,* has interesting and beautiful meanings.

It means to polish, possibly by scraping. While this might be rough treatment, it may result in making something bright and shiny. Sorrows can make the soul shine. "It is better to go to the house of mourning than to the house of feasting".

It means acceptable—Dan. 6:2. Because of an excellent spirit in Daniel he was preferred above the presidents and princes— more acceptable than the others.

It means brightness and beauty, in words for example—Gen. 49:21. How much pleasure has come by goodly words.

192

It means to garnish—Job 26:13. God's Spirit makes the heavens bright. (This is likely done by setting stars and constellations there.)

It means a throne ornament—Jer. 43:10. Pleasantness, beauty and brightness garnish thrones and also hovels. Pleasantness is a tapestry that serves as a beautiful outer garment, fitting apparel for all occasions.

חפץ

PLEASURE: "Yet it pleased the Lord to bruise Him; He hath put Him to grief: . . . and the pleasure of the Lord shall prosper in His hand", (Isa. 53:10). The word *pleasure* is in many places in the Bible but here it seems to reach its peak use. *Chaphats* is the Hebrew word and it has several meanings.

In the verse above, the principal signification is bending. The suffering Servant bent His will to God's will like a cedar bends in the wind. (See Job 40:17, where the same word is used).

In Song of Sol. 2:7 and 3:5, the word is translated *please,* meaning to be favorably disposed or inclined. Men with an Isaian disposition will come forth with Isaiah's dedication, "Here am I; send me," under the sound of God's invitation, "Whom shall I send?"

In Gen. 34:19, the word means love. For the honorable, love fills pleasure's cup with distilled delight without any dregs.

In Job 31:16, the idea is to wish or to will. When those two activities play together in the same soul, pleasure, like a parent proudly stands by.

In Isa. 54:12, this word signifies preciousness. A Christian's pure pleasure is more precious than rare gems.

In Isa. 53:10, is the idea of a cause or a weighty matter. What a cause and how weighty a matter, to arrange for the redemption of lost men. God could extend mercy but could not overlook justice's demands, neither man's sin. A price had to be paid which man could not pay but was paid by Jesus.

In Isa. 62:4, this root *chaphats* is used to build the name Hephzibah which symbolizes Zion. This would make a most appropriate name for a church, and why could not someone write a hymn using this word, and such thoughts as found in Isa. 58:3, 13; Ezek. 33:11, where this root is used?

193

רָצוֹן

PLEASURE: "Bless ye the Lord, all ye His hosts; ye ministers of His that do His pleasure", (Ps. 103:21). *Ratson* is another Hebrew word translated *pleasure* and has several honey-filled significations.

One is to delight in a person to the extent of bringing him a gift, feeling certain of a gracious reception—Gen. 33:10.

Another is to enjoy the company of a friend with whom one is on good terms—Job 34:9. What exquisite pleasure comes to those who delight in the Lord, bring Him a gift and discover themselves on good terms with Him.

Still another meaning is to satisfy, to pay off or to make compensation for—Lev. 26:41. In order to enjoy wholesome fellowship all debts must be paid and all accounts settled between those that make up that fellowship. The sin account must be settled before man can have delightful fellowship with God and that takes so much of a price that only God can pay it.

נֹעַם

PLEASURE: Another Hebrew word translated pleasure is *nam*. It also has several significations.

In Song of Solomon 7:6, it pictures the love of Jesus for the Church. The Holy Spirit used the wisdom of Solomon to tell us of the excellence of affections of the Bridegroom for the bride.

Beauty and splendor shine forth as a gorgeous color of this word in Ps. 27:4.

Grace and favor are riches in this word found in Ps. 90:17. God is ever-supplying sanctified pleasure to those who hunger and thirst for that kind but do those bring any pleasure to God?

It also means agreeable; sweet as a song—Ps. 147:1; a harp—Ps. 81:2; benign and generous; delight and loveliness. No wonder the word was employed to describe the love of David for Jonathan—II Sam. 1:26.

עָרַב

PLEDGE: "Now therefore give pledges I pray thee to my master the king . . .", (Isa. 36:8). In the word *arab* are significations which plainly show how much goes on because people do

194

make pledges and also show how much poorer we would be if no pledges were made.

First, there is the idea of exchanging, bartering and traffic. This is like bringing our tithes to the Lord and He opens the windows of heaven to pour out blessings.

Then there is the idea of becoming a surety or an exchange with someone in order to take his place—Gen. 43:9; 44:32. Jesus did just that for us.

There is also in this word the idea of mixing and mingling as in marriage—Ezra 9:2. If one is a member of the Church of the redeemed he will be as willing to make a pledge to the Redeemer, or for the Redeemer, as a bride will make a vow to the bridegroom.

יתר

PLENTEOUS: "And the Lord will make thee plenteous in every work of thine hand, in the fruit of thy body . . . for the Lord will again rejoice over thee for good", (Deut. 30:9). *Yathar,* the Hebrew root for *plenteous* is colorfully used.

First of all it is used to signify abundance—Deut. 28:11.

It means to be redundant. That is, blessings pour out beyond what is natural—they hang over profusely and may even seem superfluous.

It is used to signify what is left over—Exod. 12:10.

It means profit or gain or emolument—Eccl. 10:10.

A colorful facet of the word is excellence—Eccl. 2:13.

This root is used to build the name of Jethro—Exod. 4:18. Moses' father-in-law had a great abundance and was very generous.

ארה

PLUCK: " . . . So that all they which pass by the way do pluck . . .", (Ps. 80:12). Here the word *Pluck,* implies the gathering of fruit. The Hebrew root for it is *Arah* which has several meanings.

It means to pull off or to gather as leaves—Song of Sol. 5:1. The bride is in the garden, separated from her spouse, telling the daughters of Jerusalem how her beloved is to her, as honey, as wine, and as milk.

It means to feed by cropping or by gathering. This describes the child of God searching the Word of God.

It means a crib or a manger. The church or the trysting place may become this to the Bible student.

It means a collection of things as jewels of Gold—I Sam. 6:8; as a money-chest—II Kings 12:10; as a "mummy-chest"—Gen. 50:26; testimony box—Exod. 25:22.

פלם

PONDER: "For the ways of man are before the eyes of the Lord, and he pondereth all his goings", (Prov. 5:21). *Palas,* the Hebrew root for *ponder,* has interesting meanings with deep doctrinal implications.

It means to make level—Isa. 26:7. The Lord makes the path of the just even and smooth as a plain so that the pilgrim is never in the bush or in the ditch.

It means to weigh as in a pair of balances made level—Prov. 4:26; 5:6; 5:21. This root is used with scales, out of which grows the signification of consideration. In the corridors of eternity, God did weighing; decided in favor of fallen man; bought him back with a great price; loved that man so that He made his path with God smooth in order that the redeemed would walk with Him into the eventime of life, and eternity—John 3:16

The ancients hold that this root is used in a phrase to mean a *steel-yard.* What God thinks is the measuring stick for all of man's thoughts and actions.

חלק

PORTION: "For the Lord's portion is his people; Jacob is the lot of his inheritance", (Deut. 32:9). *Chalaq,* the Hebrew root for *portion,* has deep meanings beautifully colored by the idea of election. God divided out His people unto Himself. He appropriated this precious spoil from the conflict with the enemy and no man can pluck it out of His possession. For more on this Hebrew root see *Smooth.*

שָׁפַךְ

POUR: "I am poured out like water, and all my bones are out of joint: my heart is like wax; it is melted in the midst of my bowels", (Ps. 22:14). In this psalm is the only place in the Bible that mention is made of the piercing of the feet of our Lord. In this passage the Lord's weakness is signified by the pouring out as water. Probably it will be of special interest to Christians to study this word *shaphak,* which is the Hebrew root for *pour.*

It means to shed, as blood—Gen. 9:6. No wonder the Lord was weak on the day of His crucifixion: So much blood was lost from His veins and such a world-size burden weighted His soul.

This root is used to signify a pouring out of fury—Ezek. 22:22. God chose to pour out His wrath on the Son instead of on all sinners. No wonder the Son cried, "My God, My God, why hast thou forsaken me?" This was reported in the first verse of the psalm carrying the text for this word study.

It means to profusely expend—Ezek. 16:33. The Lord gave everything He had to save us from sin.

It signifies intercession—Lam. 2:19. In the context we discover captive Jerusalem miserable, due to her sin. As the afflicted city laments unto the Lord, a remedial command is given: Arise, cry out in the night: in the beginning of the watches, pour out thine heart like water before the face of the Lord: lift up thy hands toward him for the life of thy children. No wonder Jesus wept over Jerusalem and poured out His heart for her.

רוּק

POUR: " . . . And prove me now herewith, saith the Lord of hosts, if I will not open you the windows of heaven, and pour you out a blessing . . .", (Mal. 3:10). This word *ruq* seems to be cognate with *raqaq* and *yaraq* and the Greek verb *ereugomai* which the poets used to describe rivers as pouring out their waters. It means:

To pour out—Eccl. 11:3. He who tithes will not likely be running about to survey others' blessings or the lack thereof. He will be continually entering the gates of the sanctuary with praise and thanksgiving and going out therefrom to serve the Lord.

To empty as vessels, as sacks—Gen. 42:35. Of course God has enough vessels and sacks for His children that will tithe.

197

(Note: I found that the two next words in the Hebrew Lexicon were: *rur* which means to ooze out and *rush* which means to be poor and suffer wants. This made the word *ruq* to appear richer).

גבר

POWER: "Thine, O Lord, is the greatness, and the power and the glory, and the victory, and majesty . . . thine is the kingdom", (I Chron. 29:11). *Gabar* is the Hebrew for *power*. It is set like a "diamond of the first water" in this cluster by the chronicler where he reports on God. This sounds like the New Testament. For the colorful significations of the Hebrew word turn back to *Might*.

פלל

PRAY: "If my people, which are called by my name will humble themselves and pray . . .", (II Chron. 7:14). The several meanings of the Hebrew word *palal* will excite one as to feeling and doing.

In order to pray *palal* means, for one thing, to judge one's self and discover need for punishment for crimes committed—Ps. 106:30, (here the context is very dramatic).

Palal also means to serve, as an umpire with the added responsibility of adjusting differences. Talk of revival. This element in prayer would help bring it about.

Another meaning of *Palal* is to intercede. I suspect after the manner exemplified in John 17.

Still another duty built into this big word for pray is to think. "I never though we'd have revival", or "I never thought he'd come to church", might be honest reports of those who did not really pray for such to happen—Gen. 48:11.

בשׂר

PREACH: " . . . The Lord hath anointed me to preach good tidings unto the meek . . .", (Isa. 61:1). Preaching is such an important ministry and *Basar,* the Hebrew word translated *Preach,* is an important word. For its significations turn to *Tidings.*

Another Hebrew word *(Kara),* is translated *Preach* in Jonah 3:2. "Arise, go unto Nineveh . . . and preach unto it the preaching that I bid thee". For the various shades of meaning in *Kara* turn back to *Call*. One cannot help but note that the word for *Preach* is the same as the word for *Call* and that God calls men to preach.

יקר

PRECIOUS: " . . . And the Word of the Lord was precious in those days", (I Sam. 3:1). The Hebrew word for *Precious* is Yaqar which has several rich meanings.

It means to be heavy and on this wise it is applied to God's thoughts which are unencompassable and make up a great sum— Ps. 139:17.

Costly and dear are facets of this word that are used to describe the redemption of the soul—Ps. 49:8.

To be honored and respected grow out of this root which is used to evaluate David's name to his people—I Sam. 18:30.

How wise were the scholars that employed *Precious* to translate *Yaqar* since it further signifies *brightness*—Job 31:26; an excellent spirit of one who holds his peace and shutteth his lips—Prov. 17:27; magnificent splendor—Esther 1:4.

כון

PREPARE: "Prepare to meet thy God", (Amos 4:12). This Hebrew word *kun* is tremendously significant.

It means to ready oneself for a meeting with a person. Amos is preaching that we shall personally meet God.

This preparation shall be made in Heart—Ezra 7:10. It will not be sufficient to wash just the outside of the cup. Regardless of how much good has been done, that alone will not avail at all. Only the pure in heart will be ready to see God.

The reason for meeting God will be to face judgment—Ps. 9:7; to enjoy a place the Lord has prepared—Exod. 23:20.

The preparation shall be made only when one depends completely on divine grace. For much more on this one Hebrew word turn back to *Confirm*.

It is interesting to note that another Hebrew word translated *prepare* is *qadesh* which means to set apart or consecrate. One step in preparing to meet God, then, is to live the separated life.

עפל

PRESUME: "But they presumed to go up unto the hill top . . .", (Num. 14:44). *Aphal,* the Hebrew root for *presume,* has strong significations.

It means to be tumid—Hab. 2:4. There are those who are bombastic and distended with emptiness. They are swollen with momentary inflation. This is a strong root.

It means tumor—Deut. 28:27. Pride, according to this idea, makes a man a tumor in society, or on society: A large growth that has no function and may be offensive to eyes and to ears.

It means a tumulus or hill—Neh. 3:27. This is the kind of mound or small hill that may be found on a grave. The presumptuous resemble a sepulchre.

יכל

PREVAIL: " . . . Thy name shall be called no more Jacob, but Israel: for as a prince hast thou power with God and with men, and hast prevailed", (Gen. 32:28). Here is another interesting find. The same root word is translated *Prevail* here and *Overcome* in some other passages. The principal signification is being strong and thus able to overcome.

גבר

PREVAIL: "Moses held up his hand that Israel prevailed", (Exod. 17:11). This Hebrew word *Gabar* is translated *Prevail* here and *Might* in some other passages. How interesting to know that prevailing and might should be so closely related. For the several significations of *Gabar* turn back to *Might.*

קדם

PREVENT: "The God of my mercy shall prevent me . . .", (Ps. 59:10). This Hebrew word *Qadam* means—*What is before.* Also there is the idea of setting out to meet one that may be able to give aid. When we come into the world, there is God. For more on this Hebrew word turn back to *Eternal.*

כֹּהֵן

PRIEST: "But ye shall be named priests of the Lord: men shall call you ministers of our God . . .", (Isa. 61:6). This Hebrew word *Kahan* has quite varied shades of meaning.

One of them is to divine or celebrate God's praise. This becomes all who are God's children for they have been made priests—Rev. 1:6.

Another is to transact business for another. This is big work and requires wit and wisdom which only God can give and probably only for each occasion that arises and then only after prayer.

Still another meaning is to serve as mediator between God and man. Every Christian, even little children, feels he ought to do something to bring another or others into the right relationship to God. It has been observed that especially immediately after conversion, the redeemed share the feeling that moved Andrew—John 1:41.

And yet another meaning is to minister, as outlined so classically in Isa. 61. It is generally assumed this passage foretells of the ministry of Jesus—the Perfect High Priest. Those called to the ministry may be spiritual leaders under Him. Just like the sons of David were chief about the king, even so should all sons of God want to be at the hand of the King of kings—I Chron. 18:17.

שַׂר

PRINCE: "The everlasting Father, the Prince of peace", (Isa. 9:6). *Sarar* is the root from which the word *Prince* comes and it means:

To have dominion, to rule—Isa. 32:1. In the house or world of peace, Jesus will rule and those in His army, although at war with Satan and his angels, will have peace in their hearts. They will go out and the devils will be subject unto them but the reason for rejoicing will be because their names are written in the book of life.

Leader, commander, chief—Gen. 21:22. Here the chief announced to Abraham that God would be with him. Those who have God with them have peace even in a storm. Jesus is our Chief and has all authority and all power and this is our hope for peace.

Overseer, head shepherd—Gen. 47:6. Jesus is the Head Shepherd and He will look after His sheep and no man will be able to pluck them out of His Father's hand.

A helper, a prince of angels—Dan. 10:13. It seems that archangels acted as patrons and advocates of certain nations before God and there was one over them all. This is a wonderful use of the root word in this study. God will send angels to help particular nations and Jesus will be their Prince. This guarantees peace.

קרא

PROCLAIM: " . . . According to the word of the Lord which the man of God proclaimed", (II Kings 23:16). The Hebrew word here is *qara* having in its sound some of its meaning such as crying, clamoring and so on. For the many significations of this word turn back to *Call.*

יעל

PROFIT: "What is the Almighty, that we should serve him? and what profit should we have, if we pray unto him?", (Job 21:15). I shall set out to show that there is great profit which God provides for His own. *Yaal,* the Hebrew root for *profit,* has several significations which indicate several elements in this profit.

It signifies going up or ascending. Prayer might lead to seeing angels descending and ascending a ladder between heaven and earth.

It means to be of use. A man's worth and eminence are in proportion to his usefulness.

It means to help—Job 30:13. A praying man may obtain wisdom and the wherewithal for helping people which makes life more worth living.

God will teach a man to profit—Isa. 48:17. Therefore, it is most fitting that the unlearned in this art should pray to the Great Teacher.

This root is used to build the name Jael, for the woman that was about the most profitable soldier in the army that delivered Israel—Judg. 4, 5.

It signifies a female chamois—Prov. 5:19. This becomes an epithet for a lovely woman—Isa. 48:17.

יעל

PROFIT: "Thus saith the Lord . . . I am the Lord thy God which teacheth thee to profit, which leadest thee by the way that thou shouldest go", (Isa. 48:17). It is a thrill to make a profit but the greatest thrill comes when a profit is made for Him who giveth the power to get wealth. The meanings of *Jaal,* the Hebrew root for *profit,* are interesting.

The root has as its primary idea: to ascend, to be eminent, and to be of use, These are basic to profit but some prophets went not in that way—Jer. 2:8. There is profit in prayer—Job 21:15 and in cleansing from sin—Job 35:3.

It also means help—Isa. 30:5. A people heaped shame on themselves because they were of no help, but instead, helped another to fall—Job 30:13.

This root is used to signify a wild goat, Ps. 104:18, in which there cannot be much profit and perhaps Jesus had this in mind when he portrayed the great separation—Matt. 25:32. This root is used to build a name for a woman that was of use to God's people—Judg. 5:6, 26.

The Lord leads His people in the profitable way—Isa. 48:17, Job 21:15.

דבר

PROMISE: " . . . So will I bring upon them all the good that I have promised them", (Jer. 32:42). As certain as God will punish when He says He will so will He keep His promises to bring good. *Dabar* is the Hebrew word in this passage and for its meaning turn back to *Commandment.*

נבא

PROPHESY: " . . . And when they saw the company of the prophets prophesying . . . the Spirit of God was upon the messengers of Saul, they also prophesied", (I Sam. 19:20). The Hebrew word in this verse is *naba* which has several shades of sense.

It means to boil up or to boil forth. God's man under divine inspiration will pour forth God's words like a fountain to satisfy the spiritual thirst of God's people.

203

This word is specifically used of prophets who reveal to men the message of God whether it is to reprove the wicked or to predict future events—Joel 3:1.

It denotes raving and sounding mad—Jer. 29:26. This will give prophets license to sound off in madness against blatant evils the same as some council would encourage the same prophets to go forth proclaiming blessed good news.

Strange enough but this word also means to writhe or to make "spasmodic affections of the body", and thereby turn men to God. How many preachers "preached all over." To cool and calculating sinners some of these "hot-hearted" prophets seemed delirious and called them "mad fellows"—II Kings 9:11.

Naba also means to praise God in songs or chants that in themselves contain prophecies—I Chron. 25:2. Like the successful sermon-less Welsh Revival that came in on wings of song so have many been indoctrinated through song only.

The words *prophet* and *prophesy* are used about 600 times in the Old Testament.

צלח

PROSPER: " . . . and whatsoever he doeth shall prosper", (Ps. 1:3). This Hebrew word *tsalach* has rich significations.

It means to succeed as did God in His program of redemption—Isa. 53:10.

It means to wade through or go over as a river—II Sam. 19:18. When a man crosses his Jordans and goes over the top in his campaigns he senses a satisfaction that sweeps over his soul.

It also signifies falling suddenly upon. This nearly always is associated with the falling of the Spirit of God on men—I Sam. 10:10; 16:13: spiritual prosperity!

To finish happily is also hidden away in this good word. This is as a facet of a diamond and is dramatically employed in II Chron. 7:11. Finishing a good task gives one a feeling of prosperity.

Unbelievable as it may seem but *tsalach* is translated *promote*—Dan. 3:30 and why not since it is prosperity indeed?

204

סתר

PROTECTION: For the Lord . . . shall say, "Where are their gods . . . let them rise up and help you, and be your protection", (Deut. 32:38). *Sathar,* the Hebrew root from which *protection* derives, has several meanings.

It means to hide—Prov. 22:3. A wise man will foresee the evil of the wrong way and will hide himself in God for protection.

It means to cover as the face—Isa. 53:3. The idea here is to avert the eyes from something as if it were disgusting or abominable. Jehovah may cover His face and not regard human affairs— Ps. 10:11. Or, God may hide His face from our sins and forgive them—Ps. 51:9. Too, He may hide from us—Ps. 22:24.

It means to destroy—Ezra 5:12. Things may be hidden out of sight and thus destroyed.

It means a veil—Job 22:14. The canopy of Christ's blood protects us from the wrath of God.

It means to defend—Ps. 27:5. In time of trouble, God will care for His own by hiding them in His pavilion.

This root is used to build a proper name, Zithri—Exod. 6:22, which means, *protection of Jehovah.*

כעם

PROVOKE: "The sins . . . which he sinned . . . provoked the Lord God . . . to anger", (I Kings 15:30). *Kaas* means:

To be displeased—Neh. 4:1. Displeasure caused unfavorable action.

To be angry—Ezek. 16:42. Jerusalem sinned but the merciful God was pleased to be no more angry at her.

To irritate—Deut. 32:29. God was moved to cause his erring and sinning people to become angry with a foolish nation. (Note: Just now the Lebanese crisis or mid-east trouble has begun: Jul. 17, 1958).

To vex—Ezek. 32:9. A vexed God may bring destruction to those that vex Him.

Grief—Prov. 17:25. A foolish child of God may grieve God.

205

Sorrow—Eccl. 11:10. Has not our Lord born enough sorrow for us? Shall we crucify Him again?

קרא

PUBLISH: "Because I will publish the name of the Lord . . .", (Deut. 32:3). *Qara* is a meaningful Hebrew word and for its denotements turn back to *Call.*

שמע

PUBLISH: " . . . O Lord: That I may publish with the voice of thanksgiving, and tell all thy wondrous works", (Ps. 26:6, 7). This Hebrew word *shama* has as its primary meaning to cause to hear and understand what is published. For a fuller treatment of it turn back to *Hear.*

בשׂר

PUBLISH: "The Lord gave the word: great was the company of those that published it", (Ps. 68:11). This sounds like a theme for a pastors' convention or a missionaries' rendezvous. *Basar* is a great Hebrew word and for its significations turn to *Tidings.*

חטא

PUNISH: "Wherefore doth a living man complain, a man for the punishment of his sins?", (Lam. 3:39). This Hebrew word *chatta* sounds rough and is married to harshness.

It means to miss the mark and that at once is punishment. Like an archer who misses (Judg. 20:16) becomes the loser so does the sinner who misses God's will for his life. He loses peace, satisfaction, heaven's commendation and heaven itself.

Another signification is to make a false step, to stumble or to fall, or, all three of these in succession. Man brings calamity upon himself because he does not bring honor upon God. *Chatta* is used also to denote *sin* so a sinner gets sins for his sins or he gets punishment for his punishment. For more denotements on *chatta* turn back to *Miss.*

עון

PUNISHMENT: "And they shall bear the punishment of their iniquity", (Ezek. 14:10). The Hebrew word *avon* for punishment in this text is the same as the Hebrew word for *iniquity*. In other words, iniquity is a boomerang and when it returns to the heart whence it issued it does so with a greater force than when it emerged or spouted. Iniquity is a serpent that crawled out of man's heart only to return with more venom in its poison bags to syringe into the wounds it left. A sinner forges the tools for his punishment in the black shop of his heart where iniquity burns red like a fire. Then he cries, "My punishment is greater than I can stand"—Gen. 4:13.

For other meanings of the Hebrew word *avon* turn back to *Iniquity*.

חטא

PURGE: "Purge me with hyssop and I shall be clean", (Ps. 51:7). The Hebrew word *chatta* means missing the mark. To come around to meaning *purge* the Piel in the Hebrew is employed which denotes that the person who missed the mark is terrorized and holds himself culpable. In thus bearing the blame he craves to make an atonement for his erring; hence to be purged of his sins. In the Old Testament man made the offering for sins which was the blood of animals but in the New Testament God made the offering which was the sacrifice of *His* only Begotten. For more meanings of *chatta* turn back to *Miss*.

כפר

PURGE: "Help us, O God of our salvation, for the glory of thy Name: and deliver us, and purge away our sins, for thy name's sake", (Ps. 79:9). The Hebrew word *kaphar* means to cover, e.g., cover over our sins. This covering our sins is accomplished by the Lord in using His own blood for the cover. For the several denotements of this Hebrew word turn back to *Atonement*.

זקק

PURGE: "And he (the Lord's messenger) shall purify the sons of Levi, and purge them as gold and silver, that they may offer unto the Lord an offering in righteousness", (Mal. 3:3). *Zaqaq*, the Hebrew root for *purge,* has several meanings which indicates much will be done before these men will be used in this very high office of the Lord's work.

It means to pour—Job 36:27. Before one can make an offering

in righteousness he himself will need to be poured out on the altar first.

It means to purify—Ps. 12:6. One serving in so sacred an office ought to be first purified seven times as was the gold and silver which was to represent the Word of God.

It means to refine—Isa. 25:6. Like the wine on the lees well refined, this servant will be strained and cleaned. Then the offering that shall be made will be pleasant unto the Lord.

שׂוּם

PURPOSE: "But Daniel purposed in his heart that he would not defile himself . . .", (Dan. 1:8). This Hebrew word *sum* signifies that Daniel *stood erect* and *planted himself* so as to firmly decline the offer. He *drew himself* up into position and *set himself* against that which was not good for him. He *appointed himself* to company with the temperate ones. He *established himself* on a solid foundation, *made a pledge* and *directed himself* away from defilement.

כבה

QUENCH: "Many waters cannot quench love . . .", (Song. of Sol. 8:7). The love that cannot be quenched mentioned here is the love of the church for Christ. *Kabah* is used in Isa. 42:3, and is quoted in the New Testament—Matt. 12:20, using the Greek word *sbennumi* which means to *stifle*. *Kabah* means:

To go out like a fire—Lev. 5, 6; like a light—I Sam. 3:3.

Corresponding root in the Arabic means: To cover with ashes, to conceal by covering over.

To put out—II Sam. 21:17. The light of Israel was not to be put out but guarded and kept burning.

חיה

QUICKEN: "So will not we go back from Thee: Quicken us and we will call upon Thy name", (Ps. 80:18). The meaning of the Hebrew word *chayah* is *life*. This then helps to confirm the doctrine that he who is dead in trespasses must first be restored to life by the Lord before he can call upon the Lord to be saved (verse 19). For several significations of *chayah* turn back to *Life*.

שקט

QUIET: "For thus saith the Lord . . . In returning and rest shall ye be saved; in quietness and confidence shall be your strength", (Isa. 30:15). This Hebrew word *shaqat* has several restful shades of meanings.

It means to rest, lie down and have quiet. It is spoken of one who is never infested or troubled—Judg. 5:31. He who holds right notions of God, has scriptural beliefs and harbors Christian attitudes, will have quiet.

It means to not harass or trouble others—Judg. 18:7, 27. He who brings comfort instead of sorrow, gain instead of loss to others, will likely have peace.

Another use of this word is to describe the earth as hushing her noises in the presence of God's judgment—Ps. 76:7, 8. It is translated *fear* in this passage. There are people who freeze quiet when afraid, and there are those who gain great strength mentally, morally and spiritually in life's quiet hours.

דום

QUIETLY: "It is good that a man should both hope and quietly wait for the salvation of the Lord", (Lam. 3:26). *Dum,* the Hebrew root for *quiet,* has several meanings.

It means silent—Hab. 2:19. This is the manner of waiting. It is poor manners to wait nervously.

It means desert—Isa. 21:11. Duma is situated on the edge of the Syrian desert. Many a Pauline trail has been made to deserts: and that to pray; to wait on the Lord.

It means death—Ps. 94:17. Those that are "dead in their trespasses and sins", must wait for a quickening before they speak.

It signifies the idea of silent expectation—Ps. 62:1. The One who knew so well the richness of these Hebrew words and so often quoted them, said to His disciples, "Tarry ye . . . until ye be endued with power from on high"—Luke 24:49.

ירה

RAIN: " . . . Break up your fallow ground: for it is time to seek the Lord, till He come and rain righteousness upon you", (Hos. 10:12). Israel is punished for her sins; is exhorted to repent (6:1);

209

that there may come a watering of righteousness: "the latter and former rain". *Yarah,* the Hebrew root for *rain,* has varied meanings.

It means to lay or to found as a cornerstone—Job 38:6. The Lord asked who laid such a foundation when the morning stars sang together and the sons of God shouted for joy.

It means to sprinkle—Deut. 11:14. These showers shall water the land and a reviving will come forth when God's commandments are kept; when God is loved and worshipped and served.

It means to teach—Isa. 2:3. This teaching will take place when the law of the Lord is laid before those summoned to the house of God. The idea is that truth as it is in God's word will be sprinkled on the people.

It means to cast or shoot as an arrow—I Sam. 20:36. God's word is rained down from heaven and it enters hearts like arrows and there is a reviving.

קוּם

RAISE: "He raiseth up the poor out of the dust . . . to set them among princes, and to make them inherit the throne of glory: for the pillars of the earth are the Lord's, and He hath set the world upon them", (I Sam. 2:8). This Hebrew word *kum* has in it the idea of coming forth to exist and remain so. This sounds like the Lord Jesus after His resurrection from the chambers of darkness. For a full denotation of *kum* turn back to *Arise.*

כפר

RANSOM: "Deliver him from going down into the pit for I have found a ransom", (Job 33:24). For the meaning of *Kopher* see *Atonement.*

פדה

RANSOM: "I will ransom them from the power of the grave; I will redeem them from death: O death, I will be thy plagues; O grave, I will be thy destruction . . .", (Hos. 13:14). *Padah* means:

To buy loose, to redeem (with a price)—Exod. 13:13. This sounds like the New Testament idea of Jesus being the price to redeem man from the power of sin, or from Satan.

To set free, to let go free, e.g. from servitude—Deut. 7:8. Isreal was freed from the yoke of Pharaoh. The Greater Israel has been freed from the more tyrannical Pharaoh by the Greatest of Redeemers.

To deliver, to preserve, e.g. life from danger—Ps. 34:22. The Lord preserves His own from desolation.

Price of redemption, ransom—Num. 3:46. It is of special interest to note here that the Hebrew word is found only in the plural. Perhaps the vastness of the redemption price may be in the mind of the Holy Spirit and of the writer, a holy man.

מרה

REBEL: "But they rebelled and vexed His Holy Spirit . . . therefore He was turned to be their enemy . . .", (Isa. 63:10). This passage from the great prophet shows Christ "glorious in His apparel, traveling in the greatness of His strength" and that in order to save people who instead of yielding rebelled. For the meanings of the Hebrew word *marah* turn back to *Disobey.* No wonder that in some places this same root denotes bitterness.

גער

REBUKE: "And the Lord said unto Satan, The Lord rebuke thee, O Satan; even the Lord that hath chosen Jerusalem, rebuke thee . . .", (Zech. 3:2). *Gaar,* the Hebrew root for *rebuke,* has several powerful meanings.

It means to reprove—Jer. 29:27. This is to restrain an undesirable prophet.

It means to restrain—Isa. 17:13. It was in the case of Job that God put a restraining order on Satan.

It means to foil—Ps. 68:30. The Lord will render vain all efforts to hurt. He can stop wars. He can scatter His enemies as "smoke is driven away" so the righteous shall be glad and rejoice before God—Ps. 68:1-3.

It means to destroy—Ps. 76:6. God can put the horse and the chariot he pulls, both to sleep.

גמל

RECOMPENSE: "Say to them that are of a fearful heart, Be

211

strong, fear not: behold your God will come with vengeance, even God with a recompence; He will come and save you'', (Isa. 35:4). The Hebrew word *gamal* has quite differing denotements.

It denotes primarily the bringing of benefits for another to enjoy—I Sam. 24:17. God is always doing that, even if the situation is sad, for "all things work together for good . . ."

It also denotes the rewarding of the righteous—Ps. 18:20. Righteousness does pay. The evil doers may get intrinsic pay that lasts but for a day whereas the doers of the Word will get extrinsic rewards that will satisfy everlastingly.

Another seemingly strange denotement is the idea of cherishing or showing love for another. This has a vast sum of pay in it. To vary it, this Hebrew verb means warming so as to ripen fruit. This must be what happens when God loves His own and they ripen into stout-hearted saints. To look again, we note this word is used to describe the weaning of a child. There is cherishing here and it is good for God's child to grow up to eating "strong meat."

פדה

REDEEM: "But God will redeem my soul from the power of the grave (hell): for He shall receive me", (Ps. 49:15). This Hebrew word means to get loose by being cut loose after a deliverance price is paid. Its root is used to build a proper name, Pedaiah—II Kings 23:36, which means: Whom Jehovah preserves. For more of the meanings of *padah* turn back to *Ransom*.

גאל

REDEEM: "I have blotted out . . . thy transgressions . . . thy sins: return unto me; for I have redeemed thee", (Isa. 44:22). This Hebrew word *gaal* means to ransom as a slave or a field by paying back a price. For more of its significations turn back to *Kinsman*.

חסה

REFUGE: "God is our refuge and strength, a very present help in trouble", (Ps. 46:1). The Hebrew word for *refuge* is *chasah* and it has interesting and colorful denotements.

One is to flee as to a shelter with the idea of tarrying there for

212

protection—Ps. 57:1. The psalmist felt he would be safe when near to God so he fled until he was under the shadow of his wings. He did like the frightened chick that hurries to hide under the strong wings of the mother hen.

This leads to the second denotement which has in it the idea of trusting—Ps. 37:40. In this verse and in many others in the Psalms *chasah* is translated *trust.* The primary idea is that a place is not a refuge if you cannot trust it.

Another denotement springs from this Hebrew root. It is the idea of hope and so translated in Prov. 14:32. This embosomed hope speeds one on his flight to safety under the wings of God.

בִּין

REGARD: "Because they regard not the works of the Lord . . . He shall destroy them, and not build them up", (Ps. 28:5). The Hebrew word for *regard* is *bin.* It means to perceive, to feel and to attend. For more meanings of it turn back to *Consider.*

ראה

REGARD: "If I regard iniquity in my heart, the Lord will not hear me", (Ps. 66:18). In this passage the Hebrew word for regard is *raah* and means to see with intimacy or to be near, (Jer. 52:25). The Lord will not answer the prayers of those who have a familiarity with sin and those who are evenly planed with sin. For more on this word *raah* turn back to *Appear.*

כתב

REGISTER: "These sought their register among those that were reckoned . . .", (Ezra 2:62). *Kathab,* the Hebrew root for *register,* has several meanings.

It means to write—Num. 33:2. Moses kept a diary for the children of Israel.

It means to write up as to indicate life—Isa. 4:3. Those left in Zion, that are called holy, shall be among the living in Jerusalem.

Prescription is a meaning that derives from this root—Ezra 7:22. Directions were given on how much people should have. God's law is a prescription, and if taken as directed health will be greatly improved.

213

It is used to signify a book—Dan. 10:21. A note was made in the scripture of truth. Scripture is the word for book.

מֶלֶךְ

REIGN: "The Lord shall reign for ever and ever", (Exod. 15:18). The Hebrew word for *reign* is *malak* and for its several significations turn back to *King.*

מָאַס

REJECT: "Because thou hast rejected the word of the Lord, he hath also rejected thee . . .", (I Sam. 15:23). *Maas,* the Hebrew for *reject,* is a strong word.

It is directly opposite to choose—Isa. 7:15,16. Here it means to refuse evil and choose good but in 41:9 this root is translated *cast away* and has reference to God's children. This but endears the doctrine of election.

It means to contemn or to despise—Lam. 3:45. It is true the Lord will not cast us off (See verse 31) but the people may. Perhaps the vile ought to be loathed—Ps. 15:4.

There is the word "rejected" in Isa. 53:3, but the Hebrew for it is *chadal,* for whose significations look under *frail.*

גִּיל

REJOICE: "Be glad in the Lord, and rejoice, ye righteous: and shout for joy, all ye that are upright in heart", (Ps. 32:11). The Hebrew word for *glad* is *gil* which denotes that the heart is so full that its palpitations make the whole body tremble and dance in a circle. For more on *gil* turn back to *Glad.*

עָלַז

REJOICE: "Yet I will rejoice in the Lord, I will joy in the God of my salvation", (Hab. 3:18). Another Hebrew word translated *rejoice* is *alaz* which means to exult because of victory. The victory must be the forgiveness of sin and the saving of the soul and that quickened soul responds vigorously.

זָכַר

REMEMBER: "Remember now thy Creator in the days of thy

youth", (Eccl. 12:1). The Hebrew word for *remember* is *zakar* which means to nurture one's care for another by continually considering that one and reflecting on him. For more on this Hebrew word turn back to *Memory.*

רחק

REMOVE: "As far as the east is from the west so far hath he removed our transgressions from us", (Ps. 103:12). The Hebrew word for *remove* is *rachaq* and for its several meanings turn back to *Far.* This would allow the wording of the above text to be, as far as the east is from the west so far hath he 'farred' our transgressions from us.

קרע

REND: "Oh that Thou wouldest rend the heavens . . .", (Isa. 64:1). *Qara* means:

To tear away, to tear off—I Sam. 15:28. The Lord rent the kingdom of Israel from Saul.

To tear asunder—Gen. 37:29. Here clothes were torn as a sign of grief. Sometimes it could be wished that the heavens were torn apart as a sign of grief for sinners. Perhaps it would be more proper and profitable to pray that the heavens be parted and the earth made to tremble in order that the Name of the Lord be known.

To cut out, to cut in pieces—Jer. 36:23.

To revile, to rail at—Ps. 35:15.

Rags—Prov. 23:21. Drowsiness, drunkenness, gluttony will rend one's goods from him so that he is left in rags.

(A colorful signification of this word is in Jer. 4:30 where overpainting disfigures the face instead of making it fair.)

חלף

RENEW: "But they that wait upon the Lord shall renew their strength", (Isa. 40:31). *Chalaph,* the Hebrew root for *renew,* is like a diamond with several facets.

It means to pass, as a spirit passing by causing thought—Job 4:15-17, or, to pass, as beyond the law, hence sin—Isa. 24:5.

215

It means to change—e.g., garments to be cleaned—Gen. 35:2.
This is a renewing: God, I am waxed old like a garment, clothe
me in fresh vesture—Ps. 102:26.

It means reward—Num. 18:31. For their service in the congregation the leaders received a reward—a revival.

It means to revive—Hab. 1:11. He shall change his mind and
come over to praise God.

It means to go forward—I Sam. 10:3. For this a renewing is
a prerequisite.

נחם

REPENT: "And it repented the Lord that He had made man.",
(Gen. 6:6). With reverence approach should be made to a study
of God repenting. The word *nacham* means:

To pant, to sigh, to groan in pity of others—Jer. 15:6.

To lament, to grieve in regard to one's own deeds—Gen. 6:6.

To comfort, to console. Judah's wife died, he was comforted
and went unto others—Gen. 38:12. Could it be God finds comfort in others when we fail to love Him and serve Him as we
ought?

To avenge oneself—Isa. 1:24.

To change the mind, express grief and render aid—Isa. 12:1.

Nehemiah, comforted, aided of Jehovah—Neh. 1:1.

Note: There is ground in the root meaning of this word for believing when a nation of people becomes evil and is not separated unto God to love Him and serve Him that He will turn to a
nation that is righteous.

חסד

REPROACH: "Righteousness exalteth a nation but sin is a
reproach to any people", (Prov. 14:34). This Hebrew word
chased has puzzling significations.

It signifies disgrace while the primary idea seems to be that of
"eager desire" or zeal. Apparently these earnest and zealous people overdo it into disgrace.

It signifies jealousy that turns kindness into cruelty, which but adds reproach to reproach.

It signifies malignity that festered in an atmosphere of benignity, all because the sin of envy had its way. And what makes it worse, all of this may happen while trying to show love and good will.

It also signifies a rivalry of the wrong brand that burns beauty into ashes and turns grace into disgrace.

It is to be noticed that all of the above are very similar. They are like a bunch of thorny sticks, tied together and hard to be broken except by the power of God. For more on this word turn back to *Goodliness.*

אצל

RESERVE: "Hast thou not reserved a blessing for me?", (Gen. 27:36). *Atsal,* the Hebrew root for *Reserve,* has colorful meanings.

It means to connect or to join, as a tree is joined to the ground by roots. The ancients metaphorized on this by wishing themselves to be joined to noble stock. We could spiritualize by greatly desiring to be joined to Him from Whom comes all that we have and are.

It means near or by the side of—I Kings 3:20. Always the child of God will want to be near to Him to Whom he is vitally connected.

It means to reserve—II Chron. 34:8. Azaliah did not reserve himself but God reserved him. We cannot do God's reserving for Him; but if by Him we are reserved we have but to sing and serve.

נוח

REST: "Blessed be the Lord that hath given rest unto His people . . .", (I Kings 8:56). This word *nuach* is also translated rest and has several significations.

It signifies to settle down after drawing a good breath. It is used to report Noah's ark settling—Gen. 8:4; the Holy Spirit descending upon men—Num. 11:25.

It signifies a settling down for quietness and gentleness that does not offend—Eccl. 10:14. At once there is the thought of criminals, neighbors and oneself all of whom need the Lord's rest.

217

It also signifies a bequeathing to one's heirs—Ps. 17:14. Surely the most comforting rest Christians enjoy is to imagine what it will be to be joint-heirs with Christ.

דמם

REST: "Rest in the Lord and wait patiently for Him", (Ps. 37:7). This Hebrew word *damam* is onomatopoetic in that its sound imitates its meaning. When it is pronounced *dmammmm* the lips are closed so that the mouth is neither taking in nor giving out. The word signifies being silent in the presence of someone and listening. This is the key for getting help from the Lord. It also describes an important part of prayer.

שׁוּב

RESTORE: "He restoreth my soul: He leadeth me in path's of righteousness . . .", (Ps. 23:3). This Hebrew word *shub* means to turn back or return, as a soul which has gone away from God. It also means to bring back to the source of health and refreshment, that life which has become weary and faint in wandering in the wrong direction.

For more on this Hebrew word turn back to *Backsliding*.

גרף

RESTRAIN: "Yea thou castest off fear, and restrainest prayer before God". Blameful man that, which withholds adoration of his God. *Garaph* is the Hebrew root for *restrain* containing several meanings.

It means to shave or to diminish—Jer. 26:2. The idea is to preach the whole word, unshaven, unaltered, unscratched.

It means to attract to oneself—Job 36:27. Here God attracts or draws up drops of rain. He can make it rain upside down, stop all rain, or send rain.

It means to abate—Num. 9:6. There is little telling how many things Satan uses to keep people back from worshipping God. Here the men inquired, What is it that holds us back?

צפר

RETURN: " . . . Whosoever is fearful and afraid, let him return and depart early from mount Gilead . . .'', (Judg. 7:3). *Zaphar*, the Hebrew root for *return*, has very colorful and dramatic meanings.

It means to go in a circle or to revolve. These thousands that were discharged from Gideon's army had been feverishly milling around like frightened gazelles hemmed in by hunters rather than great steeds roaring forward with war chariots.

It means to leap or to spring like a he-goat. They leaped at the first chance to go home, war or no war, honor or no honor.

It is used to build the word for frogs—Exod. 7:27. A frog is most timid and will leap in a circle if you walk in a circle around him.

It means to twitter like birds. That is about all the work birds do and they are probably the most easily frightened and will take to flight, away from any activity. Gideon's 300 were not like that. They leaped not over marshes on the way home, but leaped on the enemy on the way to victory.

שׁוּב

RETURN: "Return thou backsliding Israel, saith the Lord, and I will not cause mine anger to fall upon you . . .'', (Jer. 3:12, 22 and 4:1). This Hebrew word *shub* means *backsliding* and therefore the verse above could be translated freely, thus reporting God as saying, "Backslide back to Me, my backsliding people." The rebels are to rebel against their rebellion. It is used in Ps. 23, to signify restoration and refreshment. For more on it turn back to *Backsliding*.

גָּלָה

REVEAL: "It was revealed in mine ears by the Lord . . .'', (Isa. 22:14). This Hebrew word *galah* has several shades of meaning:

For one thing, it means to make naked, especially the ear by removing hair or a veil in preparation for communication with God as a revealer of secrets—Dan. 2:22, 28. (Obviously to them with unstopped ears). God discovers secret things to mortal eyes which are uncovered and causes wonder—Ps. 119:18.

It means migration—Ezra 5:12. To apply this to the text above it would mean that what God has in His mind has migrated to the mind of man.

219

In Josh. 15:19, this Hebrew word is translated *spring.* God's mind is like a spring flowing with thoughts sweeter than honey.

It also means a bowl or a reservoir which serves to remind us that God has something in store to be revealed.

It means to loose or to break, e.g. news, confidential matters, secrets. John on Patmos was in on a spiritual scoop—Eccl. 12:6.

ירא

REVERENCE: "Ye shall keep my sabbaths, and reverence my sanctuary: I am the Lord", (Lev. 19:30). *Yare,* the root from which *reverence* is derived, has several meanings.

It means to fear—Gen. 3:10. Fear, man's terrific enemy, shows up in Scripture reports before any of the other great emotions. Here, Adam is afraid when God, whom he had disobeyed, walked into this first garden. The root carries the idea of trembling.

It means to hesitate—Gen. 46:3. God assured Jacob all would be well for him in Egypt and that he should not demur to go down.

It means to be godly—Job 1:1. Fearing God involved being upright, perfect and eschewing evil.

It means terrible or holy—Ps. 99:3; Deut. 10:21. God's Name and works are so great that awe and holy fear are excited in the hearts of His people.

It means timidity—Deut. 20:8. This is an element in approaching God in acceptable worship.

It means wonderful—Ps. 139:14. In one breath the psalmist sings about the marvelous works of God and how wonderfully he himself is made.

חיה

REVIVE: "Wilt Thou not revive us again that Thy people may rejoice in Thee", (Ps. 85:6). In this text the Lord is spoken of three times and in each case the life and happiness of His people are affected and this depends on being revived. This Hebrew word translated *revive* is *chayah.* For its meaning turn back to *Life.*

סרה

REVOLT: "Turn ye unto him from whom the children of Israel have deeply revolted", (Isa. 31:6). *Sarah,* the Hebrew root for *revolt,* has several meanings. (Also see "Rebel").

It means fault or crime—Deut. 19:16. We could, along with ancient Rabbins, hold that criminals are thorns and nettles in society's path.

It means apostasy or defection from Jehovah—Jer. 28:16.

It means cessation—Isa. 14:6. This is quite a factor in refractions.

This root may be related to *sur,* (see *eschew*), which signifies degenerate shoots of a strange vine—Jer. 2:21. This well describes rebels from righteousness.

גמל

REWARD: "The Lord rewarded me according to my righteousness", (II Sam. 22:21). Another Hebrew word translated *reward* is *gamal.* Its primary meaning is helping another by helping him to bear fruit. This ought to be a great word for ministers, Christian education leaders, music leaders—in fact, all who willingly strive to enlarge the Lord's reign (kingdom). For more on this word turn back to *Recompense.*

פרה

REWARD: " . . . Verily there is a reward for the righteous . . .", (Ps. 58:11). This word *parah,* translated *reward* here, signifies the result or consequences of actions and endeavors. It is used to describe fruit of fields, trees and man (offspring). It has been said that the greatest product of a Christian life is another Christian. For the meaning of *parah* turn back to *Fruit.*

צדק

RIGHTEOUS: "If I find in Sodom fifty righteous within . . .", (Gen. 18:26). This Hebrew word *tsadaq* is the big word for righteousness. It means to be straight, justified, pronounced innocent and happy. For more of its fullness turn back to *Just.*

ישר

RIGHTEOUS: "Let me die the death of the righteous, and let

221

my end be like his!'', (Num. 23:10). *Yashar* is another Hebrew word for righteous and has several significations.

It means to be straight in the way and not traveling sideways or crossways—I Sam. 6:12. Whether it be horse, plane, ship, train or man, there is not much worth if not straight in the way.

It means to be level like an aqueduct through which water is to flow. Where the gospel quenches thirsty nations it has come to them through righteous men.

It means to be even, as a mind that is on an even keel showing contagious poise. How many a Sodomic situation has been saved by the presence of a Righteous man.

It also means to possess integrity. One's self, one's thoughts, one's words and actions are to so shine before men that God will be glorified.

סלע

ROCK: "The Lord is my Rock . . . my God . . . in whom I will trust", (Ps. 18:2). *Sala,* the Hebrew root for *rock,* is used interestingly.

It is used to signify God as a Rock—Ps. 31:3. Those making God their refuge have an everlasting security.

It is used to name a city between the Dead Sea and the Elanitic Gulf in a deep valley surrounded by lofty rock. People lived in dwellings hewn out in the rock. The ruins of the ancient city are reported as still existing under the name that means, Valley of Moses. The name of that original city, Sela, would make a good title for a hymn, a church and our eternal home.

צור

ROCK: " . . . Lead me to the Rock that is higher than I. For thou hast been a shelter for me . . .", (Ps. 61:2, 3). Although there are five Hebrew words translated *rock, Tsur* is most often used which has several meanings.

It means a refuge—Ps. 18:2. If God is our defense and high tower we will need not spend time and energy encountering enemies. Jesus, "opened not His mouth", and was as a Lamb "dumb before the shearers" likely because He was hid in God.

It describes the origin of God's people—Isa. 51:1.

It means to bind up. Security is enjoyed by those bound up with God.

It means to form or to fashion. *Tyre* is a derivative of this word. Alexander the Great fashioned a mound between an island and his continent to make Tyre a richer and greater city. We shall never enjoy true opulence until we are joined to God—and Jesus is the Mound of connection.

רוּץ

RUN: "I will run the way of thy commandments, when thou shalt enlarge my heart", (Ps. 119:32). He is to run and not pace like a hesitating snail. *Ruts,* the Hebrew root for *run,* is excitingly used in several scriptures.

In Prov. 18:10, it is used to mean run to anyone for refuge. The Name of the Lord is perfect security and man should always keep himself near it.

In Esther 8:14, it is used to tell of posts who hasted. Posts of the Great King, being pressed by His commandment, ought to hasten to the ends of the earth with the good tidings.

In Gen. 41:14 it is used to tell that Joseph is brought hastily to the king to interpret his dreams. Preachers are interpreters of God's Word and are sorely needed around the world.

In I Sam. 17:17, the root is used to tell that bread and cheese need to be delivered quickly to the camp for David's brothers. Messengers of Christ must speed spiritual bread and meat to their brother men.

In Ps. 68:31, it is used to tell of men running (stretching hands) to God.

שׁבת

SABBATH: "For today is a sabbath unto the Lord . . .", (Exod. 16:25, 26). *Shabath,* the Hebrew root for Sabbath has interesting meanings and uses.

It means to rest—Exod. 34:21. The idea is to lie by, to keep holiday, to be sitting down and to be sitting still as opposite to labor.

The root is used to tell of elders resting from the gate—Lam. 5:14. That is they did not go to the public place or the forum.

It means to desist or cease—Hos. 7:4. The dough that is full of activity, rising, stops all activity when put in a heated oven. Even so should man stop all activity on the day of rest and gladness.

It carries the idea of celebration—Lev. 23:32. This important day called Sabbath is to be properly celebrated. It is to be kept holy since it was set up by Him who is Holy.

It means to restrain—Ps. 8:2. The Lord made the enemy to desist, to be still and to rest from his wickedness. God makes wars to cease—Ps. 46:9.

It is used to tell of land not tilled—Lev. 26:34, 35. Our days are plowed so much that our souls at their best selves would want that one day a week should not be plowed.

It means interruption—Exod. 21:19. Glorious interruption: A day of rest in seven. The time lost on the Sabbath will be more than paid for to those who keep the Sabbath holy as a day of rest.

It carries the idea of great solemnity—Exod. 16:23. This day was the day of rest of the holy Sabbath unto the Lord and the people made special preparation for it on the day before.

אשה

SACRIFICE: "An atonement for all the congregation . . . they shall bring their offering, a sacrifice made by fire unto the Lord . . .", (Num. 15:25). The Hebrew word *issheh* means an offering (made unto God) and along with it a fire which consumes it. This is saying to us that we are to make gifts, (even ourselves), to the Lord and if the Lord pleases to receive them and burn them we are to furnish the fire.

זבח

SACRIFICE: "For the Lord hath prepared a sacrifice . . .", (Zeph. 1:7). When the Lord made a sacrifice a feast followed. When He gave His only begotten Son the whole world was invited to eat of Him who is the bread of life and thus not to perish. This Hebrew word *zabach* denoted a sacrifice offered as a blood atonement for sin. Could it be Zephaniah was moved to tell of the sacrifice on Calvary which was to take place centuries later?

קדש

SAINT: "He came with ten thousands of saints . . . Yea, he loved the people; all his saints are in thy hand . . .", (Deut. 33:2, 3). The Hebrew word for *saint* is *qadash* which is the same elsewhere translated *sanctify, sanctuary*. For the denotements of *qadash* turn back to *Dedicate*.

חסד

SAINT: "Precious in the sight of the Lord is the death of his saints", (Ps. 116:15). The Hebrew word for saint in this verse is *chasid* which signifies being beautiful and graceful because what one does is actuated by kindness and love. Thus we note that the Psalmist is saying that precious in the sight of the Lord is the death of His people who are beautiful and graceful because their deeds are prompted by kindness and love. For more denotements of *chasid* turn back to Goodliness.

ישע

SALVATION: "Behold, God is my salvation; I will trust and not be afraid . . . He also is become my salvation", (Isa. 12:2). Salvation is a grand doctrine and the Hebrew word for it is *yasha* which is very colorful.

The first denotement is to be broad, ample and spacious which to the Hebrews was an emblem of deliverance from dangers and narrow straits.

Then along with this extra elbow room are riches and opulence which make a most blessed set of circumstances.

Further, *yasha* means to deliver; (Ps. 34:6) as from dangerous straits to restful spaciousness.

Add to all of this the idea of succor; (Isa. 45:20) and the result is a full and perfect salvation; indeed a grand doctrine.

Isaiah's name comes from this root and means; "Salvation of Jehovah." How appropriate since it was he who predicted clearly, deeply and richly the saving ministry of the suffering Servant—Isa. 52:13, 53:12.

קדש

SANCTIFY: "The Lord spake, saying, "I will be sanctified in

225

them that come nigh me, and before all the people I will be glorified . . .", (Lev. 10:3). "I the Lord do sanctify Israel", (Eze. 37:28). The Hebrew word for *sanctify* is *qadash* and for its significations turn back to *Dedicate*.

מקדש

SANCTUARY: "When I thought to know this, it was too painful for me; until I went into the sanctuary of God; then understood I their end", (Ps. 73:16, 17). The Hebrew word for *sanctuary* is *miqdash* which means to be pure, clean, holy and separate. This well describes the place where God meets His people. For a full signification of this word turn back to *Dedicate*.

שטן

SATAN: "The sons of God come to present themselves before the Lord, and satan came also among them", (Job 1:6). The Hebrew word for Satan is *satan* and it has been transliterated into the Greek as Σαταν. The Hebrew root has several significations.

It signifies lying in wait as an enemy to oppose all that is high and good—even the Lord.

It signifies accusing, calumniating and resisting men in the presence of God—Zech. 3:1, 2; Job 1:6.

This root is used to build a name for a well for which strove the herdsmen of Gerar and of Isaac—Gen. 26:21. Then there is basis for the conclusion that Satan has come into the midst of a people when they are quarreling and breaching concord.

רוה

SATISFY: "They shall be abundantly satisfied with the fatness of thy house; and thou shalt make them drink of thy river of pleasures", (Ps. 36:8). The soul may be satisfied with the meanings of *ravah*, the Hebrew root for satisfied.

It means to water—Ps. 65:10. God enriches the earth with His river and softens it with showers which causes it to spring up. This is poetical for God blessing the soul.

The root is used to signify the sword drinking blood—Jer. 46:10. The day of God's vengeance will give the sword a drink of blood from the veins of the adversaries.

226

It is used to signify one being satisfied with his spouse—Prov. 5:19. One will be so satisfied with the love of the wife of his youth that he will not desire the company of a strange woman.

It is used to signify a soul being satisfied—Jer. 31:25. The Lord promises to satiate the weary soul and also to replenish it.

It means to irrigate—Jer. 31:12. The soul of the languishing shall become as a watered garden and it shall rejoice from its sorrow. The Lord will, like the prophet—Isa. 16:9, water with His tears.

יׁשע

SAVIOUR: ". . . All flesh shall know that I the Lord am thy Saviour and thy Redeemer . . .", (Isa. 49:26). The Hebrew root for *Saviour* is *yasha* which is used to over 100 times in the Old Testament. It means to have room enough to harbor and supplies enough for succor after being delivered from dangerous straits. For more on this root turn back to *Salvation*.

פוּץ

SCATTER: ". . .And they were scattered, because there is no shepherd: . . .", (Ezek. 34:5). In this chapter we have reflected God's concern for His flock which became scattered because of poor shepherding. *Puts*, the Hebrew root for scatter, has strong meanings.

It means to break in pieces and scatter as dust—Hab. 3:6. God may drive asunder nations until one emerges who will bring Him Glory.

It means to hammer—Job 16:12. When Job was at ease the Lord shook him up for His own purpose.

It means to harass any one—Job 18:11. Terrors agitate.

It means to pour abroad—Job 40:11. A person can spread hinself abroad like the east wind—Job 38:24; or like a missionary—Ps. 126:6.

It means to scatter as seed—Isa. 28:25. God's people must sow God's seed over God's world. Persecutions may make God's people into missionaries.

It means to desolate—Nahum. 2:2. There is a desolation when purses are emptied to money but not like that when the land is emptied of people.

זרה

SCATTER: "And I scattered them among the heathen, and they wre dispersed through the countries: according to their way and according to their doings I judged them", (Ezek. 36:19). The Lord scattered them because they had idols; they had done wrong and they had profaned God's name (verses 18, 20). *Zarah,* the Hebrew root for *scatter,* has several meanings.

It means to search—Ps. 139.2. The psalmist is sifted or proven in his walk and in his rest.

It means to fan—Isa. 41:16. God's chosen ones will be able to rout the enemy as with a great fan.

It is used to describe the duty of a good sovereign—Prov. 20:8. The king will disperse evil out of his domain as did Jesus out of the temple; out of evil-possessed people.

שׁוֹט

SCOURGE: "And the Lord of hosts shall stir up a scourge. . .", (Isa. 10:26). God punished the enemy of His people with a scourge. *Shut,* the Hebrew root from which *scourge* comes has several meanings.

It means to whip or lash as the sea with oars—Ezek. 8:26. God used a paddle.

It signifies running in haste up and down the land lashing with the arms as with oars—II Sam. 24:2, 8. The purpose here was to visit and inspect. God may visit His people and inspect them.

It signifies running the eyes over a book—Dan. 12:4. The eyes of the Lord may run up and down the earth—Zech. 4:10. People may run to and fro looking for the word of the Lord—Amos 8:12.

It means a whip—Prov. 26:3. This whip may be a tongue—Job 5:21. Or, it may be a calamity or a plague or a scourge the Lord whips out—Isa. 10:26. About all we can say is to quote the Lord's word which says He will chastise whom He loves.

הרשׁ

SEARCH: " . . . For the Lord searcheth all hearts . . .", (I Chron. 28:9). The verb *to search* comes from the Hebrew root *darash* which means to tread something for a purpose. The Lord comes seeking, loving, inquiring and demanding. If He is pleased or provoked He may tread on the object of His search for His own pleasure or for the benefit of the object.

חקר

SEARCH: "The heart is deceitful . . . wicked, who can know it? I the Lord search the heart . . .", (Jer. 17:9-10). *Search* comes from the Hebrew root *chaqar* which means to examine with capacity to number the innumerable and discover that which is past finding out. This God can do for He knows "the balancings of the clouds", (Job 37:16) and hast "walked in the search of the depth", (Job 38:16). There will nothing be hidden from the Discoverer of secrets.

סוד

SECRET: "Surely the Lord God will do nothing, but He revealeth his secret unto his servants the prophets", (Amos 3:7). *Sod* the Hebrew root for *secret*, has several hidden meanings.

It means circle or divan—Jer. 15:17. While this setting is not wholesome, the idea prevails that persons sit together and converse familiarly.

It means a consulting with others—Jer.23:18. God and His children consult confidentially with each other.

It means a deliberation—Prov. 15:22. Purposes are established by groups who think together over a matter; and this may not be revealed to the larger community.

It means an intimate conversation—Prov. 3:32. This wonderfully transpires between the righteous ones and their God.

ראה

SEE: "God saw everything that He had made . . .", (Gen. 1:31). *See* comes from a Hebrew root *raah* which means to view and behold in order to discover the appearance. After the review a visit is made for the prupose of enjoying the find. To translate this meaning into the first chapter of Genesis one sees God making; then visiting and delighting in what He made. For more on this Hebrew root turn back to *appear*.

בָּקַשׁ

SEEK: "I have gone astray like a lost sheep; seek thy servant
...", (Ps. 119: 176). *Seek* in this verse comes from the Hebrew
root *baqash* which means to find in order to draw near unto and
to touch. For more on this root turn back to *Beseech*.

דָּרַשׁ

SEEK: "Seek ye the Lord while He may be found", (Isa. 55:6).
Seek in this verse comes from the Hebrew root *darash* which means to find someone to love, to inquire of and to make requests
to. For more on this root turn back to *Search*.

סָלָה

SELAH: "I acknowledged my sin unto thee . . . Lord; and thou
forgavest the iniquity of my sin. Selah", (Ps. 32:5). *Salah*, the
Hebrew root for *Selah*, has several probable meanings and uses.

It means to be silent or cease using the voice or an instrument.
Think what God has done for thee.

Thus it comes to mean pause; a little while the instruments play
an interlude, which may serve as meditation music.

Or, it may mean to raise the voice or strike up a symphony
on the instruments. It seems to be thus used in Ps. 32 and in the
prayer by Habakkuk (Chap. 3).

It is used many times in Psalms and the end of certain sections
or strophes which report a high spiritual experience.

שָׁלַח

SEND: "I AM hath sent me unto you", (Exod. 3:14). Send
comes from the Hebrew root *shalach* which means a missile
weapon, a dart or a spear to be sent against an enemy. A child
of God ought be willing to be cannon "fodder" to be thrust
against the chief enemy of them both. Another signification of
this root is shoots or sprouts—Isa. 16:8. Every child of God ought
be like a shoot that blooms and bears fruit.

For more on this root turn back to *Cast*.

בדל

SEPARATE: "Now therefore make confession unto the Lord . . . and do His pleasure; and separate yourselves from the people of the land . . .", (Ezra 10:11). *Separate* comes from the Hebrew root *badal* which has several rich denotements.

It denotes a division as by a curtain or a wall. Confession unto God and doing His pleasure will separate one from those who never do either.

It denotes the capacity to distinguish and to discern like knowing the difference between the holy and the unholy—Lev. 10:9, 10. This is a picture of a separating out like the cowhands do among cattle.

It denotes one's activity in putting a distance between oneself and a place, or a condition, or an atmosphere. In the midst of temptations as also in God's service the separated man or woman will be observed as diligently laboring to rightly positionize himself or herself.

It also denotes a precious article of merchandise. *Bdellium*, a derivative of this root, is the name for a precious stone costly in nature and ranks close to gold. Some ancients hold that this root signifies a pearl. In any event, there is prominent the idea of preciousness which evaluates the one separated from the world unto God for His pleasure.

שרף

SERAPHIMS: "I saw also the Lord sitting upon a throne . . . Above it stood the seraphims: each one had six wings . . .And one cried to another, and said, Holy, holy, holy, is the Lord of hosts . . .", (Isa. 6:1-3). *Saraph*, the Hebrew root for *seraphim*, has several meanings.

It means to be noble and of a high birth like a prince. Any one faithfully serving the Lord is a "Noble of Heaven". These heavenly courtiers become leaders in the worship of the Lord of heaven.

It means angels who minister—Isa. 6:6. Their ministry is total and it becomes difficult to know when and where the ministry of the Lord stops and ministry of the angels begins.

It means a serpent, likely having wings—Num. 21:6. These winged creatures were a symbol of wisdom and healing to the

Hebrews. Man needs these two blessings and any sign of them would be most welcome.

It means a priest—Isa. 43:28. These angels were not only princes of heaven but also "princes of the sanctuary" here on earth revealing God to man and aiding that man in fitting him for that revelation. They brought God down to man and brought man up to God.

עבד

SERVE: ". . . Choose you this day whom ye will serve . . . but as for me and my house, we will serve the Lord", (Josh. 24:15). The word *serve* derives from the Hebrew root *abad* which is used over 1,000 times in the Old Testament. For its denotements turn back to *Bondage*.

צבא

SERVICE: ". . .All that enter in to perform the service, to do the work in the tabernacle of the congregation", (Num. 4:23). Here we have *Zaba*, the Hebrew root for *service*, which is used many times in this chapter and in chapter 8. It has colorful meanings.

It means to go forth to war—Num. 31:7. Israel warred against Midian as the Lord commanded Moses.

It is used to report that the Lord came down to fight for Mount Zion—Isa. 31:4. Horses and horsemen cannot help but the Holy One can.

It means service in the temple (church)—Num. 4:23; 8:24. The teachers and officers make sort of a *militia sacra*.

It means an army—Num. 1:3. These holy soldiers are set to go forth to war against the enemy of the soul. They are a consecrated host.

This root is used to report a host of angels in heaven around the throne of the Lord—I Kings 22:19.

It is used to report the sun, moon and stars make up the powers to the heavens that are subject to the command of the Lord—Isa. 45:12, Matt. 24:29.

This root is employed to show God as the leader and patron of Israel's armies—I Sam. 17:45.

It has the idea of shining in it and possesses splendor and beauty—Isa. 28:5. Christian service is a light set high to be seen and to bring glory to God.

It means will or pleasure. This may be the highest use of the root. The Lord's soldier wants to do the will of the Lord.

In Dan. 11:45 the root is used to describe the mount of holy beauty, i.e. Mount Zion. In Dan. 11:41 the root appears in connection with the glorious land of the kings. In such prophetic elegance the simple word for *service* finds its way and place.

פרר

SHAKE: "I was at ease, but . . . he hath taken me by my neck and shaken me to pieces . . .", (Job 16:12). Likely Job was shaken up by the Lord more than any man. *Parar*, the Hebrew root for *shake*, is very colorful.

It is used to mean a broken promise—Isa. 33:8. A shake up usually follows a broken promise.

It means to bring to nought—Ps. 33:10. God frustrates peoples' Babelic devices. They will be so shook up they can hardly talk, if at all.

It means to annul or to abolish—Ps. 85:4. The sinner's hope is that God will cease His anger toward him.

It means to fail—Eccl. 12:5. When one fails he ought tremble— on his knees.

It means to rend—Ps. 74:13. The Red Sea must have been shook up when it was parted to its depths. The earth was "moved exceedingly" when it suffered a concussion—Isa. 24:19. Job's afflictions cause him a violent shaking.

מחסה

SHELTER: "for thou hast been a shelter for me, and a strong tower from the enemy", (Ps. 61:3). *Shelter* derives from the Hebrew root *chasah*, whose denotements are given under *Refuge*.

רעה

SHEPHERD: "The Lord is my Shepherd . . .", (Ps. 23:1). *Shepherd* is a derivative of the Hebrew root *Raah* which has several denotements and also has a two-way spiritual satisfaction in it. It means at the same time to feed and the one doing the feeding. Jesus not only provides bread for his hungry flock but at the same time He is that Bread. He not only leads the thirsty to water but He is that Water. He guards, governs and "leads His dear children along" and rules them with benignity.

For more on this Hebrew root turn back to *Feed*.

מגן

SHIELD: "But thou, O Lord, art a shield for me", (Ps. 3:3). *Shield* is a derivative of the Hebrew root *magan* which has two significations.

It signifies a protector and in this verse relates for our comfort and calming that the Lord is the Protector. This root was used to tell of princes and chiefs who protected their people by force of arms. Our Prince has a limitless arsenal with which to guarantee perfect protection personally.

It signifies a covering as of the heart—Lam. 3:65. Jehovah religion has first to do with the heart, where, because of noticeable vulnerableness, very desparately needs a shield.

אור

SHINE: "Arise, shine, for thy light is come, and the glory of the Lord is come", (Isa. 60:1). *Shine* derives from the Hebrew root or which has several denotements.

It denotes a light that can shine only after being surrounded and illumined by another light.

It denotes a freshening and a gladding. The child of God has received a freshening and a Joy from heaven and he is now to become a gladdener by letting his light shine. Any nation will rejoice when God's people within it hold up their torches of righteousness.

It denotes knowledge, doctrine and revelation. There is one derivative of this root that indicates a sapphire as the symbol of truth and often this gem was worn as a neck piece.

It denotes a flame of fire and verdure and flowers. As if prismatically, colors spray from this rich root, which colors brighten the world. God's people are to do that spiritually—Isa. 58:11.

It denotes happiness. This is the crown for God's elect.

234

קצר

SHORTENED: "Behold, the Lord's hand is not shortened, that it cannot save . . .", (Isa. 59:1). *Qatsar*, the Hebrew root for *shortened*, has meanings that bring out more riches of this text.

It has in it the idea of weakness, i.e., the hand shortened so it cannot accomplish—Isa. 50:2. But the text teaches that God is not weak.

It means impatience, i.e., shortness of spirit—Exod. 6:9. But God is the most excellent example of patience for He has no shortness of spirit.

It means an end, like the end of man whose days are few—Job 14:1. God's days are not shortened but are from everlasting to everlasting.

It means to reap coming from the idea of cutting down—Lev. 19:9. But the text says that God's hand is not cut down so that it cannot save.

Often is man weak, impatient, unable and beat down. But this is never true with God.

כתף

SHOULDER: "Because the service of the sanctuary belonging unto them was that they should bear upon their shoulders", (Num. 7:9). But some men had rebellious shoulders—Neh. 9:29. They hardened their necks and would not hear—Zech. 7:11.

Kathaph, the Hebrew for *shoulder*, also means side of a building—I Kings 7:39. Some men's shoulders are like a side of a building for bearing a load.

It also means the pieces on the high priest's ephod—Exod. 28:7. Moses' shoulder-pieces were the two men holding up his arms—Exod. 17:11.

It means sides of a gate or a door—Ezek. 4:12. Good is it for a church when good men stand about her doors to serve.

רוע

SHOUT: "The pastures . . . the valleys; they shout for joy, they also sing", (Ps. 65:13). *Rua*, the Hebrew root for *shout*, has strong meanings.

It means to make a loud noise like shouting for a battle—I Sam. 17:20. The Christian life is a warfare and loud cryings out against evil and the evil one may be in order. It is also in order to "make a joyful noise to the Lord . . ."—Ps. 95:1.

It means to sound an alarm—Joel 2:1. At the prospect of the coming of God's terrible judgment, faithful prophets blew faithfully warnings on the trumpets.

It means to suffer and come off ill—Prov. 11:15. In this chapter is the report that the wicked, the hypocrite, the talebearer and others will come off ill in the judgment.

It also rings with triumph—Judg. 15:14. The Spirit of the Lord can loose all the cords and bands that hobble and keep one from living abundantly—Ps. 47:1.

שׁגה

SIN: "And if the whole congregation of Israel sin . . .", (Lev. 4:13). *Sin* in this passage derives from the Hebrew root *shagah*, which means to wander as sheep—Ezek. 34:6; to wander from a way or from divine precepts—Ps. 119: 118; to reel from the way because of wine—Isa. 28:7. For more on this Hebrew root, turn back to *Err*.

שׁגג

SIN: ". . . The soul that sinneth", (Num. 15:28). *Sin* in this passage derives from *shagag*, which is a slight variation of the one above—Lev. 4:13, means to make a mistake—Eccl. 5:5 or to do wrong. Mistakes may be very costly and wrongdoing is never right. For more on this Hebrew root, turn back to *Err*.

עון

SIN: "O thou man of God? art thou come unto me to call my sin to remembrance . . .", (I Kings 17:18). *Sin* in this verse derives from the Hebrew root *aiwon*, which means perverseness, wrongness, crime, calamity, and misery—Ps. 31:10. For more on this Hebrew root, turn back to *Iniquity*.

חטא

SIN: ". . .In sin did my mother conceive me", (Ps. 51:5). *Sin* in this passage derives from the Hebrew root *chatah*, which is

236

used near 400 times in the Old Testament and means to miss like an archer—Judg. 20:16; like feet that make a false step—Prov. 19:2. For more on this Hebrew root, turn back to *Miss*.

פשע

SIN: "He that covereth his sins shall not prosper", (Prov. 28:13). *Sin* in this passage derives from the Hebrew root *pasha*, which has several significations.

It signifies breaking up an alliance with another. A sinner is a poor, foolish man who withdraws fellowship with a rich and loving God.

It signifies revolt and rebellion—II Kings 1:1.

It signifies apostasy as man from God—Isa. 1:2, 28.

אשם

SIN: "Yet it hath pleased the Lord to bruise him . . . make his soul an offering for sin . . .", (Isa. 53:10). *Sin* in this verse derives from the Hebrew root *asham*, which means to fail in duty and to transgress. Man not only failed to carry out God's commands, but willfully went past the "OFF LIMITS" sign. For more on this root, turn back to *Guilty*.

שיר

SING: "I will sing unto the Lord . . .", (Ps. 13:6). *Sing* in this verse derives from the Hebrew root *shir* which means to sing an address to someone. The song is not for telling *of* or *about* the Lord or His works but is to be addressed, or better, sung *to* the Lord—Ps. 96:1, 2.

This Hebrew root signifies that a song may be a recitation or even a declamation; it may be classed as a beautiful ornament—Ezek. 16:7 or as a parable—Isa. 5:1; it may be used to communicate comfort, doctrine and inspiration to the afflicted or to the discouraged.

זמר

SING: "Sing unto the Lord ye saints of his", (Ps. 30:4). *Sing* in this verse comes from the Hebrew root *zamar* which means to prune or to cut off. The ancients concluded that at intervals in celebrations, discourse was cut off and communications were

237

uttered in rhythmical tones.

The root means also to play an instrument and be accompanied by singing—Isa. 12:5; which well describes a popular spiritual activity of the Church of God.

רפה

SLACK: "In that day it shall be said to Jerusalem, Fear thou not: and to Zion, let not thine hands be slack", (Zeph. 3:16). Slackness in God's work issues in several sad states which are found in the different meanings of *rapha,* the Hebrew root for *slack.*

One of these is weakness—Neh. 6:9. Slackness among the Lord's servants results in not getting the work done and also losing the strength to do the work.

Another is discouragement—Jer. 49:24. Slackness leads to discouragement and discouragement to more slackness.

Another is idleness—Exod. 5:17. Here the root is used to report idleness which means that a slack hand is or will be idle soon.

Another is omission—Neh. 6:3. There is the idea in this root that slackness means that some of the work will not get done.

Still another is slothfulness—Prov. 18:9. Slackness leads to laziness and laziness to waste.

Perhaps the worst is forsakefulness—Deut. 4:31. When one lets up in God's work it looks like he is about to quit it and let God's garden go untended.

ישן

SLEEP: "I will both lay me down in peace, and sleep; for thou, Lord, only makest me to dwell in safety", (Ps. 4:8). *Yashen,* the Hebrew for *sleep* in this verse, has colorful meanings and uses.

It is used to build a name for a little town, Jeshnah (Modern: Ain Sinai) which lies about three miles North of Bethel and has "a spring and interesting ancient remains". It is rightly named *sleepy.*

It means to be lax, languid and weary—Eccl. 5:12. A working man's sleep is sweet but a rich man may have trouble sleeping.

It means to rest—I Kings 19:5. Elijah slept, was awakened and fed by an angel. After more rest he enjoyed a good meal and journeyed forty days to Horeb, the mount of God to hear that still small voice.

It means to be old, as one who has dwelt long in a place—Deut. 4:25; also as an old crop—Lev. 25:22,—grain that had been asleep a long time. Such restful sleep would be desired in a day of so much sleeplessness. Lord, as in the day of the psalmist, lay us down in peace to sleep.

נכה

SMITE: "Surely he hath born our griefs . . . smitten of God", (Isa. 53:4). Some hold that the intensity of the sufferings of Jesus are more fully portrayed in Isaiah than in the New Testament. The Hebrew root *nakah,* of which *smitten* is a dcrivative, helps to firm up this position with its several denotements.

It denotes slander with a tongue.

It denotes harm such as a plant may receive from a worn, or a man from the sun; or a city from a hord of violent besiegers.

It denotes hurting in the area of the spirit or in the body as with a plague. It has been said, "They plagued him to death."?

It also denotes transfixing—I Sam. 18:11.

The intensest intensity denoted by *nakal* is to evict or to drive out—Num. 22:6. A son may suffer many injuries but the worst of them all is to be driven out of his father's sight and then forsaken.

For still more on this Hebrew root turn back to *kill.*

כתת

SMITE: "For I will no more pity the inhabitants . . . they shall smite the land", (Zech. 11:6). Guilty possessors and pitiless shepherds will not longer have the Lord's pity but shall be smitten. *Qathath,* the Hebrew for *smite,* is used in a variety of situations.

It is used to mean hammer—Isa. 2:4. War is over and swords shall be beaten into plowshares.

It is used to describe the destruction of idols that are worshipped—Mic. 1:7.

It describes despair—Jer. 46:5. Fear beat men down and they "fled apace".

It describes nations dashing themselves against each other—II Chron. 15:6. Civil and international discord are so wasteful but God has used this means to bring down nations who forgot Him.

חלק

SMOOTH: "Which say to the seers, See not; and to the prophets, Prophesy not unto us right things, speak unto us smooth things . . .", (Isa. 30:10). There are several ideas in *Chalaq,* the Hebrew root for *smooth.* In this passage it is opposite to *right.*

In Ps. 36:2 it means to flatter. That is, to make his tongue smooth in his own eyes even though his image is thereby made rough.

In Isa. 57:6 it means bare as far as trees are concerned in that portion along the stream. Flattering is usually barren.

It means slippery ways—Ps. 73:18. The wicked who may be barren flatterers deserve to have the skids under them.

It means to divide—Josh. 22:8. This dividing is done by casting a smooth reckoning stone to discover lots, thus when the Hebrew thought of lots he thought of *smooth* stones.

Finally it comes to mean that divided—II Isa. 9:36. Here a certain portion of ground was used for Jezebel's dishonorable burial.

חבל

SORROW: "The sorrows of death compassed me, and the pains of hell gat hold upon me. I found trouble and sorrow", (Ps. 116:3). If *sorrow* derives from the Hebrew root *dabal,* it means to press together as if into a round cake—1 Sam. 25:18. Sorrow can do that for God's child but for such an one it is a sweet cake from heaven's bakery.

If the Hebrew root here is *chabal* (and more likely it is), it has different denotements.

It denotes a tightening and twisting to tighten still more. God may cast a rope about His child and bind that child to Himself by the experience of sorrow. Sorrow may become the Great Shepherd's crook—Zech. 11:7, 14.

It denotes writings, pain and pangs. As the young is brought forth with throes so may good fruit yield from a be-griefed life—Job 39:3.

Silver cord is a derivative of this root—Eccl. 12:6. Sorrow is like a precious metal band that binds one to God.

דאב

SORROW: "Therefore they shall come and sing in the height of Zion . . . they shall not sorrow any more at all", (Jer. 31:12). *Daab,* the Hebrew root for sorrow here, has several meanings.

It means to melt, languish or pine away—Ps. 88:9. The idea is that the fever of it all makes one flow down. Perhaps this is due to old age, sickness or weakness following fright.

It means to dread—Job 41:14. When these Job-like clouds come they turn one's sunshine into sorrow.

It means faintness as in the spirit—Deut. 28:65. When rest and ease flee sorrow causes one to melt away.

But the Lord replenishes and satiates—Jer. 31:25. If weeping Jeremiah enjoys restoration why should not all men.

יגה

SORROWFUL: "I will gather them that are sorrowful for the solemn assembly . . .", (Zeph. 3:18). In the midst of Zion's song of joy God promises to gather all of those who are grieved because they cannot go to church. *Jagah,* the Hebrew root for *sorrowful,* reveals the deep feeling of those prohibited from the sacred assembly.

It means to be pained in mind and have the soul vexed—Job 19:2.

It means to be crippled in spirit or otherwise afflicted—Lam. 3:33.

It means to be separated—II Sam. 20:13. It is sad to be separated from the sanctuary where one is wont to go but sadder to be deprived of the fellowship of others who frequent the sacred precincts. But, the promise is the Lord will reconvene the pilgrims and give them more than they enjoyed before. (Comp. Zeph. 3:17-20).

נֶפֶשׁ

SOUL: "And the Lord God . . . breathed into his nostrils the breath of life; and man became a living soul", (Gen. 2:7). *Soul* derives from the Hebrew root *naphash* which has several denotements.

It denotes breath, vital spirit or the principle of life—Gen. 35:18; I Kings 17:17. When this breath is absent there is death. At death the spirit is departed.

It denotes mind and rationality—Ps. 57:1. The idea is that the soul not only discovers the trustworthy but persuades the whole person to place his trust in it or cast his all upon it.

It denotes the seat of affections, feelings and emotions—Ps. 35:9. The soul, which the Lord breathed into the body, feels after the Lord and upon discovering Him is moved to rejoice in Him.

It signifies a person—Exod. 5:1. That which can love or hate; that which can sing or be sad; that which can be excited by the right or by the wrong makes up the total personality. The body is only clay and will one day return to the ground from which it came.

זָרַע

SOW: "And I will sow them among the people: and they shall remember me in far countries", (Zech. 10:9). This is a definite instance of foreign missions, by which the number of the Lord's redeemed increased (comp. verse 8). *Zara,* the Hebrew root for *sow,* is full of colors.

It means to disperse, as righteousness—Prov. 11:18; as iniquity, 22:8. A nation may be sowed down with saints or with sinners.

It means to bear seed—Gen. 1:11, 29. That is, a Christian ought let his light so shine that men seeing his good works would glorify the Father.

It means to conceive seed—Lev. 12:2. Of course God's people cannot reproduce themselves as God's children but they can be instruments of such reproduction. The goal of a Christian: another Christian.

242

It means children—Gen. 13:16. Paul calls Onesimus, Son (Philemon).

It means a field of grain—Isa. 23:3. Ask a minister if his congregation does not look a field of Golden grain for God's granary. In Ps. 22:24 God's people are, by this Hebrew root signified a family.

חשׂך

SPARE: "Spare not, lengthen thy cords and strengthen thy stakes", (Isa. 54:2). *Chasak* means:

To restrain, to hold back—II Sam. 18:16. This is the year of world missions and instead of holding back there ought be daring and abandon in giving the gospel to the world.

To preserve—Ps. 78:50. Life or money thus preserved will not be a blessing at all. Both must be placed on the altar.

To deny anything to anyone—Gen. 22:16. Since God gives everything how can anyone hold back anything from Him.

Not to use or not to give out freely—Prov. 13:24. Here it tells that he who spares the rod hates the child. Those who give freely to God's work love the God of that work.

To reserve—Job 38:23. Niggardly indeed is he who reserves anything for him self which ought go to others.

To use tenderly, to treat with pity—II Kings 5:20. The cause of the Lord must not be approached tenderly and looked on with pity. Martyrs did not support the cause thusly.

רוח

SPIRIT: "Not by might, nor by power, but by my Spirit, saith the Lord", (Zech. 4:6). The Hebrew word *ruach* used here has several meanings.

It means to breathe, to blow through the nostrils; hence to smell—Gen. 8:21.

It means to touch—Judg. 16:9. Here fire touched the widths which bound Samson. On pentecost the Lord touched the disciples with His fire.

It means breeze of the day—Song of Sol. 4:6. God's breath upon His people becomes a welcome and transforming breeze.

It means hurricane, tempest—Job 1:19. Sometimes God sweeps the earth with the rough wind of His spirit.

It means a Spirit that animates the whole universe—Ps. 33:6; moves men to live uprightly and do righteously—Ps. 51:10-12; gives unusual capacities to men—Exod. 31:3; inspires preachers—Num. 24:2; enables Joseph to interpret Pharaoh's dreams—Gen. 41:37; gives a ruler courage and victory—Judg. 3:7-10; causes righteousness and justice to reign—Isa. 11:1; that shall be given even to this generation—Isa. 59:21.

מקל

STAFF: "And thus shall ye eat . . . your shoes on your feet, and your staff in your hand . . .", (Exod. 12:11). *Maqal,* the Hebrew root for *staff* here, means a sprout, a twig, a walking stick with an overtone of punishment. In Hos. 4:12 it signifies a divining rod while in I Sam. 17:40 it seems to signify a courage item in the scant arsenal of David as he faces the giant.

שען

STAFF: "For thou art with me, thy rod and thy staff, they comfort me", (Ps. 23:4). Several Hebrew words are translated *staff,* but the one used here is *Shaan,* which has several meanings.

It means to lean upon one as a king who leaned upon his high officers—II Kings 7:17. We that are "kings and priests" here below lean upon Him who is King of kings in heaven and in earth.

It means to rely upon or to trust in—Isa. 10:20. Man learns well who trusts naught else but on the Lord. He does not even lean on his own understanding but on the Lord—Prov. 3:5.

It means to be adjacent or to adjoin, Num. 21:15. Here one country was near to another. It is good to always be near to the Lord.

It means to recline and to rest—Gen. 18:4. Those pilgrims that travel by still waters, leaning upon the Lord will have peace and rest.

מטה

STAFF: "Moreover, he (Lord) said unto me, Son of man, behold, I will break the staff of bread in Jerusalem", (Ezek. 4:16). *Mattah,* the Hebrew root for *staff* here has in it the idea of

244

strengthening the heart. In Mic. 6:9 the root is translated *rod* and there carries the signification of chastisement. So, the very staff that may comfort or strengthen may be used for punishing.

יצב

STAND: "And the Lord said unto Moses, Gather unto me seventy men of the elders of Israel, whom thou knowest . . . and bring them unto the tabernacle of the congregation, that they may stand there with thee", (Num. 11:16). Men, known to be qualified, were chosen to stand before the congregation and share the burdens of the people (Comp. verse 17). *Jatsab,* the Hebrew root for *stand,* has several significations.

One is to set in place. God, or one commissioned by Him, must direct the recruiting and the installing. Perhaps the best example would be a pastor and his church staff, both paid and volunteer.

Another is for one to take a stand—Num. 22:22. Here one of God's ministering angels stood in the way to oppose Balaam, who finally admitted he sinned, and changed his course. There shall always be a need for ministers who, like their Lord, will take a stand in the way of money changers in the house of prayer.

Another signification is to stand up for anyone—Ps. 94:16. Many of God's people have been blessed by the ministry of a courageous advocate.

דגל

STANDARD: "And the children of Israel shall pitch their tents, every man by his own camp, and every man by his own standard", (Num. 1:52). *Dagal,* the Hebrew root for *standard* has much in it.

It means ensign—Num. 2:2, 3, 10, 18. The flag was an indication of allegiance, dedicative and determinative.

It was given first place always—Num. 10:14. Before Israel was seen, their flag was seen showing they were on God's side.

The Hebrew root means to be under cover, as under love—Song of Sol. 2:4; as under protection—Ps. 20:6. Christians should have a sign going before them announcing they are under grace, and, that to God they will be loyal.

חקה

STATUTE: " . . . From evening to morning before the Lord:
It shall be a statute for ever . . .", (Exod. 27:21). This is an ever-
binding law. *Chaqah,* the Hebrew root for *statute* is interesting.

In the first place, it means to carve or engrave—I Kings 6:35.
Carving and engraving carry with them a for-everness.

Then it means painted or portrayed—Ezek. 8:10. Placing thus
God's law on door posts, ceiling, etc. will make certain their pub-
licity.

Also, it means to dig as with a hoe in the ground. A mark was
made on the ground beyond which one was not to go. The ancients hold this to be the explanation of Job 19:8; 13:27; Lam. 3:7.

Finally, it comes to mean law—Exod. 27:21. One may go so
far but no farther for God has drawn a line.

גנב

STEAL: "Thou shalt not steal", (Exod. 20:15). The Hebrew
word for *steal* is *ganab* which has several meanings.

It means to take secretly. It is thought this verb comes from
the Arabic root meaning *side:* to do on the side, to put aside pri-
vily. The storm carries away to the side; the chaff—Job 21:18.

It means to deceive—Gen. 31:20. This sort of lie was first met
with in the Garden of Eden and was named serpent.

It means a thief—Exod. 22:2, 7, 8. It seems the program of res-
titution outlined here would reduce thievery.

באש

STINK: "Ye have troubled me to make me to stink among the
inhabitants of the land", (Gen. 34:30). The Hebrew for *Stink* is
Baash—so much like the English of about the same meaning—
has several meanings.

It means to have a bad smell—Exod. 7:18. There are sins that
make men a stench to society.

It means to be bad and abominable—I Sam. 13:4. The wicked
need a holy bath.

It means to be loathesome—I Sam. 27:12. How precious becomes He Who is able to make us acceptable in God's society.

It means a weed—Job 31:40. Is not the world better off when men and women become flowers and fruits in God's garden?

סער

STORM: "Thou shalt be visited of the Lord of hosts with thunder, and with earthquake, and great noise, with storm and tempest . . .", (Isa. 29:6). *Saar,* the Hebrew root for *storm,* has several uses. (While doing this word a storm of thunder, great noise and high wind came to this Christian encampment by the water course among great trees where I often serve as camp pastor).

It is used to tell of comfortless Israel who was afflicted and tossed with tempest whom God comforted—Isa. 54:11.

It is used to tell of a king who was sore troubled—II Kings 6:11.

It is used to tell of the Lord's storm that altered Jonah's life—Jonah 1:4.

It is used to report on how God scattered His disobedient people by a whirlwind—Zech. 7:14.

It is used to tell of great Ephraim who sinned greatly and became little and was driven like chaff in a whirlwind—Hos. 13:3.

כחר

STRENGTH: "And Delilah said to Samson, Tell me, I pray thee, wherein thy great strength lieth . . .", (Judg. 16:6). Samson had strength unequaled on earth. For a study of it, the several meanings of *koach,* the Hebrew root for strength, shall be given.

It means to be able to break with violence—Judg. 16:30.

It means angelic strength—Ps. 103:20.

It means strength gotten from the earth—Gen. 4:12.

It means ability—Dan. 1:4. This is an area of man beyond that which is physical.

It means substance or wealth—Job 6:22; 36:19. There is strength in wealth—Prov. 5:10; Ezra 2:69.

It means fierce and cruel—Isa. 13:9. This, as well as most of those significations listed above, well describes Samson.

עזז

STRENGTH: "The Lord will give strength unto his people; the Lord will bless his people with peace", (Ps. 29:11). *Azaz,* the Hebrew root for *strength,* has powerful meanings.

It means vehement, as a wind—Exod. 14:21. As the strong wind divided the waters of the sea so would the Church want to disperse the tide of unrighteousness. God is over both.

It means heroes—II Sam. 6:14; Judg. 5:21. Those who have been strong spiritually and morally will be heroes to succeeding generations.

It means security—Judg. 9:51. Strength and security go hand in hand to give a hand to pilgrims of the way.

It means defence and refuge—Ps. 28:7, 8. Though the big waters are troubled, God's children should never be—Ps. 46:1, 2.

It means splendor—Hab. 3:4; Ps. 96:6. The usual concomitants of God's power are honor, majesty and brightness.

This root carries in it the idea of praising—Ps. 68:34. He whose excellency is over Israel shall have the praise of Israel.

This root is used to describe activity in deep waters—Isa. 43:16. We will be in deep waters often and then desperately need God's strength.

עצם

STRONG: "And He increased his people greatly; and made them stronger than their enemies", (Ps. 105:24). *Atsam,* the Hebrew root for *strong,* has strengthful meanings.

It means to bind up and to bind fast—Isa. 33:15. Eyes were closed tightly against evil.

It means to bind the eyes in sleep—Isa. 29:10. There are times it takes strength to close the eyes in good sleep.

It means to be numerous—Ps. 38:19. There is strength in numbers.

It means body—Ps. 139:14. That is, the human body which is wonderfully made and is composed of a million projects bound together.

Tropically, it means "arguments with which disputants defend their cause"—Isa. 41:21.

סמך

SUSTAINED: "I laid me down and slept; I awaked; for the Lord sustained me", (Ps. 3:5). "Sustained" comes from the Hebrew root *samak* which has several colorful denotements.

It denotes leaning upon for support—Amos 5:19. Amos needed aid for his people for they were as one fleeing from a lion, met by a bear, hiding in a house and bit by a serpent there.

It denotes being unmoved—Ps. 112:8. Firmly stand the faithful.

It denotes bestowment—Gen. 27:37. Isaac informed Esau that Jacob was made Lord and much would be provided for him. God has informed sinners that saints are heirs of God and joint-heirs with Jesus.

It denotes drawing near to form an attachment. God's children have such connections as provide total sustenance.

It is used to build the name Semachiah for a man who was strong. All who have God's provisions can be strong. They shall lie down, sleep, arise strong!—I Chron. 26:7.

בלע

SWALLOW: "Enemies . . . the Lord shall swallow them up in His wrath . . . for they intended evil", (Ps. 21:8-11). *Bala* is the Hebrew for *swallow* and it has several meanings.

It means to destroy as Korah's wicked were swallowed by the earth—Exod. 15:31.

It means to be devoured because God's wrath has been excited—Ps. 21:8.

It means to be consumed by wrong desire—Isa. 28:7.

It means to be confined for instruction and disciplining—Jonah 1:17.

249

It means to overcome as death is swallowed up in victory—
Isa. 25:8.

שׁבַע

SWEAR: "And they sware unto the Lord . . .", (II Chron.
15:14). In this great passage (verses 12-15) it is colorfully reported that the people sought the Lord with heart and soul, found
Him, rejoiced and the Lord gave them rest. *Sabaa,* the Hebrew
root for *swear,* is used variously.

It is used to declare allegiance unto God as in the passage
referred to above. When one finds the Lord he will find Him so
wonderful that he will desire to bind himself by oath to Him; and
will discover that the Lord will help him keep the pledge.

It is used to commit oneself to fear and serve the Lord—Deut.
6:13. It is something like one vowing to be faithful to his life mate.

It is used to promise something to any one—Gen. 50:24. God
swore to give certain blessings to His people and we should swear
to give certain blessings to God.

It is used to bind with an oath—Gen. 50:5. A son, Joseph, was
bound to do a certain deed for his father.

It is used to express adjuration—I Kings 22:16. This means to
charge or appeal solemnly. Ever and always solemn appeal will
have its place, an important place, in the Lord's work.

לוּחַ

TABLET: "Let not mercy and truth forsake thee . . . write them
upon the table of thine heart", (Prov. 3:3). *Luach,* the Hebrew
root for *tablet* has interesting meanings.

It means to be polished smooth; to glitter and shine. This was
true of Moses' tablets, heart and face.

It means tablet of the heart—Prov. 3:3. Here was an exhorta-
tion to write the commandments on the table of the heart and
not to forget them.

It means a surface that is doubled or there may be two surfaces
as on the deck of a ship—Ezek. 27:5. It seems this is the notion
of having two surfaces so that more may be written and more
remembered.

This root is used to build a name for a city in Moab. It means floored or made smooth by use of boards—perhaps the streets thereof. Could this be applied to mean that a city should be so constructed so as to receive the impress of God's law?

לוּן

TARRY: "When the man rose up to depart . . . he said unto him, Behold now, the day draweth toward evening, I pray you tarry all night", (Judg. 19:9). *Lun,* the very colorful root for *tarry,* has several meanings and uses.

Surely the oustanding use of it is in Deut. 21:23, (which is quoted in John 19:13). It means to remain or to stay as the body all night on the tree.

It means to stay all night—Gen. 19:2. The would be host persisted and the would be guest resisted.

It means abide—Ps. 91:1. This is to restfully dwell under the shadow of the Almighty.

This root has in it a shade of beautiful stubbornness—Ps. 55:6,7. The psalmist betroubled insisted if he could fly he would go to and remain in the wilderness.

It is used to say what is mine shall remain with me—Job 19:4.

It is used to teach the sinner that judgment will remain in the midst of his house—Zech. 5:4.

זהר

TEACH: "And thou shalt teach them ordinances and laws and shalt shew them the way wherein they must walk, and the work that they must do", (Exod. 18:20). This ought be a great text for Sunday School teachers. The Hebrew word for *teach* is *zahar* which has several meanings.

It means to be bright, to shine—Dan. 12:3.

It means to make light, to enlighten, to teach—Exod. 18:20.

It means to admonish, to warn—II Kings 6:10. To admonish the wicked to turn from his evil way—Ezek. 3:18, is a further use.

It means to warn with authority from God—Ezek. 3:17.

251

It means to receive instruction—Eccl. 4:13. This is the opposite of foolishness.

It means brightness, splendor—Ezek. 8:2. God's teachers will make a singular appearance.

It means beauty, especially of flowers. A Hebrew month, (parts of May and June), Zif, comes from this root to represent that time of the year when flowers bloom.

ידה

THANKSGIVING: "Enter into His gates with thanksgiving", (Ps. 100:4). The Hebrew word for *thanksgiving* is *yadah* which is employed in the Old Testament to signify different activities.

In Ps. 32:5 it is translated *confess* with the idea that sins are pointed out with the hand or projected to be seen or shown with the hands extended. Imagine David thus acting in the presence of the sin-forgiving God. (The first two letters of the root means hand).

In the above-quoted verse and many others it means to first acknowledge receipt of benefits and then celebrate and give thanks. Usually God is named as the Person to be celebrated.

In Dan. 9:4, the action is quite different. Here is a confession of sin and an acknowledgement of quilt and then an inventory made of God's benefits. This makes a required prelude to an oratorio of Thanksgiving.

In the first part of Ps. 45 (In the ascription) it means a *lovely* song or in Ps. 84 it is translated *amiable.* In I Chron. 25:1 the root is used to build a pronoun which is given as a name to one of David's choristers and musicians. Now, putting all of this together we have a sinner who confesses his sins to God, is forgiven, joins the choir and sings lovely songs of thanksgiving to Him who is full of grace and mercy. This sinner joins a choir like the one mentioned in Neh. 12:8 where this word is used again.

דמה

THINK: "We have thought of thy loving-kindness, O God, in the midst of thy temple", (Ps. 48:9). *Damah,* the Hebrew root for *think,* has several meanings.

It means to become like—Song of Sol. 2:9. Thinking upon God may make us more like Him.

It means to use similitudes—Hos. 12:11. The idea is to liken in one's mind the object of meditation. That is, imagine.

It has in it the idea of aspiration—Isa. 14:14. O, to be more like the Master.

It signifies purpose—Isa. 14:24. Think, and then do something.

This verb also signifies silence and rest—Ps. 83:1. While here there is a negative indicated but the idea of silence, peace, etc. goes along with thinking.

חוּט

THREAD: "Delilah therefore took new ropes, and bound him therewith . . . And he brake them off his arms like a thread", (Judg. 16:12). *Thread* here signifies less than little but the Hebrew verb *chut,* from which it comes is variously used.

It is used to signify sewing, hence, *thread.*

It is used to signify repairing, as a wall—Ezra 4:12. Mending little by little, as if with threads, the historic walls of Jerusalem were restored.

It is used in an ancient proverb, "Not even the least; not a thread nor a sandal-thing"—Gen. 14:23.

It is used, on the other hand, to signify a matter of life and death—Josh. 2:18. The cord that lowered to safety the two spies become the scarlet thread in the window which vouch-safed the sparing of Rahab's family.

רעם

THUNDER: "Lo, these are parts of his ways: . . . but the thunder of His power who can understand?", (Job. 26:14). What great sound can, better than thunder, represent the whole compass of the divine power and all the mighty deeds which can be predicated to God? *Raam,* the Hebrew root for *thunder,* has deep meanings.

It means to roar like the sea—Ps. 96:11. When the Lord reigns the heavens rejoice; the earth is glad; the sea roars and the fulness thereof.

It represents God's judgment—I Sam. 2:10. The Lord shall thunder upon His adversaries and they shall break to pieces but the horn of His anointed shall be exalted.

It means to provoke—I Sam. 1:6. Here the adversary irritated Hannah in order to make her fret because the Lord had shut up her womb.

It is used to describe the ways of God—Ps. 77:18. In this poetic passage, verses 13-19, the Power and ways of God are described rising to a high pitch when this root is employed in verse 18.

It means the best—Gen. 47:1 1. The best land, represented by the loudest noise, was given Joseph's brethern, i.e., the land of Rameses, which name is built on the above root.

בשׂר

TIDINGS: "How beautiful upon the mountains are the feet of him that bringeth good tidings", (Isa. 52:7). There is an interesting and reasonable relation between *beautiful* and *tidings*.. The root for *tidings* has in its primary meaning the idea of fairness and beauty. It is *basar* and has several meanings.

It means to be cheerful on account of good news. Well, of course, the Christian ought to be joyful because he has received the gospel.

It means to cheer with glad tidings—II Sam. 18:19. Here the messenger ran to tell one that God had avenged that one of his enemies. Many sad ones are gladdened when told that in Christ there is reconciliation with God and that Christ has won the victory over man's three chief enemies: sin, death and the grave.
It means to satisfy—Job 31:31. This is in praise of one's hospitality that satisfies his guests with flesh. The followers of the Lord, like their Lord, have meat to eat that the unconverted know not of.

It means a healthy body with quiet heart—Prov. 14:30. One can be glad if he has this and he that tells him that it comes from the Lord (the only source) has beautiful feet.

לפיד

TORCH: "In that day will I make the governors of Judah . . . like a torch of fire . . .", (Zech. 12:6). Very interesting are the different significations in *lapeed,* the Hebrew root for *torch*..

254

There is the idea of a lamp shining—Judg. 7:16. Many of our barriers and walls would fall if God's people would flash gospel truth and power from their lamps.

Much like this is the burning lamp—Gen. 15:17. Christians often hide their lamps under a bushel where they may suffer for lack of air and airing.

Then there is the striking thought of a man being a torch despised—Job 12:5. That is, though once in high consideration, he is now vile and condemned.

This root is used to build the name for Deborah's husband—Judg. 4:4. Since Deborah was such a lambent flame of right and song—Judg. 5:1, why could not she have chosen for a husband one of common interest.

רגז

TREMBLE: "The Lord reigneth; let the people tremble: He sitteth between the cherubims; let the earth be moved", (Ps. 99:1). The Hebrew word for *tremble* is *ragaz* which has several meanings.

It means to be moved, to be disturbed, to be thrown into commotion—Isa. 64:2. People and mountains are to quake and to melt in the presence of the Lord.

It means to rejoice—Jer. 33:9. People are to be moved with joy over the coming of certain persons or a certain Person.

It means to trouble—Job 3:17. Disturbances may be trouble to some people and to others it may become a blessing in bringing them to God.

It means to provoke to anger—Job 12:6. Such provocation may lead to salvation.

חרד

TREMBLE: " . . . Saith the Lord: But to this man will I look . . . that . . . trembleth at my word", (Isa. 66:2). *Charadh,* the Hebrew root for *tremble,* is used colorfully.

It is used to describe the assemblage before God's law-teacher—Ezra 9:4.

255

It is used to express fear—I Sam. 14:15. There was a very great trembling in that quake-shaken area.

It is used to describe reverence for God's word—Isa. 66:5. The Lord shall appear to the joy of those who have a regard for God's word.

It is used to portray concern and care—II Kings 4:13. The widow was "careful for us with all this care." This sort of attention given to God's word and workmen will build up God's kingdom in the earth.

מעל

TRESPASS: "Because they trespassed against me, therefore hid I my face from them, and gave them into the hand of their enemies", (Ezek. 39:23). *Maal,* the Hebrew root for *trespass,* has some purging preachments in it.

It means treacherous sin—II Chron. 29:6. These people did evil in the eyes of God, forsook God, turned from the church and went away from God and all that was holy.

It means disobeying God—I Chron. 10:13. Saul kept not the word of the Lord and transgressed against it.

It means stealing—Josh. 22:20. The idea seems to be that trespassing is robbing God of allegiance. To further aggravate the situatuion, Saul showed faith in a foreign spirit instead.

It means falsehood—Job 21:34. Trespassing against God and His word is to be untrue to God, to one's self and to one's people-casting shame on all.

אגדה

TROOP: "It is He that hath builded His stories in the heaven, and hath founded His troop in the earth", (Amos 9:6). The Hebrew root for *troop* is *agudah* and it has interesting denotements.

It denotes a band—Isa. 58:6. This served as sort of a hobble.

It denotes a bundle—Exod. 12:22. One straw alone would not do this work of mercy and emergency. It took a bunch tied together.

256

It denotes a troop of men—II Sam. 2:25. The children of Benjamin formed a troop on a hill. God's children are needed everywhere forming troops on all hilltops.

It denotes an arch—Amos 9:6. God can build, out of His men, a rainbow across the heavens.

עכר

TROUBLE: "And Joshua said, Why hast thou troubled us? the Lord shall trouble thee this day", (Josh. 7:25). *Akar,* the Hebrew root for *trouble,* has interesting meanings.

It means to make turbid or to afflict any one—Judg. 11:35. There are many who bring evil upon the country or upon a church. This root is the same as *acan,* which is the name for the Israelite who by his sacrilege brought defeat upon the people— Josh. 7:1; 22:20.

It means to be moved with grief—Ps. 39:2. Troubles stir our sorrows.

It is employed to describe a cruel man afflicting his own flesh— Prov. 11:17. This is strong preaching to those who dissipate their bodies which are the temple of God.

בהל

TROUBLE: "And the woman came unto Saul, and saw that he was sore troubled . . .", (I Sam. 28:21). *Bahal,* the Hebrew for *trouble,* has striking meanings.

It means to be amazed—Exod. 15:15. This is to be trepidation or struck with terror.

It means to be vexed or to tremble—Ps. 6:2, 3. The body and the soul are both reported by this word as shaking.

It means to flee because of fear—Judg. 20:41. This comes to mean haste—Prov. 28:22.

It means to suffer sudden destruction—Zeph. 1:18. The people sin; this excites God's wrath and moves Him to destroy and to hide His face—Ps. 104:28. This kind of trouble is the worst of all or the sum of all troubles.

257

המה

TROUBLED: "I remembered God and was troubled", (Ps. 77:3).

The psalmist was deeply moved for *hamah,* the Hebrew root for *troubled,* has several meanings.

It means to roar like a bear—Isa. 59:11; growl like a dog, Ps. 59:6; mourn as a dove—Ezek. 7:16; cry aloud—Ps. 55:17; to be tossed like great waters—Ps. 46:3; to have his soul stirred like pipes of a great musical instrument—Jer. 48:36.

It is used figuratively to describe disquietude of soul—Ps. 42:5,11; also internal tumult—Jer. 4:19.

It is used to picture a rambling or buzzing about—Prov. 7:11.

It is used to describe the sound of rain—I Kings 18:41; of singing—Ezek. 26:13; of a tumultuous multitude—Isa. 13:4; of an army imposingly outfitted—Judg. 4:7.

It is used to build a name—Ezek. 39:16, for the city where prophecy says the slaughter of Magog will take place.

יחד

UNITE: "Teach me thy way, O Lord: I will walk in thy truth: unite my heart to fear thy name", (Ps. 86:11). By exchanging places with two letters in *unite,* one has *untie.* The psalmist desired supremely union with the Lord. *Jachad,* the Hebrew root for *unite,* has dramatic meanings.

It carries the idea to knit together—I Chron. 12:17. David's heart was that to those of the children of Benjamin and Judah.

It contains the idea "When it rains it pours"—I Chron. 10:6. Saul, his sons, his family all died at the same time.

It signifies simultaneousness—Ps. 4:9. Indeed this was a confluence of blessings that a man may lie down to rest and also enjoy peaceful sleep.

It means same mindedness—I Sam. 17:10. While in this verse there is an expression of emotional collusion, it might have been to be of the same mind which was in Christ.

This root is used to build a name, Jahdo—I Chron. 5:14. This was a good man: all together.

258

נבב

VAIN: "For vain man would be wise . . .", (Job 11:12). *Nabab* and *abab,* the Hebrew root for *vain,* has very interesting meanings.

One is, to bore through and make hollow. A vain man is hollow or empty.

Another is to be stupid and foolish. A man is quite stupid when he goes around empty since there are so many good things to fill a man's life, mind and heart.

And another is to be without heart because one's heart is ravished—Song of Sol. 4:9. Indeed is a man empty when he has no heart. No heart issues in no friends.

Still another is to lack understanding. A man is not only vain but is only part of a man if he does not understand.

שׁוא

VANITY: "God will not hear vanity", (Job 35:13). *Shava,* the Hebrew root for vanity here, has colorful meanings.

It means false and falsehood—Ps. 12:2. Vanity is a lie.

It means evil and wickedness—Job 11:11. Vanity is a wicked deceiver.

It means nothingness and uselessness—Mal. 3:14. Here, of course, the opposite is implied but everywhere vanity is less than a puff of wind.

און

VANITY: "He that soweth iniquity shall reap vanity", (Prov. 22:8). For the meanings of *aven,* the Hebrew root for *vanity* here, see *iniquity.*

הבל

VANITY: "Vanity of vanities, saith the Preacher, vanity of vanities; all is vanity", (Eccl. 1:2). *Habal,* the Hebrew root for *vanity* here and in about 50 other passages, has several meanings.

It means a breath as of air or a breeze—Isa. 57:13. This shows that vanity is something that is here now and then gone.

It means to become vain or to act foolishly—II Kings 17:15. These people followed the vain hopes they cherished.

It means evanescent, transient and frail—Job 7:16. Job's days left him like a breath. This life evanesces like a vapor.

It means empty and fruitless—Lam. 4:17. Why would man make an idol of something which is worthless—Jer. 2:5.

It means an abortion—Eccl. 6:3, 4. It is to end valuelessly.

This root was used to name Abel—Gen. 4:2. He was probably so called from the shortness of life according to the ancients.

It means idleness—II Kings 17:15. The lesson here is: No matter how much man works if he works not for God, he is idle.

תֹּהוּ

VANITY: "They are counted to him less than nothing and vanity", (Isa. 40:17). *Tohu,* the Hebrew root for vanity here, means ruin, vacancy, desolateness. For more on it see *form.*

כֶּרֶם

VINEYARD: "My beloved hath a vineyard in a very fruitful hill", (Isa. 5:1). *Karam,* the Hebrew root for *vineyard,* is used colorfully.

It means to be noble and of a generous nature: applied to persons and to fertile soil as producing fine fruits. A vineyard would be a field or garden of vines or trees *or persons* producing such fruits.

This root is used to build a name: Carmel—Josh. 19:26—which is a fertile mountain adorned with groves and trees. This name is good for a church full of fruitful Christians.

Vineyard is "a frequent emblem of the people of Israel"—Isa. 3:14, 51; Matt. 20:1. Israel was a fruitful bough in God's vineyard, a spiritual promontory across the centuries.

It means a vinedresser—Isa. 61:5. Then the root was employed to build a name for a son of Reuben—Num. 26:6. Carmi (vinedresser) would make a good title for God's minister.

עלם

VIRGIN: "Therefore the Lord himself shall give you a sign. Behold a virgin shall conceive, and bear a son, and shall call his name Immanuel", (Isa. 7:14). *Alam,* the Hebrew root from which stems the word *virgin,* is used to speak of young men and young women of marriageable age. *Almah,* the feminine derivative in this passage means a virgin, girl, maiden of marriageable age, the age of puberty.

This virgin, as Delitszch points out, was a maiden of the house of David as was prophesied, who was selected for an extraordinary end. She was to bear a son full of promise whom she would name Immanuel.

This nameless maiden of low rank God "singled out and now showed to the prophet in the mirror of His counsel, would give birth to the divine deliverer of His people."

Not only does the root carry the idea of strength and vigor which served well in this unusual occurrence but also *eternity* suggesting that the virgin would be forever spoken of.

Likely the reasons that she would forever be spoken of are first, that her child would be virgin-born—Isa. 7:14; second, that He would be the Wonderful One—Isa. 9:6; and third, that He would be the Reigning One—Isa. 11:1.

חזה

VISION: "I (the Lord) will pour out my spirit upon all flesh; and your sons and daughters shall prophesy, . . . your young men shall see visions", (Joel 2:28). *Chazah,* the Hebrew root for *vision,* has exciting meanings.

It means contemplation—Ps. 27:4. The psalmist very much desired to behold the beauty of the Lord in the sanctuary.

It means feeling—Job 27:12. In this passage a spiritual experience is described.

It signifies an agreement—Isa. 28:18. The heart of the Hebrew religion is an agreement between God and His people.

It means to see—Job 19:26-27. Job felt sure he would see God.

It means a prospect—Dan. 4:8, 17. One having a grand idea

261

may be one who has a perception of what things are going to be like.

It signifies a vision—Dan. 4:2, 7, 13. The king had visions which only Daniel could interpret.

It means a revelation—II Sam. 7:17. God will reveal to His men that which He wants spoken unto them and to their audiences.

A derivative of this root signifies valley of visions which was Judah and Jerusalem in particular which became the seat and the home of divine revelation—Isa. 2:3. The derivative *hazion* seems to be an allusion to *hatsion* which the Septuagint put into the Greek *Zion*. This great word was not translated into English but transliterated and reads today *Zion*—the valley of people who have seen God or at least have had a vision of God's convenant dealings with them.

פָּקַד

VISIT: "And the people believed: and when they heard that the Lord had visited the children of Israel . . . they bowed their heads and worshipped", (Exod. 4:31). Here God visited the people and in Jer. 23:2 He wants His pastors to visit the people. *Paqad,* the Hebrew root for *visit,* has several meanings.

It means providence, care—Job 10:12. God gives life, canopies it with His favor and visits in order to inspire.

It means to go to any one in kindness to see how they do—I Sam. 17:18. God comes to visit us in kindness which convinces us He does not neglect His own even if a mother should neglect her sucking child—Isa. 49:15. Pastors ought to visit, for the Great Shepherd visits His flock.

It means to appoint others to visit—Num. 27:16. The Lord set a man over a congregation to lead them; to bring them in; and, this in such a manner as to make them feel they have a shepherd.

It means to muster—Isa. 13:4. Enumeration of the flock can be well done when visiting the flock.

It means to deposit—Jer. 36:20. When a visit is made a deposit is made in the purse or in the life of the visited or the visitor. In fact, this root is used to mean stores or wealth—something laid up—Isa. 15:7.

It means to punish—Jer. 44:13. In several scriptures this root is used to tell how the Lord visits in order to punish men and nations. In Ps. 111:7 the root is used to build a word that means mandates or precepts which come about after God's visit and punishment.

קוֹל

VOICE: "And they heard the voice of the Lord God walking in the garden in the cool of the day", (Gen. 3:8). *Qol,* the Hebrew root for *voice,* has several meanings.

It means to call—Gen. 3:8. This voice the first pair heard had a summoning sound. This is kin to *Qahal,* the Hebrew root for *congregation.*

It means thunder—Ps. 29:3. Even thunder in full tone is not great enough to represent the voice of God.

It means to weep—Gen. 45:2. The weeping one has a voice of his own.

It means to sing—Ps. 104:12. The happy and contented ones have a voice of their own.

It means to thunder—Ps. 77:18. Struggling, the psalmist found victory and remembering it was God who gave it he needed the elements in their sounds to help tell of it.

It means words or a discourse—Eccl. 5:2. A common use of the word but very uncommon here and in verse 5.

It means rumor or report—Gen. 45:16. This could be a hurtful use of the word.

It means sound as of a trumpet—II Sam. 15:10. This shall always be an effective sound.

It means noise—Ezek. 24:1. This is an interesting use of the root.

This root is used to build a name, *Kolaiah,* which means "voice of God". What if Bible teachers and preachers could bear this name?

נדר

VOW: "Then there shall be a place which the Lord your God shall choose to cause his name to dwell there: thither shall ye

bring . . . all your choice vows which ye vow unto the Lord'',
(Deut. 12:11). The Hebrew word for *vow* is *nadar* which has
varied meanings.

It means to drop down as grain falling on a threshing floor
when winnowed. The promises of God's people may be like gold-
en grain for his grainery—and the crop may be more prolific when
those people are threshed by trials and tribulations.

It means to promise voluntarily—without the threshing.

It means scattering or sowing. How much good and sunshine
has been scattered by God and man when making promises.

אסר

VOW: "If a man vow a vow unto the Lord, or swear an oath
to bind his soul with a bond . . .", (Num. 30:2). *Asar* is a strong
Hebrew root and has several meanings.

It means to bind or make fast—Neh. 4:18. These sword-and-
trowel people had a mind to work and the wall was finished.

It means to put in bonds or become a captive—Song. of Sol.
7. Here we have a bride and bridegroom bound by love and
promise. The kingdom has its best days when its subjects serve
in Pauline-like slavery.

It means to harness or to yoke—I Sam. 6:7. The Church is a
chariot bringing people to the Lord—rolling most beautifully
when there are yoked to it strong men and faithful women.

It means discipline or prohibition—Dan. 6. Vows become
fences along the highway of life.

ספד

WAIL: " . . . And they shall weep for thee with bitterness of
heart and bitter wailing", (Ezek. 27:31). The Hebrew word for
wailing is *sapad* which has several denotements.

It denotes smiting the breast as a gesture of mourning—
especially for the dead. Children of the living God ought so mourn
for those dead in their sins. Jesus did.

It denotes continuity. This is the desperate need for those who
"weep for the erring" only during revival efforts or only in Sunday services.

In one case this root is used to build a word that denotes those mourned for. This gives the activity a new dimension.

קוה

WAIT: "They that wait upon the Lord shall renew their strength", (Isa. 40:31). The Hebrew word for *wait* is *qawah* which means to await with the notion of holding on strongly; and during the time becoming wound together with the object of the waiting. For more on it turn back to *Hope.*

הלך

WALK: "And Enoch walked with God: and he was not; for God took him", (Gen. 5:24). The Hebrew word for *walk* is *halak* which means to go forth and also to go through as a way of life or conduct. This going is to result in an increase of such blessings as grace and knowledge. For more on this Hebrew word and its relative *yalak,* turn back to *Go.*

נוד

WANDER: "Thou tellest my wanderings: put thou my tears into thy bottle: are they not in thy book?", (Ps. 56:8). The significations of *nud,* the Hebrew root for *wander,* portray some of the elements of wandering.

One is afflicted—Job 2:11. Affliction will get people on the road. They get shaken and they move.

One is to pity or to commiserate—Job 16:4. Pitying some who are pitiful but pushes them out.

One is to deplore or to bemoan—Jer. 22:10. This favors the signification above but is stronger. The bemoaned wants to leave his native country and return no more.

Another is to wag the head as expressing hissing—Jer. 18:16. Elders who practice this will increase the number of prodigals.

Another is to thrust out—II Sam. 23:6. This is the most unpardonable cause of vagabondage.

Still another is to flee—Gen. 4:12, 14, 16. Cain hastily wandered off to the land of Nod (wandering). The proper name, *Nod* derives from the Hebrew root for *wander.*

תעה

WANDER: "The man that wandereth out of the way of understanding shall remain in the congregation of the dead", (Prov. 21:16). By "way of understanding" is meant *wisdom* the sum of which is in Christ. By "dead" is meant sheol, grave, hades—that place of waste and darkness where the only light is more darkness. This verse implies that man is already in the assembly of the dead and will stay there if he misses the way of understanding. *Taah,* the Hebrew root for *wander,* has several meanings and uses.

It is used to describe homelessness—Gen. 21:14. Even as Hagar and her son were sent away into the wilderness even so will the sinner be homeless until he comes to God who builds a home without hands.

It is used to speak of drunk persons—Isa. 28:7. Strong drink and sin both make men reel, go astray and miss the true way.

It is used to tell of the mind and heart that reel in giddiness—Ezek. 14:11. These that erred from paths of virtue and piety and God shall bear their iniquity—Ezek. 44:10. One language at this passage calls them heretics and another says they are given to idolatry.

It means to be deceived—Job 15:31. The world's greatest deception is to entice a man to wander and miss the way that leads to the assembly of God's people who shall enjoy eternal happiness.

As a metaphor, it means to cause to err from the paths of virtue and piety as a nation into ungodliness—Isa. 3:12, II Kings 21:9. When a man wanders from God he is voting for his nation to do so and God will bring such evil upon him *and* his nation that whosoever hears of it, "both his ears shall tingle"—II Kings 21:12.

זהר

WARN: "So thou, O son of man . . . shalt hear the word at my mouth, and warn them for me", (Ezek. 33:7). The Hebrew word for *warn* is *zahar* which means to be bright and shine like the moon in his splendor or flowers in their beauty for the purpose of admonishing others to turn from the wrong way. For more on this Hebrew root turn back to *Teach.*

היה

WAS: "And God said, Let there be light: and there was light", (Gen. 1:3). *Hayah,* the Hebrew root for *was,* is used variously and colorfully.

It means existence—Exod. 3:14. Here it is used to make the great prounouncement, I AM THAT I AM. That is, just as light was there so was God: except God was not created or was not spoken into existence.

This verb is coupled with the idea of possession—Exod. 20:3. Man is to be owned by Jehovah, the only God.

It is used with the idea of purposeful existence—Exod. 4:16. We are here for a reason.

It is used to help express companionship—I Kings 1:8. Men were not with Adonijah but walked with God and received unusual blessings.

It is used to tell of being like another—Gen. 3:22. To be more like the Lord is the noblest reason and the highest goal for existence.

חרב

WASTE: " . . . The wind of the Lord shall come up from the wilderness, and his spring shall become dry, and his fountain shall be dried up . . .", (Hos. 13:15). *Waste* here signifies that the fountain shall fail and the treasure of pleasant vessels shall be spoiled. *Charab,* the Hebrew root used here, has other significations.

It signifies wasted sanctuaries—Amos 7:9. This is the number one waste in the land.

It signifies one nation wasting another—Jer. 50:21. Soon would this reduce the whole world to nothing.

This root is used to mean sword—Deut. 13:15, which is an instrument of waste.

It signifies nations that waste themselves by not serving God—Isa. 60:12. A garden will go to weeds without any planting or cultivation.

Horeb, built on this root, names a peak of Mount Sinai but likely would not be used by a thriving church.

צפה

WATCH: "The Lord watch between me and thee, while we are absent one from another", (Gen. 31:49). The Hebrew word for *watch* is *tspha* which has several significations.

It signifies being bright and shining like the Light of the world who is watching over His own.

It signifies looking around for a distance and upon discovering any danger, warning those who might be affected.

It signifies prophets—Ezek. 3:17, who have been called of God to hear God's word and warn the people. If the warning does not take place and the people die in their sin, their blood will be on the hands of those who were called.

יבל

WATER COURSES: "And they shall spring up as among the grass, as willows by the water courses", (Isa. 44:4). *Yabal* is the Hebrew root for *water courses* which has interesting meanings.

It means flowing stream—Isa. 44:4. Water was promised thirsting Israel; God's Spirit was to come upon her seed; blessings would flow upon her offspring. This was revival. The spiritual garden would grow again.

It means rain. If there is not a cloud in the spiritually dry sky the Elijahs must pray.

It means produce or increase—Job 40:20. God can cause the mountains to bring His man food while he rests under the shades of the fens that also double as a covert. When the Lord is Shepherd the pilgrim will be often at the table of plenty for his soul.

שקה

WATERETH: "He watereth the hills from His chambers: the earth is satisfied . . .", (Ps. 104:13). *Shaqah,* the Hebrew root for *watereth,* has rich meanings.

It means to give to drink—Gen. 24:43. Many of humankind stand and wait at spiritual wells trusting that some spiritual minister will give them a draught to quench their parching thirst.

It means to irrigate—Ps. 104:13. Some have declared there is as much water above in the firmaments as there is below in the seas. This is hard to believe but it is easy to believe that only God can water the hills, the fields and the pastures.

It signifies the moistening of the marrow of the bones—Prov. 3:8; 15:30; 17:22. The psalmist's sin dried his bones (Ps. 32:1-4) which only God could relieve and then only when the sufferer confessed his sins unto God.

ארח

WAYFARER: "And when he lifted up his eyes he saw a wayfaring man in the street of the city", (Judg. 19:17, 18). The Hebrew for *Wayfarer* is *Arach* and has several meanings.

It means to be on the way—Job 34:8. But he may not be on the right way.

It means travelers in a caravan as merchants—Gen. 37:25. Servants of the Lord travel over land and sea taking the priceless which may be had without price.

It means a manner of conduct and life—Isa. 2:3. He who has this mode of life will please God and be preserved by Him.

It means destiny—Dan. 5:23. The teaching here is that in thy walk thou art to please God in Whose hand thy breath is.

לאה

WEARY: "Thou, O God, didst send a plentiful rain, whereby thou didst confirm thine inheritance, when it was weary", (Ps. 68:9). God's people were weary unto fainting but He sent a reviving rain. As to how serious was their condition is revealed in the several aspects of *laah,* the Hebrew root for *weary.*

It means to labor or to struggle so as to lead to exhaustion—Job 4:5. This suffering man was reminded that whereas he aforetimes strengthened those with feeble knees was now himself fainting.

It means to make effort and that in vail—Jer. 20:9. Cannot this become very wearisome? God's word was as a burning in the bones and to try keeping quiet was in vain.

It means to be sick—Jer. 15:6. God was grieved or made sick at putting up with Judah's backward goings.

It means to tire one's patience—Mic. 6:3. The Lord brought

His people out of slavery and redeemed them and yet they controverted.

This root is used to build Leah's name—Gen. 29. Much patience and weariness are shown in this dramatic story.

Scholars hold that this root is the same as *labah,* which means to thirst and languish because of famine—Gen. 47:13.

ארג

WEAVER: "My days are swifter than a weaver's shuttle", (Job 7:6). Very colorful meanings are in *Arag,* the Hebrew root for *Weaver.*

It means quick and regular motion. Time rocked on, back and forth, like a rocking chair for regularity and a weaver's shuttle for speed.

It means to plait or to braid—Judg. 16:13. Ropes of hair are caressed back and forth like the steps of a camel on his slow journey—first to one side then the other.

It means a chest or coffer, moving and shaking in the cart in which it is hauled. The vibration may be like "a sack of stones suspended from a camel by way of equipoise".

בכה

WEEP: "He that goeth forth and weepeth, bearing precious seed, shall doubtless come again with rejoicing, bringing his sheaves with him", (Ps. 126:6). The Hebrew word for *weep* is *bakah* whose sound imitates falling drops. It has several significations.

It signifies falling as of tear drops: in one case after public calamities—Num. 11:10; in another in mourning for the dead. A nation in sin or in straits may cause the falling of many of these drops and that from the eyes of God's children.

It signifies the sorrow as of a penitent—Ezra 10:1. This sorrow may sweep the heart of an individual for his own sins or the sins of another or the sins of a nation.

It signifies weeping in some one's embrace—Gen. 45:15. There usually is rejoicing in heaven and in earth when God's word is born forth to accomplish God's purpose.

תכן

WEIGH: "Talk no more so exceedinging proudly . . . for the Lord is a God of knowledge, and by him actions are weighed", (I Sam. 2:3). *Takan,* the Hebrew root for *weigh,* has heavy meanings.

It means to examine—Prov. 21:2. The Lord ponders the heart thus making a full examination into it as if to prove it.

It means to be equal—Ezek. 18:29. When God weighs something or someone He seems to do an evening up with a true and established measure. His norm is Truth as it is in Christ and Christ Himself. He who does not measure up to this Truth is a liar and he who does not measure up to Christ is short of the glory of God.

It means to try or to prove—Isa. 40:13. Who can direct the Holy Spirit or who can be His counsellor and teach Him?

It means to tell—II Kings 12:10. They "told the money that was found in the house of the Lord" which deed likely was marked with accuracy.

It means a task—Exod. 5:19. Their work was measured or weighed out unto them so that this became their task.

It means perfection of beauty—Ezek. 28:12. When things measure out even, are arranged precisely and balance perfectly, there is a beauty of symmetry. How beautiful are those that walk uprightly; serve man unselfishly and love God devotedly.

לחש

WHISPER: "But when David saw that his servants whispered, David perceived that the child was dead", (II Sam. 12:19). The use of *lachash,* the root for *whisper,* in this passage is very simple and obvious. But, in Isa. 26:16 (where it is translated *prayer*), there is much more depth and color.

It means an ornament. Prayer is a gorgeous gem easily discovered on those who wear it.

It means an inscribed plate of gold. When afflictions bow one down he is not to scream complaints but pour out whispers of willingness to the One who gives permission to those afflictions to come.

It means magic. Prayer does work like magic. It is a miraculous

271

mystery how an unseen God performs impossibilities before our eyes.

It means charm. Prayer is an infinitely more important charm than a rabbit's foot, or a figurine.

This exciting root also means incantation. I walked this evening along a beach and saw the moon pour a silver trail toward me. The Prayer I prayed seemed to be an enchanting and tuneful song in which God seemed to whisper acceptance.

לבן

WHITE: " . . . Though your sins be as scarlet, they shall be as white as snow . . .", (Isa. 1:18). *Laban,* the Hebrew root for *white* is variously used.

It is used to mean cleanse or purify—Ps. 51:7. The singer of Israel was born a sinner—Ps. 51:5. When he became aware of it he pleaded with God to make him white.

It was used poetically to signify the moon and the sun—Isa. 24:23. The moon and sun with their whiteness shall be darkened into confusion when the Lord reigns gloriously.

It is used to describe trees with whitish leaves, like the poplars in Hos. 4:13.

It is used to describe the clearness of the sapphire clearness of the pavement under God's feet—Exod. 24:10.

It means frankincense for its white color which marks it as being very pure—Lev. 2:1.

It is used to describe the two lofty parallel ridges of Lebanon which are topped with eternal snows.

It is used to give name to a son of Gershon—Num. 3:18, because he was white.

זנה

WHOREDOM: "The land hath committed great whoredom, departing from the Lord", (Hos. 1:2). *Zanah* the Hebrew word for *whoredom* has several meanings.

It means to play the harlot—Gen. 38:24. Loathesome is a paramour and in the end he may be burnt.

It means to commit idolatry—Lev. 20:5. When man leaves God, God may leave him. Even a nation, like Tyre, may commit fornication with other nations—Isa. 23:17.

It means to seduce, to cause to commit fornication—Exod. 34:16. Seduction that breaks up the conjugal union is one of society's top crimes but what sort of crime it must be when a man leads another to leave God and go after pleasure, business, family or some other god. A man may not perform an overt act to cause in another man a breach of fidelity towards God but he is as seditious as he who excites a rebellion against constituted authority if he lures a man away from God, from worshiping God, from serving God in church or out of it.

רע

WICKED: "But the men of Sodom were wicked and sinners before the Lord exceedingly", (Gen. 13:13). In this verse the Hebrew word for *wicked* is *ra* which means to make a noise and sound off with loud crying while doing evil. For more on it turn back to *Evil.*

עול

WICKED: ". . . As a man falleth before wicked men, so fellest thou", (II Sam. 3:34). In this verse the Hebrew word for *wicked* is *aval* which means to turn away, to distort and to be wrong. For more on the Hebrew root turn back to *Iniquity.*

עמל

WICKED: ". . . Every hand of the wicked shall come upon him", (Job 20:22). In this verse the Hebrew word for *wicked* is *amel* which means to labor at being troublesome, to be wretched and miserable. For more on this Hebrew root turn back to *Iniquity.*

הוה

WICKED: "Wickedness is in the midst thereof . . .", (Ps. 55:11). In this verse the Hebrew word for *wicked* is *havvah* which means to strive until breathless and rush headlong into ruin. For more on this root turn back to *Calamity.*

Thus we see wickedness is tragic and terrible; intensive and extensive and a sizable catalogue of Hebrew words—with many

273

and varied significations—was employed to tell of it.

רֹשַׁע

WICKED: "I will early destroy all the wicked of the land: that I may cut off all wicked doers from the city of the Lord", (Ps. 101:8). The word *wicked* appears twice in this verse but each derives from a different Hebrew word. The first comes from *rasha* which means to make a noise, cause a disturbance and at the same time be ungodly and impious. For more of its significations turn back to *Iniquity*.

The second comes from *aven* which has interesting denotements.

It denotes nothingness or non-existence. This is quite a different appraisal of the wicked.

It denotes having a negative power which can be expressed by privatives such as, *non, no, not, un, in*. The appraisal is lessening.

It denotes being empty and fruitless. This wicked company produces nothing, weighs nothing and amounts to nothing. They depreciate the ground they occupy.

עֶצֶב

WICKED: "And see if there be any wicked way in me, and lead me into the way everlasting", (Ps. 139:24). In this verse the Hebrew word for *wicked* is *etseb*. For its meaning turn back to *Idol*.

זִמָּה

WICKED: "The instruments of the churl are evil: he deviseth wicked devices to destroy the poor with lying words . . .", (Isa. 32:7). In this verse the Hebrew word for wicked is *zamah* which means mischief or crime devised in the mind and carried out in deed.

אָנַשׁ

WICKED: "The heart is deceitful above all things, and desperately wicked", (Jer. 17:9). In this verse the Hebrew word for *wicked* is *anash* which means to be sick incurably and ill at ease with a malignant disposition.

274

רָצוֹן

WILL: "I delight to do thy will, O my God . . .", (Ps. 40:8). *Ratson* is the Hebrew word for *will*. It means delight, satisfaction and acceptance. The psalmist wanted to give Him delight; satisfy Him; do that acceptable to Him. For more on this Hebrew word turn back to *Pleasure.*

אָבָה

WILLING: "If ye be willing and obedient ye shall eat the good of the land", (Isa. 1:19). *Abah* is the Hebrew for willing and it has several meanings.

It means to consent—Prov. 1:10. If sinners entice, one is not to consent but if God ordains, one is to bow willingly.

It means to desire. One is to breathe after the Lord, desiring always to please Him.

It means to be disposed, as in the text. The Lord changes the heart so that it is inclined to do His will.

It means poverty or want—Prov. 23:29. The starving one is hungering and thirsting after righteousness. He exclaims in pain until the Lord moves into the vacuum of misery.

It means a bulrush—Isa. 18:2. This notion seems to grow out of the fact that a bulrush bows its head in the wind—Isa. 58:5. This is what God wants of His child whether in the whirlwind of troubles or in the gentle breeze of the Spirit's leading.

נָדַב

WILLINGLY: "And now have I seen with joy thy people, which are present here, to offer willingly unto thee", (I Chron. 29:17). This passage, verses 9-17, is a masterpiece on giving to the Lord. *Nadabh,* the Hebrew root for *willingly,* has exciting significations.

It means to impel or to incite—Exod. 25:2, 35:21. The heart is to be moved to give willingly. Two forces may move the heart: God's Spirit and man's love.

It means to volunteer—II Chron. 17:16. Seeing the need, the willing soul volunteers to give before the appeal is made because he senses the need the same as the one making the appeal. He gives the tithe before God collects it.

275

It means to give spontaneously—Ezra 2:68. Some who came to the house of the Lord in Jerusalem, offered freely for the house of God to set it up.

It means abundance—Ps. 68:9. God sent a plentiful rain. If His people would give plentifully with joy there would be rejoicing over plenty.

This root is used to build a name: Nadabiah which means Jehovah is liberal—I Chron. 3:18. How blessed to be able to put *nadab* in front of one's name.

In the Oriental mind nobility is closely connected with liberality in giving—Isa. 32:8. Also this root is used to indicate a happy state of excellency or welfare—Job 30:15. Generosity signifies magnanimity.

ארב

WINDOWS: "And prove me now herewith, saith the Lord of hosts, if I will not open you the windows of heaven . . .", (Mal. 3:10). This word *windows* is always in the plural except in Hos. 13.3. The Hebrew for it is *arubbah* which has several meanings.

It means a window closed by a lattice and not by glass—Eccl. 12:3. Somehow one would feel he is not quite as shut out by a lattice as by a glass; or, the lattice affords a warmer and more intimate relationship.

It means a dove house as shut in with lattice work—Isa. 60:8.

It means a chimney—Hos. 13:3. One might think of God as being a peerless patron that pours out benefits upon us all.

It means sluices, flood-gates—Gen. 7:11. This seems to be the primary idea in the word. God pours out His blessings upon those that so love Him and so love His program for redeeming the world that they tithe—which amount, if given by all Christians, would open the gates of our churches, sending out missionaries with the Gospel to the uttermost parts of the earth.

The other Hebrew word for window is *challon* and usually is in the singular and means an opening in a house—Josh. 2:15, 18, 21.

חכם

WISDOM: " . . . And in the hearts of all that are wise hearted

I have put wisdom, that they make all that I have commanded thee", (Exod. 31:6). Here, *chakam* is the Hebrew word for *wisdom*. It is used over 300 times in other passages in the Old Testament which may be indicative of the importance of wisdom in God's work. For the several rich denotements of this Hebrew root turn to *Wise*.

שׂכל

WISDOM: "Only the Lord give thee wisdom . . .", (I Chron. 22:12). In this passage, the Hebrew word for *wisdom* is *sakal*— a very dramatic word. It means to look at self, circumstances and others thoroughly in order to prudent behavior which is a most vital step to success and prosperity—Josh. 1:7, 8. This root is also used to signify a *song* —Ps. 47:7. For more on it turn back to *Instruct*.

טעם

WISDOM: "O taste and see that the Lord is good . . .", (Ps. 34:8). The Hebrew word for *taste* is *team* which is translated *wisdom* in Dan. 2:14. The connection is very interesting. *Team* means to taste in order to discover flavor, palatability and delectation. The tasting may be done with the mind or soul.

בנה

WISDOM: "To him that by wisdom made the heavens . . .", (Ps. 136:5). In this passage, the Hebrew word for *wisdom* is *banah* which means to erect. God's servants possess the highest wisdom when they build for him. One derivative of *banah* means to build a family as the family of the Lord.

לב

WISDOM: "He that getteth wisdom loveth his own soul", (Prov. 19:8). Another Hebrew word for *wisdom* is *leb* which means *heart, hollow* and *mind*. It becomes more evident that God means for his children to possess *wisdom* that has heart, mind, soul and warmth in it.

חכם

WISE: "Surely this great nation is a wise and understanding people", (Deut. 4:6). *Chakem,* the Hebrew word for *wise,* has several denotements.

It denotes decision and judgment. These two are basic in bringing and keeping a nation in front.

It denotes cunningness which is used to outwit and outdistance.

It denotes skill as in arts—Isa. 3:3.

It denotes the capacity to be a magician—Exod. 7:11.

It denotes sensibleness, such as possessed by those endued with reason.

It denotes dexterity, especially in connection with work in God's house—Exod. 36:1,2. "The wicked shall be turned into hell, and all nations that forget God"—Ps. 9:17.

It has derivatives that denote wisdom of the angels—II Sam. 14:20; wisdom of leaders—Deut. 34:9. A nation cannot long be great apart from God.

פלא

WONDER: "And Joshua said unto the people, Sanctify yourselves; for tomorrow the Lord will do wonders among you", (Josh. 3:5). *Pala* the Hebrew word for wonder in this passage, means to separate or to distinguish. God's people have always been a wonder to the world because of separation from it and because of being distinguished by peculiarities. This Hebrew root means also to be great. When God's own come out and are separated unto him, *he* will do the wonders and make them great. For more on this word turn back to *Marvelous.*

יפה

WONDER: "And I will shew wonders in the heavens and in the earth . . .", (Joel 2:30). *Yapha,* the Hebrew word for *wonder,* means to be bright and shine forth in beauty. For more on this root turn back to *Beautiful.*

פלא

WONDERFUL: "For unto us a child is born, unto us a son is given: and the government shall be upon his shoulder: and his name shall be called Wonderful . . .", (Isa. 9:6). *Pala,* the Hebrew root for *Wonderful* has wonderful meanings.

It means to be "wonderful great"—II Chron. 2:9. Solomon announced that the temple he was about to build would be so but Jesus' body, which He Himself called a house, was a much greater blessing to many more people.

It means to show great kindness—Ps. 31:21. Was ever one so kind as the One to wear this name: Wonderful.

It means wonderful counsel—Isa. 28:29. Is not the Lord's counsel above the counsel of all others as the sun is above the candle in brightness?

It means strong for or against any one—Job. 10:16. When the Lord is for us who can be against us but equally true is it that when the Lord is against one who can save him.

It means supernatural—Judg. 13:19. His conception was from heaven; His ministry was to prepare souls for heaven; and when that was done He returned to heaven. There was so much about Him and His work that was supernatural we shall always remember Him as the Wonderful Wonder.

אָמַר

WORD: "My son, if thou wilt receive my words . . .", (Prov. 2:1). *Amar,* the Hebrew word for *word* has rich significations.

It signifies that which has been brought into the light and this God wants his children to receive.

It signifies thinking purposefully. God wants His own to walk with him and discover what he shall reveal out of his heart.

It signifies commanding. God's word is the first and final fiat.

These commands form a song for victory—Ps. 68:11, and a promise—Ps. 77:8.

For more on this root turn back to *Command.*

מַלְאָךְ

WORK: "And on the seventh day God . . . rested . . . from all his work . . .", (Gen. 2:2). In this passage *Melak* is the Hebrew word for *work.* It means to wait upon and to minister. When God creates He also ministers to that which He has created and since no time limit is put on the services rendered it means for the lifetime of that created.

יד

WORK: "And Israel saw that great work which the Lord did . . .", (Exod. 14:31). *Yad,* a Hebrew word for work, means power as shown by the hand. What wonders have been wrought by the hand of God. How safe is His child in His hand. For more on this root turn back to *Hand.*

שׂוּם, שִׂים

WORK: "How he had wrought His signs in Egypt", (Ps. 78:43). *Work* or *wrought* in this passage derives from *sim* or *sum.* The Lord set up many symbols of His power in Egypt. God's name and power were to be related to all areas and activities. For significations of these roots turn back to *Purpose.*

דָּבַר

WORK: "I will speak of the glorious honor of thy majesty, and of thy wondrous works", (Ps. 145:5). *Dabar,* the Hebrew word for *work,* is, in other passages, translated *word;* showing that with God the word and the deed are much the same matter. For the significations of this root turn back to *Command.*

חוה

WORSHIP: "I and the lad will go yonder and worship . . .", (Gen. 22:5). *Chavah* the Hebrew word for *worship,* means to bow down or to prostrate oneself before anyone to do him honor and reverence. Bowing oneself at church or worshipping in order to be seen of men, or of God for that matter, is not full worship even if done in Jesus Name. The worship must honor God. This calls for praying to get oneself ready to worship and paying all debts of money, gratitude, respect and love to everyone due and more especially to God. One can at once see how a worship service may be long although the sermon may be short.

Also, this word means to humble oneself and to submit. Acceptable worship in God's sight would include the presenting of oneself as a "living sacrifice". One, would need to submit himself, give himself away to the Lord and to be sure to label the act by saying, "Here am I, Lord, send me." Those disobedient to the heavenly vision are hardly ready to worship the God of the heaven from whence cometh the vision.

More than all of this, in order to really worship, neither great

280

demonstrations nor loud noises are necessary. In fact, another facet of this same word tells that one's voice shall be low as if coming out of the dust—Isa. 29:4. So, it appears improbable that one can hurry in late to a worship service and hope to leave soon and in the meantime to have worshipped God acceptably.

This word *Shachah* is used about a hundred times in the Hebrew Old Testament and is the only one to describe the act of worshipping Jehovah. Daniel uses a word a few times which is translated *worship* but in connection with idols only. In II Kings 10 a word is used five times which is translated *worship* but not in connection with the worship of Jehovah.

חיל

WORTHY: "If he will shew himself a worthy man, there shall not an hair of him fall to the earth: but if wickedness shall be found in him, he shall die", (I Kings 1:52).

Chayil, the Hebrew root for *worthy,* signifies strength and worthiness because of a man's valour not his horses or his chariots—Ps. 33:16. This strength lies also in man's capacity for leadership in some worthy expedition or campaign. An honest man is worthy, says the Hebrew of this word. A man of integrity, virtue and good quality is a worthy man according to the meaning of this great word. It is used to describe Ruth as being virtuous—Ruth 3:16. Other uses of this word in the Bible indicate that a nation is in line for a blessing from God when its men are worthy. They form the best army. They make the best entrenchment. They are the safest fortification. For another view of this word see *Able.*

כאב

WOUND: "For he maketh sore, and bindeth up; he woundeth and his hands maketh whole", (Job 5:8). Suffering is the inexplicable blow God deals man and healing the unfathomable mercy. Whom He loves, He chastens. *Kaab,* the Hebrew for *wound* in this verse, has other meanings.

It means to mar—II Kings 3:19. A field may suffer from stones thrown and so can man be pained.

It means to gossip—Ezek. 13:22. God may permit His child to be wounded by lies, but the very wounds may be constant reminders to walk blamelessly.

281

It means a grieving thorn—Ezek. 28:24. This pricking may humble and lead one to know God more fully.

חלל

WOUND: "But He was wounded for our transgressions", (Isa. 53:5). No estimate can yet be made of the sufferings of Christ on the cross but *Chalal,* the Hebrew root for wounded, has several significations that help describe the ordeal.

It means to bore through. The twisting spear went into His side, through His heart, on out through His hands and His feet into the far reaches of His impassioned soul.

It means to loose as a covenant—Ps. 89:34. Christ's wounds hurt like broken promises hurt a conscientious person.

It means to profane or to defile—Lev. 19:8. He who profanes anything holy will suffer intolerably. These may be profaned: sanctuary—Lev. 21:9; the Sabbath—Exod. 31:14; God's name—Mal. 1:11,12.

It means to prostitute or to make common—Lev. 19:29. The iniquitous court convened covertly by Pilate and Associates set out to make a common criminal of the Uncommon Friend of man.

חלה

WOUND: "But he (was) wounded for our transgressions", (Isa. 53:5). Be prepared for a feast spiritual. *Chala,* the Hebrew root for *wound,* has many facets and each reflects a different posture of the Suffering Servant. It means for one to be rubbed and worn down until he is polished. No wonder we think of His face as having shone. It means to be diseased from a hurt, which disease causes pain and this pain becomes a metaphor of concern, anxiety and grief—I Sam. 22:8. In another place this word is employed to tell of one who strove to please the King. How Jesus worked at pleasing His Father. Also it means to be made weak. Right are the singers who tell: "I am weak, but Thou art Strong" and we are right too if we sing: "He was made weak that we might be strong". That is, sin made Him weak instead of us who are in Him who "cannot sin". There is another and an exciting use of this word—II Sam. 6:19. Here it is translated *cake* and in Leviticus it means a cake offered for sacrifice. Jesus was so offered and became not only the "Bread of life" but also a "Cake of Bread." Little children like cake better than bread. John endearingly calls us "little children" so why cannot we feast on this "Cake" of heaven? For more on this word see *Grief.*

אף

WRATH: "The wrath of the Lord was kindled against the people, and the Lord smote the people with a very great plague", (Num. 11:33). This Hebrew word *aph* means the member with which one breathes, hence: nose. In Job 4:9, it is used to signify the consuming blast from the nostrils of God. Could the artists who have sketched the blasting and snorting North wind draw for us a semblance of what it might be when a Mighty God becomes angry at sinning man or sinning nations?

Another Hebrew word translated *Wrath* is *chemah,* and means Sun, Heat, and Wrath. First we note the poetical use of it in Job 30:28 to denote the sun. Next in Gen. 27:44, *Chemah* means fury, heat, anger. In this passage one is to fear the fury of his brother. How much more should that person fear, or group of persons fear who have excited the wrath of Almighty God. Further this Hebrew word signifies *Poison*—Deut. 32:24. The context describes the terribleness of the Lord towards the people that have caused Him to abhor them. In another Scripture—I Chron. 4:26, this word is used to name a son and means the "Wrath of God". Let us hope, pray and so live that this name shall never be put as a label on us or on ours. *Kaas* is another Hebrew word translated *Wrath* and means *Sadness* in addition to other things. Wrath is cruel and causes much weeping. How many suffer losses and shed tears because their sins excited the wrath of God? Habakkuk prayed "I Lord . . . in wrath remember mercy." The Hebrew word for wrath here is *Rogez* and signifies trembling and trouble. It is used also to describe one as being thrown into commotion. All of this and more besides can God cause to come to pass. How very careful ought we to be to sin not and always please God in all things. No wonder that men tremble, suffer tensions and sadly sail their little skiffs upon the rocks. They have fallen short of the glory of God and have not the righteousness of God as it is in Christ Jesus. For more on *Rogez* see *Tremble.* For more on *Kaas* see *Provoke.* Wrath, wrath, is a big word with many shades of meaning. We must flee the wrath of God and flee to Him whom we have offended, beg His forgiveness, and take our punishment.

Index of English words whose significations are unfolded in HEBREW HONEY.

Index to Scripture Texts wherein are found all of the words exegeted in HEBREW HONEY.

(First is chapter and verse, then the word)

GENESIS

EXODUS

LEVITICUS

4:13 . . . . Sin	19:30 . . . . Reverence
10:3 . . . . Sanctify	23:3 . . . . Convocation
16:2 . . . . Mercy Seat	24:11, 16 . . . . Blaspheme
19:11 . . . . Lie	24:17 . . . . Kill
19:15 . . . . Neighbour	

NUMBERS

1:52 . . . . Standard	14:44 . . . . Presume
4:23 . . . . Service	15:25 . . . . Sacrifice
5:5, 6 . . . . Guilty	15:28 . . . . Sin
5:8 . . . . Atonement	15:28 . . . . Ignorance
7:9 . . . . Shoulder	16:3,4 . . . . Congregation
7:84 . . . . Bowl	21:16 . . . . Gather
8:9 . . . . Assembly	23:10 . . . . Righteous
11:4 . . . . Lust	27:20 . . . . Obedient
11:16 . . . . Stand	27:23 . . . . Command
11:33 . . . . Wrath	30:2 . . . . Vow
13:30 . . . . Overcome	32:11, 12 . . . . Follow
14:18 . . . . Mercy	32:16 . . . . Fold
14:22 . . . . Miracle	

DEUTERONOMY

1:5 . . . . Declare	20:1 . . . . Bring
3:24 . . . . Might	26:18, 19 . . . . Honour
4:6 . . . . Wise	28:11 . . . . Goods
4:23 . . . . Forbid	30:9 . . . . Plenteous
4:26 . . . . Perish	31:7, 8 . . . . Go
5:16 . . . . Bondage	32:2, 3 . . . . Doctrine
6:12 . . . . Bondage	32:3 . . . . Publish
8:14 . . . . Bondage	32:6 . . . . Buy
8:15 . . . . Lead	32:9 . . . . Portion
11:16 . . . . Deceive	32:29 . . . . Consider
11:18 . . . . Lay Up	32:38 . . . . Protection
12:11 . . . . Vow	33:1 . . . . Man
13:5 . . . . Bondage	33:2, 3 . . . . Saint
14:23 . . . . Learn	33:27 . . . . Eternal

JOSHUA

1:5 . . . . Forsake	10:10 . . . . Discomfit
1:6, 9, 18 . . . . Courage	13:33 . . . . Inherit
1:9 . . . . Dismay	23:10 . . . . Chase
3:5 . . . . Wonder	24:15 . . . . Choose
7:25 . . . . Trouble	24:15 . . . . Serve

JUDGES

2:3 . . . . Weigh	14:19 . . . . Expound
3:20 . . . . Message	16:12 . . . . Thread
5:26 . . . . Hammer	16:16 . . . . Strength
6:6 . . . . Impoverish	19:9 . . . . Tarry
7:3 . . . . Return	19:17, 18 . . . . Wayfarer
13:6 . . . . Countenance	20:16 . . . . Miss

RUTH

1:8 . . . . Kindly	3:12 . . . . Kinsman

I SAMUEL

2:3 . . . . Weigh	19:20 . . . . Prophesy
2:8 . . . . Raise	21:13 . . . . Mad
2:29 . . . . Kick	25:29 . . . . Bound
3:1 . . . . Precious	25:30 . . . . Appoint
7:12 . . . . Ebenezer	28:21 . . . . Trouble
15:23 . . . . Reject	30:6 . . . . Encourage
17:26, 36 . . . . Army	

II SAMUEL

3:34 . . . . Wicked	19:34 . . . . Live
7:24 . . . . Confirm	20:6 . . . . Harm
7:27 . . . . House	22:21 . . . . Reward
12:19 . . . . Whisper	

I KINGS

1:52 . . . . Worthy	8:57 . . . . Leave
3:3, 4 . . . . High Place	13:21 . . . . Disobey
3:7 . . . . Little	15:30 . . . . Provoke
3:9 . . . . Discern	17:18 . . . . Sin
6:7 . . . . Axe	18:37 . . . . Hear
7:51 . . . . Dedicate	19:19 . . . . Mantle
8:56 . . . . Rest	21:28, 29 . . . . Humble
8:57 . . . . Forsake	

II KINGS

17:27	Manner	24:15	Mighty
23:16	Proclaim	25:28	Kindly

I CHRONICLES

4:10	Grant	28:29	Give
22:12	Wisdom	29:11	Power
28:9	Search	29:17	Willingly

II CHRONICLES

6:13	Kneel	24:6, 16	Chief
6:26	Confess	25:19	Home
7:14	Pray	28:13	Offend
11:17	Kingdom	30:18	Pardon
15:14	Swear	32:23	Gift
19:7	Fear	33:19	Entreat

EZRA

2:62	Register	8:23	Beseech
7:28	Hand	10:11	Separate

NEHEMIAH

2:9	Letter	5:16	Continue
4:6	Mind	9:21	Lack
4:21	Labour	13:26	Beloved

ESTHER

2:17	Crown	10:2	Declaration
3:8	Disperse		

JOB

1:1	Perfect	22:23, 24	Gold
1:1	Eschew	26:14	Thunder
1:6	Satan	27:5	Integrity
2:3	Perfect	32:8	Inspiration
4:7	Innocent	33:9	Innocent
5:2	Envy	33:23	Interpreter
5:8	Wound	33:24	Ransom
5:17	Correct	34:32	Iniquity
7:6	Weaver	35:13	Vanity
11:12	Vain	36:7	Establish
15:11	Consolations	36:22	Exalt
16:12	Shake	37:14	Harken
20:22	Wicked	42:9	Accepted
21:15	Profit		

PSALMS

48:9	Think	85:6	Revive
49:15	Redeem	86:11	Unite
50:23	Conversation	86:9, 12	Glorify
51:5	Sin	86:17	Comfort
51:7	Purge	91:11	Angel
51:10	Clean	92:5	Deep
51:12, 13	Free	92:13	Flourish
55:11	Wicked	94:12	Chasten
56:8	Wander	95:6	Come
58:11	Reward	95:8	Harden
59:10	Prevent	96:3	Declare
61:2, 3	Rock	96:7, 8	Give
61:3	Shelter	96:8	Bring
65:13	Shout	99:1	Tremble
66:13, 15	Offer	99:9	Hill
66:18	Regard	100:4	Thanksgiving
68:7	March	101:8	Wicked
68:9	Weary	102:7	Alone
68:11	Publish	103:12	Remove
68:34	Excellency	103:21	Pleasure
69:5	Hide	104:2	Cover
71:1	Confusion	104:13	Watereth
71:5	Hope	105:24	Strong
73:16, 17	Sanctuary	105:43	Chosen
73:23	Hold	106:48	Amen
75:10	Cut Off	108:2	Awake
76:11	Pay	109:16	Break
77:3	Troubled	111:4	Compassion
77:14, 18	Lightning	115:3, 4	Idol
78:38	Forgive	116:3	Sorrow
78:43	Work	116:10, 11	Liar
79:9	Name	116:15	Saint
79:9	Purge	118:23	Marvelous
80:1	Lead	119:32	Run
80:12	Pluck	119:63	Companion
80:18	Quicken	119:81	Fainteth
81:4	Law	119:112	Incline
81:16	Honey	119:176	Seek
84:2	Cry	125:5	Crooked
84:9	Behold	126:6	Weep

PSALMS — (Continued)

127:1	Labour	145:5	Work
127:3	Heritage	147:3	Bind
136:5	Wisdom	147:2, 3	Break
139:24	Wicked	149:3	Dance
142:6	Attend		

PROVERBS

2:1	Word	17:5	Mock
3:3	Tablet	17:22	Merry
5:21	Ponder	18:24	Friend
10:7	Memory	19:8	Wisdom
10:24	Granted	19:13	Calamity
11:8	Deliver	21:16	Wander
12:22	Lying	22:8	Vanity
14:28	Honour	23:4	Labour
14:34	Reproach	28:13	Sin
15:15	Merry	29:1	Harden
15:16	Fear	29:2	Authority
15:29	Far	29:22	Man
16:20	Happy		

ECCLESIASTES

1:2	Vanity	3:18	Manifest
2:5	Garden	7:26	Escape
2:24	Enjoy	11:1	Cast
3:16	Iniquity	12:1	Remember

SONG OF SOLOMON

1:16	Beloved	4:16	Blow
2:4	Love	6:4	Beautiful
2:16	Beloved	7:6	Pleasure
4:7	Fair	8:7	Quench

ISAIAH

1:10	Hear	9:6	Wonderful
1:18	White	9:6	Counsellor
1:19	Willing	9:6	Government
2:3	Law	9:6	Prince
5:1	Vineyard	9:7	Increase
6:1-3	Seraphims	10:26	Scourge
7:14	Virgin	11:1	Branch
8:16	Disciple	12:2	God

12:2 . . . . Salvation	44:6 . . . . King
13:11 . . . . Iniquity	44:22 . . . . Redeem
14:1 . . . . Join	45:20 . . . . Near
21:4 . . . . Affrighted	45:22 . . . . Look
21:11 . . . . Night	45:23 . . . . Bow
22:14 . . . . Reveal	48:17 . . . . Profit
24:1 . . . . Empty	48:21 . . . . Cleave
26:3 . . . . Peace	49:1 . . . . Listen
28:7 . . . . Err	49:3 . . . . Israel
28:16 . . . . Foundation	49:18 . . . . Bind
28:29 . . . . Counsel	49:26 . . . . Saviour
29:6 . . . . Storm	51:3 . . . . Eden
29:11 . . . . Learn	51:11 . . . . Obtain
30:2 . . . . Ask	52:1 . . . . City
30:10 . . . . Smooth	52:7 . . . . Tidings
30:12 . . . . Perverseness	52:7 . . . . Beautiful
30:15 . . . . Quiet	52:13 . . . . Exalted
30:15 . . . . Confidence	53:4 . . . . Smite
31:5 . . . . Defend	53:4 . . . . Grief
31:6 . . . . Revolt	53:4, 12 . . . . Bear
32:6 . . . . Hypocrisy	53:5 . . . . Wound
32:7 . . . . Wicked	53:5 . . . . Heal
33:22 . . . . Judge	53:7 . . . . Dumb
35:4 . . . . Recompense	53:10 . . . . Pleasure
35:8, 9 . . . . Highway	53:10 . . . . Sin
36:8 . . . . Pledge	54:2 . . . . Enlarge
38:14 . . . . Oppress	54:2 . . . . Spare
38:17 . . . . Love	54:5 . . . . Husband
40:6 . . . . Goodliness	54:7 . . . . Gather
40:14 . . . . Instruct	55:6 . . . . Seek
40:17 . . . . Vanity	55:6 . . . . Found
40:25 . . . . Equal	55:11 . . . . Accomplish
40:31 . . . . Wait	57:15 . . . . Inhabit
40:31 . . . . Renew	58:11 . . . . Guide
42:1 . . . . Elect	58:13 . . . . Delight
42:4 . . . . Judgment	59:1 . . . . Shortened
42:4 . . . . Fail	60:1 . . . . Arise
42:16 . . . . Crooked	60:1 . . . . Shine
43:24 . . . . Father	60:1 . . . . Light
44:4 . . . . Water courses	61:1 . . . . Anoint

296

ISAIAH (Continued)

61:1	Preach	63:10	Rebel
61:1	Liberty	64:1	Rend
61:6	Priest	65:7	Measure
61:10	Clothe	65:20	Accursed
62:5	Marry	66:1, 2a	Heaven
63:9	Pity	66:2	Tremble

JEREMIAH

1:5	Ordain	16:17	Hide
2:9	Plead	17:7	Hope
3:12, 22	Return	17:9	Wicked
3:15	Pastor	17:9, 10	Search
3:15	Feed	23:8	Lead
3:22	Backsliding	26:17	People
4:22, 23	Evil	27:18	Intercession
6:8	Depart	30:17	Outcast
7:3	Amend	31:12	Sorrow
11:17	Plant	32:42	Promise
12:17	Destroy	33:3	Call
14:15	Give	33:4, 6	Cure
15:9	Ghost	50:5	Join
15:16	Eat		

LAMENTATIONS

3:26	Quietly	3:55, 56	Hide
3:39	Punish		

EZEKIEL

4:16	Staff	27:31	Wail
11:5	Fall	33:7	Warn
11:19	Heart	34:5	Scatter
14:10	Punishment	34:16	Lost
18:4, 20	Die	36:19	Scatter
18:31	Heart	36:26	New
21:2	Drop	39:23	Trespass
21:26	Low	44:4, 5	Going

DANIEL

1:8	Purpose	6:24	Accuse
1:15	Fair	7:14	Dominion
3:4, 5	Herald	9:25	Messiah
5:11	Man	11:38	God
5:26	Number		

HOSEA

1:2	Whoredom	11:7	High
4:16	Backslide	13:14	Grave
5:7	Deceit	13:14	Ransom
9:7	Mad	13:15	Waste
10:12	Rain	14:1	Fall

1:2 . . . . Whoredom   11:7 . . . . High
4:16 . . . . Backslide   13:14 . . . . Grave
5:7 . . . . Deceit   13:14 . . . . Ransom
9:7 . . . . Mad   13:15 . . . . Waste
10:12 . . . . Rain   14:1 . . . . Fall

JOEL

2:7 . . . . March   2:28 . . . . Vision
2:17 . . . . Minister   2:30 . . . . Wonder
2:27 . . . . Ashamed   3:20 . . . . Generation
2:28 . . . . Dream

AMOS

3:7 . . . . Secret   9:6 . . . . Troop
4:12 . . . . Prepare

OBADIAH

18 . . . . Kindle

MICAH

3:7 . . . . Answer   6:8 . . . . Justly

HABAKKUK

1:13 . . . . Iniquity   3:2 . . . . Mercy
2:4 . . . . Faith   3:18 . . . . Rejoice
2:4 . . . . Just

ZEPHANIA

1:7 . . . . Sacrifice   3:17 . . . . Love
3:16 . . . . Slack   3:18 . . . . Sorrowful

HAGGAI

2:7 . . . . Desire

ZECHARIAH

3:2 . . . . Brand   10:4 . . . . Nail
3:2 . . . . Rebuke   10:9 . . . . Sow
3:18 . . . . Sorrowful   11:6 . . . . Smite
4:6 . . . . Spirit   12:6 . . . . Torch

MALACHI

Index of Hebrew roots whose significations are unfolded in
HEBREW HONEY.

א—Aleph—'

אב—Father
אבד—Destroy
אבד—Lost
אבד—Perish
אבה—Willing
אבן—Ebenezer
אבר—Abram
אגדה—Troop
אגר—Letter
אדון—Lord
אדם—Man
אדר—Excellent
אדר—Mantle
אהב—Beloved
אהב—Love
אהב—Friend
אוד—Brand
אוה—Lust
אויל—Mighty
און—Vanity

אור—Shine
אור—Light
אות—Miracle
אזן—Hearken
אזר—Gird
אחז—Hold
אחר—Follow
איב—Enemy
איש—Man
אכל—Eat
אל—God
אלוה—God
אלהים—God
אלה—Bring
אלם—Dumb
אמן—Amen
אמן—Believe
אמן—Faith
אמץ—Courage
אמר—Word

אנה—Answer
אנוש—Man
אנש—Wicked
אסף—Gather
אסר—Vow
אף—Wrath
אצל—Reserve
ארב—Windows
ארג—Weaver
ארה—Pluck
ארר—Curse
ארח—Wayfarer
אש—Fire
אשה—Sacrifice
אשם—Guilty
אשם—Offend
אשם—Sin
אשר—Happy
אשר—Blessed

ב—Beth—b

באר—Declare
באן—Stink
בגד—Deceit
בדד—Alone
בדל—Separate
בהל—Trouble
בוא—Enter
בוא—Come
בוא—Grant
בוא—Lead
בור—Pit
בוש—Ashamed
בוש—Confound
בוש—Confusion
בחן—Examine
בחיר—Elect
בחר—Choose

בטח—Hope
בטח—Confidence
בין—Consider
בין—Instruct
בין—Discern
בין—Regard
בית—Home
בית—House
בכה—Weep
בלע—Swallow
במה—High Place
בנה—Wisdom
בעט—Kick
בעל—Husband
בעל—Man
בעל—Marry
בער—Burn

בעת—Afrighted
בצר—Gold
בקע—Cleave
בקק—Empty
בקר—Enquire
בקש—Beseech
בקש—Seek
ברא—Create
ברית—Covenant
ברך—Kneel
ברך—Bless
ברק—Lightning
ברר—Manifest
בשר—Tidings
בשר—Preach
בשר—Publish

300

ג—Gimel—g

גאה—Excellency
גאל—Kinsman
גאל—Redeem
גבורה—Might
גבה—Exalted
גבר—Power
גבר—Man
גבר—Prevail
גדל—Magnify

גרע—Cut Off
גדר—Fold
גור—Abide
גיל—Glad
גיל—Joy
גיל—Rejoice
גלה—Reveal
גלל—Commit

גמל—Recompense
גמל—Reward
גנב—Steal
גנן—Defend
גער—Rebuke
גרז—Axe
גרף—Restrain
גרש—Drive

ד—Daleth—d

דאב—Sorrow
דבק—Cleave
דבר—Command
דבר—Work
דבר—Promise
דבר—Message
דבש—Honey
דגל—Standard

דוד—Beloved
דום—Quietly
דור—Generation
דין—Judge
דכא—Contrite
דלה—Draw
דלל—Impoverish
דלק—Kindle

דמה—Think
דמם—Rest
דרור—Liberty
דרך—Conversation
דרך—Lead
דרש—Search
דרש—Seek

ה—He—h

הבל—Vanity
הגג—Muse
הגה—Meditate
הדר—Honour
הוה—Calamity
הוה—Wicked

היה—Was
הלך—Lead
הלך—Go
הלך—March
הלך—Walk
הלל—Boast

הלל—Mad
הלם—Hammer
המה—Troubled
המם—Discomfit
הר—Hill

ז—Zayin—z

זבח—Sacrifice
זהר—Teach
זהר—Warn
זכר—Memory

זכר—Remember
זמה—Wicked
זמר—Sing
זנה—Whoredom

זקק—Purge
זרה—Scatter
זרע—Sow

ח—Cheth—ch

חבל—Sorrow
חבר—Companion
חבש—Bind
חגג—Feast
חדל—Frail
חדש—New

חוה—Live
חוה—Worship
חוט—Thread
חול—Dance
חזק—Encourage
חזק—Continue

חזה—Vision
חטא—Miss
חטא—Sin
חטא—Punish
חטא—Purge
חיה—Quicken

301

חיה—Revive
חיה—Life
חיל—Able
חיל—Worthy
חי—Live
חכם—Wise
חכם—Wisdom
חלה—Grief
חלה—Wound
חלל—Wound
חלם—Dream
חלף—Renew
חלץ—Deliver
חלק—Portion

חלק—Smooth
חמד—Desire
חמל—Pity
חנה—Encamp
חנן—Grace
חנן—Mercy
חנף—Hypocrisy
חסד—Goodliness
חסד—Kindly
חסד—Saint
חסד—Reproach
חסד—Mercy
חסה—Refuge

חסר—Lack
חפה—Innocent
חפף—Innocent
חפץ—Pleasure
חפץ—Delight
חקה—Statute
חקר—Search
חרב—Waste
חרד—Tremble
חשך—Spare
חשב—Impute
חשק—Love
חתת—Dismay

ט—Tet—t

טהר—Clean
טוב—Merry
טוב—Fair

טוב—Kindly
טוב—Good

טוב—Goods
טעם—Wisdom

י—Yod—y

יכל—Water Courses
יכל—Prevail
יכל—Overcome
ינה—Sorrowful
ינע—Labour
יד—Hand
יד—Work
יד—Consecrate
ידה—Confess
ידה—Thanksgiving
ידע—Know
ידע—Learn
יהב—Give
יהוה—Lord

יחד—Unite
יטב—Amend
יכח—Correct
יסד—Foundation
יסר—Chasten
יעד—Meet
יעל—Profit
יעץ—Counsel
יעץ—Counsellor
יעץ—Guide
יפה—Beautiful
יפה—Fair
יפה—Wonder
יצא—Going
יצב—Stand
יצר—Form

יקע—Depart
יקר—Precious
ירא—Reverance
ירא—Fear
ירד—Descend
ירה—Rain
ירש—Inherit
ישראל—Israel
ישב—Dwell
ישב—Establish
ישן—Sleep
ישע—Salvation
ישע—Saviour
ישר—Righteous
יתד—Nail
יתר—Plenteous

כ—Kaph—k

כאב—Wound
כאה—Break
כאר—Honour
כבד—Glorify
כבד—Honour

כבה—Quench
כבם—Fuller
כהה—Fail
כהן—Priest
כון—Confirm

כון—Prepare
כום—Cup
כף—Bowl
כור—Pierce
כוב—Liar

כחר—Strength
כחד—Hide
כחש—Lie
כלה—Fainteth
כנע—Humble
כסה—Cover
כעם—Provoke
כפר—Atonement

כפר—Mercy Seat
כפר—Purge
כפר—Ransom
כפר—Forgive
כפר—Pardon
כרוז—Herald
כרם—Vineyard

כרע—Bow
כרח—Cut
כשל—Fall
כתב—Register
כתף—Shoulder
כתר—Crown
כתת—Smite

ל—Lamed—l

לאה—Weary
לב—Mind
לב—Wisdom
לבב—Heart
לבן—White
לבש—Clothe
לוה—Join

לוז—Perverseness
לוח—Tablet
לון—Tarry
לוץ—Interpreter
לחם—Fight
לחץ—Oppress
לחש—Whisper

ליל—Night
למד—Disciple
למד—Learn
לעג—Mock
לפיד—Torch
לקח—Doctrine

מ—Mem—m

מאם—Reject
מגן—Shield
מדד—Measure
מחסה—Shelter
מות—Die
מות—Kill
מטה—Staff
מלא—Fulness
מלאך—Angel
מלאך—Work
מלאך—Messenger

מלט—Escape
מלך—King
מלך—Kingdom
מלך—Reign
מנה—Number
מנח—Gift
מעל—Trespass
מערכה—Army
מעקשים—Crooked
מצא—Found
מקל—Staff

מקנא—Jealous
מקרא—Convocation
מקדש—Sanctuary
מראה—Countenance
מרה—Disobey
מרה—Rebel
משיח—Messiah
משפט—Justly
משפט—Law
משפט—Judgment
משח—Anoint

נ—Num—n

נאה—Beautiful
נבא—Prophesy
נבב—Vain
נכה—Smite
נבט—Behold
נבל—Fool
נגר—Expound
נגש—Near
נדב—Willingly
נדיב—Free

נדח—Outcast
נדר—Vow
נהג—Lead
נהל—Lead
נוד—Wander
נוח—Rest
נוח—Lay Up
נחה—Guide
נחה—Lead
נחל—Heritage

נחל—Inherit
נחם—Comfort
נחם—Repent
נחש—Learn
נטה—Incline
נטע—Plant
נטף—Drop
נטש—Forsake
נכה—Kill
נסע—Journey

נעם—Pleasure	נקה—Cleanse	נשׂג—Obtain
נפל—Fall	נקה—Innocent	נשׂא—Beguile
נפשׁ—Ghost	נשׂא—Accepted	נשׂם—Inspiration
נפשׁ—Soul	נשׂא—Bear	נשׁק—Kiss
נצח—Chief	נשׂא—Bring	נתן—Give
נצל—Deliver	נשׂא—Forgive	נתן—Granted
נצר—Branch	נשׂא—Lift	נתן—Ordain
נקב—Blaspheme		

ס—Samech—s

סבב—Compass	סלע—Rock	ספר—Declare
סגל—Jewel	סלה—Selah	ספד—Wail
סוד—Secret	סמך—Sustained	סרה—Revolt
סור—Eschew	סער—Storm	סרר—Backslide
סלל—Highway	ספח—Join	סתר—Protection

ע—Ayin—o

עבד—Bondage	עיר—City	ענה—Hear
עבד—Serve	עכר—Trouble	ענו—Meek
עבר—Hebrew	על—High	עפר—Dust
עדה—Assembly	עלה—Ascend	עצב—Idol
עדן—Eden	עלה—Offer	עצב—Wicked
עול—Wicked	עלז—Rejoice	עצה—Counsel
עול—Iniquity	עלם—Hide	עצם—Strong
עולם—Everlasting	עלם—Virgin	עקלקל—Crooked
עון—Iniquity	עם—People	ערב—Pledge
עון—Punishment	עמל—Iniquity	ערה—Empty
עון—Sin	עמל—Labour	עשה—Accomplish
עור—Awake	עמל—Wicked	עשה—Do
עזז—Strength	עפל—Presume	עשה—Made
עזב—Forsake	עמם—Neighbour	עשה—Labour
עזב—Leave	עמק—Deep	עשק—Oppress
עזר—Help	ענג—Delight	עתר—Entreat
עטה—Cover	ענה—Gentleness	

פ—Pe—p

פגע—Intercession	פחד—Fear	פלם—Ponder
פדה—Ransom	פלא—Marvelous	פנה—Look
פדה—Redeem	פלא—Wonder	פסל—Image
פוח—Blow	פלא—Wonderful	פעם—Bell
פוץ—Scatter	פלט—Deliverer	פקד—Visit
פזר—Disperse	פלל—Pray	פתח—Door

פתח—Open   פרה—Reward   פרש—Declaration
פקה—Open   פרח—Flourish   פשע—Sin
פרד—Garden   פרר—Shake   פתה—Deceive
פרה—Fruit

צ—Tsade—ts

צבא—Service   צור—Rock   צפן—Hide
צדק—Just   צלח—Prosper   צפר—Return
צדק—Righteous   צעד—March   צרר—Enemy
צוה—Appoint   צפה—Watch   צרר—Bound
צוה—Forbid

ק—Qoph—q

קבץ—Gather   קוה—Hope   קרא—Meet
קבר—Grave   קוה—Wait   קרא—Publish
קדם—Eternal   קול—Voice   קרא—Proclaim
קדם—Prevent   קום—Arise   קרא—Call
קדש—Dedicate   קום—Raise   קרן—Horn
קדש—Holy   קטן—Little   קרע—Rend
קדש—Sanctify   קלל—Accursed   קרץ—Accuse
קדש—Hallow   קנא—Envy   קשב—Attend
קדש—Saint   קנה—Buy   קשה—Harden
קהל—Congrega-   קצר—Shortened   קשר—Bind
      tion

ר—Resh—r

ראה—Appear   רוץ—Run   רעה—Shepherd
ראה—See   רוק—Pour   רעה—Pastor
ראה—Enjoy   רחב—Enlarge   רעם—Thunder
ראה—Regard   רחק—Remove   רעע—Harm
ראש—Chief   רחק—Far   רפא—Heal
רבה—Authority   רחם—Compassion   רפא—Cure
רבה—Increase   רחם—Mercy   רפה—Slack
רגז—Tremble   ריב—Plead   רצון—Pleasure
רדף—Chase   רנן—Cry   רצון—Will
רוה—Satisfy   רע—Evil   רצח—Kill
רוה—Spirit   רע—Wicked   רשע—Iniquity
רום—Exalt   רע—Neighbour   רשע—Wicked
רוע—Shout   רעה—Feed

שׂ—Sin—s

שָׂגַב—Exalt	שִׂיחַ—Commune	שָׂמַח—Merry
שׂוּם—Purpose	שִׂים—Work	שַׂר—Prince
שׂוּם—Work	שָׂבַל—Instruct	שָׂרָה—Government
שָׂטָן—Satan	שָׂכַל—Wisdom	שָׂרָף—Seraphims

שׁ—Shin—sh

שְׁאוֹל—Grave	שׁוֹבֵב—Backsliding	שָׁמַע—Hear
שְׁאוֹל—Hell	שָׁוָה—Equal	שָׁמַע—Publish
שָׁאַל—Ask	שׂוּחַ—Meditate	שָׁמַע—Obedient
שָׁבַע—Swear	שׁוֹט—Scourge	שָׁמַע—Listen
שָׁבַר—Break	שָׁחַת—Corrupt	שָׁמַר—Keep
שַׁבָּת—Sabbath	שִׁיר—Sing	שָׁעַן—Staff
שָׁגַג—Ignorance	שִׁית—Foundation	שָׁפַט—Judge
שָׁגַג—Sin	שָׁכַן—Inhabit	שָׁפַט—Manner
שָׁגָה—Err	שָׁלַח—Cast	שָׁפַךְ—Pour
שָׁגָה—Sin	שָׁלַח—Send	שָׁפֵל—Low
שָׁגַע—Mad	שָׁלַט—Dominion	שָׁפַר—Pleasant
שָׁוְא—Vanity	שָׁלַם—Peace	שָׁקָה—Watereth
שׁוּב—Return	שָׁלַם—Pay	שָׁקַט—Quiet
שׁוּב—Restore	שֵׁם—Name	שָׁקַר—Lying
שׁוּב—Convert	שָׁמַי—Heaven	שָׁרַת—Minister

ת—Tav—th

תֹּהוּ—Form	תָּכַן—Weigh	תֹּם—Perfect
תֹּהוּ—Vanity	תַּנְחוּמוֹת—Consolations	תָּמַם—Perfect
תּוֹרָה—Law	תֹּם—Integrity	תָּעָה—Wander

THE HEBREW ALPHABET (SQUARE LETTERS)

Letter	Name	English	Value	Signification
א	Aleph	'	1	Ox
ב	Beth	b	2	House
ג	Gimel	g	3	Camel
ד	Daleth	d	4	Door
ה	He	h	5	Latticewindow
ו	Vav	v	6	Hook
ז	Zayin	z	7	Weapon
ח	Cheth	ch	8	Fence
ט	Tet	t	9	Snake
י	Yod	y	10	Hand
כ	Kaph	k	20	Bent Hand
ל	Lamed	l	30	Ox-Goad
מ	Mem	m	40	Water
נ	Num	n	50	Fish
ס	Samech	s	60	Prop
ע	Ayin	'	70	Eye
פ	Pe	p	80	Mouth
צ	Tsade	ts	90	Fish Hook
ק	Qoph	q	100	Back of Head
ר	Resh	r	200	Head
שׂ	Sin	s	300	Tooth
שׁ	Shin	sh	—	''
ת	Tav	th	400	Cross

The TEN COMMANDMENTS ... EXODUS 20

I: Thou shalt have no other gods before me.

לא יהיה לך אלהים אחרים על פני

II: Thou shalt not make unto thee any graven image.

לא תעשה לך פסל

III: Thou shalt not take the name of the Lord thy God in vain.

לא תשא את שם יהיה אלהיך לשוא

IV: Remember the Sabbath day, to keep it holy.

שמור את יום השבת לקדשו

V: Honour thy father and thy mother.

כבד את אביך ואת אמך

VI: Thou shalt not kill.

לא תרצח

VII: Thou shalt not commit adultry.

לא תנאף

VIII: Thou shalt not steal.

לא תגנב

IX: Thou shalt not bear false witness.

לא תענה עד שוא

X: Thou shalt not covet.

לא תחמד

BIBLIOGRAPHY

Analytical Concordance of the Bible, Robert Young. Philadelphia: Judson Press.

Commentaries on the Old Testament, Carl F. Keil and Franz Delitzsch. Grand Rapids, Mich.: Wm. B. Eerdmans Publishing Co.

Hebrew and English Lexicon of the Old Testament, Gesenius, (Tr. by Edward Robinson). Boston: Crocker & Brewster, 1836.

Hebrew Text of the Old Testament, New York: Hebrew Publishing Co., 1912.

The Holy Bible.

Unpublished class and sermon notes.